AutoCAD 2022 Training Guide

"If you have any big goal.
So, divide it into small goals.
And then achieve step by step goal."

Linkan Sagar

www.bpbonline.com

FIRST EDITION 2022
REPRINT 2026

ISBN: 978-93-5551-280-2

Distributors:

BPB PUBLICATIONS
20, Ansari Road, Darya Ganj
New Delhi-110002
Ph: 23254990/23254991

DECCAN AGENCIES
4-3-329, Bank Street,
Hyderabad-500195
Ph: 24756967/24756400

MICRO MEDIA
Shop No. 5, Mahendra Chambers,
150 DN Rd. Next to Capital Cinema,
V.T. (C.S.T.) Station, MUMBAI-400 001
Ph: 22078296/22078297

Published by Manish Jain for BPB Publications, 20 Ansari Road, Darya Ganj, New Delhi-110002 and Printed by him at Manipal Technologies Limited, Manipal

www.bpbonline.com

Dedicated to

Late Adarsh Sagar

About the Author

Mr. Linkan Sagar has done B.tech from UPTU Lucknow .Currently, He live in Delhi, India. His first book is Autocad, Revit, 3ds Max, He had extensively worked on various other software like Solidworks, Catia, Staad-pro and Revit. He is having wide industry experience. He has worked on more than 50 major live projects and delivered approx. 280 presentations in sector of engineering and designing. He is also a motivation speaker as a profession. Currently working furniture industry as a senior design engineer.

Blog links: *https://cadgenius.blogspot.com/*

LinkedIn Profile: *https://in.linkedin.com/in/linkan-sagar-4b16a7a7*

Acknowledgement

While writing this book, I was constantly supported and guided by many wonderful people. Their extended support will always be priceless for me. My mother, Archana Sagar, is a woman of substance. Like any other mother in the world, her unconditional support, caring nature, never-ending faith in me, and motivation encouraged me to finally realize that I can transfer my knowledge through writing for various other people who seek the same knowledge. And, this is how my book writing began. I would like to thank my sister, Shivani Sagar and My Daughter, Jessica Sagar , who always lovingly supports, motivates, and inspires me. Many thanks to my wife, Mansi Sagar, who is a wonderful partner. she not only understands my dreams and aspirations, but is equally involved in internalizing and living it up with me. It's wonderful how she was took on all the responsibilities.

So that I can get space and comfort for writing this book with dedication. She stands strong with me in all the highs and lows of my life. These two women are the sources of continuous energy that keep me going. This book is about technical skills precision and perfection in the engineering field. My special thanks to Manveer Singh

And, last but not least, thanks to BPB Publications.

Preface

This book carriers a lot for you if your starting AutoCAD this book extremely simple to understand and Can enlighten this time with better projects easy language. My vigorous effort toward the understanding of students and their problems in AutoCAD. Mechanical engineer will be solved after my attempt for this book. So far, my earlier book AutoCAD 2015 REFERENCES AND THEN AutoCAD 2017 references followed by Autocad2018, 3DMAX 2019, Revit 2019, Autocad2019, SolidWorks 2019, Inventor and now AutoCAD 2022 references have been asuccess for my beloved reader. As I receive positive feedback, and numerous peoples are benefitting from it, I am being more eloquent for this book with novel project and easy language. This book carries a lot for you If you are starting AutoCAD for the first time. This book is extremely simple understand and will enlighten you with fundamental of solid works. You can easily learn AutoCAD as it is a basic step-by-step book. The main objective of writing this book, after being inspired from my previous edition, is to make student enthusiastic about learning the concept of AutoCAD, I wish you a great future in designing.

Coloured Images

Please follow the link to download the *Coloured Images* of the book:

https://rebrand.ly/joy26v5

We have code bundles from our rich catalogue of books and videos available at **https://github.com/bpbpublications**. Check them out!

Errata

We take immense pride in our work at BPB Publications and follow best practices to ensure the accuracy of our content to provide with an indulging reading experience to our subscribers. Our readers are our mirrors, and we use their inputs to reflect and improve upon human errors, if any, that may have occurred during the publishing processes involved. To let us maintain the quality and help us reach out to any readers who might be having difficulties due to any unforeseen errors, please write to us at :

errata@bpbonline.com

Your support, suggestions and feedbacks are highly appreciated by the BPB Publications' Family.

Piracy

If you come across any illegal copies of our works in any form on the internet, we would be grateful if you would provide us with the location address or website name. Please contact us at **business@bpbonline.com** with a link to the material.

If you are interested in becoming an author

If there is a topic that you have expertise in, and you are interested in either writing or contributing to a book, please visit **www.bpbonline.com**. We have worked with thousands of developers and tech professionals, just like you, to help them share their insights with the global tech community. You can make a general application, apply for a specific hot topic that we are recruiting an author for, or submit your own idea.

Reviews

Please leave a review. Once you have read and used this book, why not leave a review on the site that you purchased it from? Potential readers can then see and use your unbiased opinion to make purchase decisions. We at BPB can understand what you think about our products, and our authors can see your feedback on their book. Thank you!

For more information about BPB, please visit **www.bpbonline.com**.

Table of Contents

CHAPTER 1
Introduction

WHAT IS AutoCAD?

Autodesk Company who develops software named AutoCAD, stands for Autodesk's Computer aided design. It's a drafting and designing software. There is several software for drafting and designing available in market, out of them The AutoCAD is best, because it Works on co-ordinate system that help's in survey drawing and drafting.

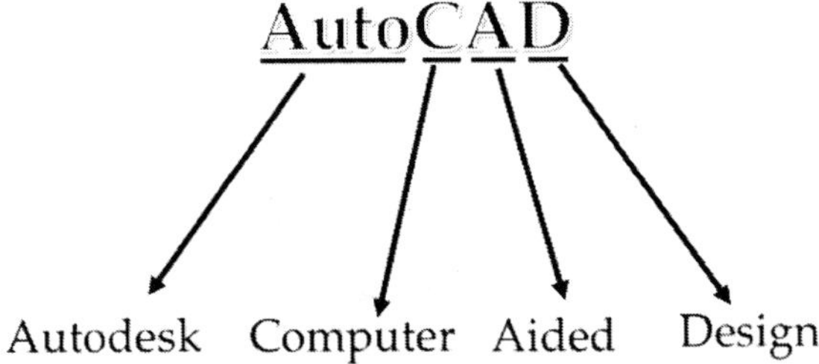

Figure 1 *full form of AutoCAD*

HISTORY OF AutoCAD?

AutoCAD was Came in concept during 1977, and it's first commercial release was in 1979 with the name Interact CAD. Later on Autodesk Company develop it and Release in 1982 for Microcomputer. Gradually the lighter version for small PC and Notebook were release. In 2010 AutoCAD 360 app was released for mobile.

AutoCAD in 1982 OLD AutoCAD in 2022 NEW

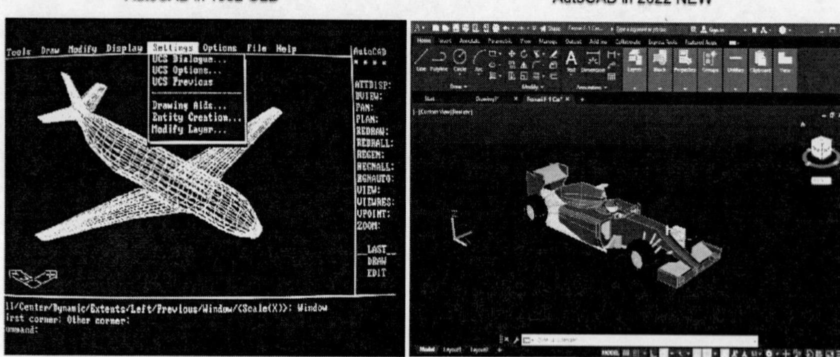

Figure 2 AutoCAD version

USAGE OF AutoCAD

AutoCAD is used for 2D and 3D design, mostly for Civil, Mechanical, Electrical, Interior & Architecture domain. You can design & draw layout, building plan, mechanical part etc. This software is very popular among small to large scale Companies.

AutoCAD stands for Automatic Computer Aided Design.

1. As an Architectural planning tool.

Figure 3 Architectural

2. As an Engineering drafting tool.

***Figure 4** Drafting*

3. As a Graphic design tool.

***Figure 5** Graphic design*

4. In the fashion industry.

***Figure 6** Fashion industry*

5. As an industrial design tool.

***Figure 7** Industrial design*

Important command/short cut of CAD

In AutoCAD, there are more than 1000 commands. But some commands are like this. Which are used mostly. That's why I am telling some important commands here.

Open page - Ctrl + O
New page - Ctrl + N
Save - Ctrl + S
Save As - Ctrl + Shift + S
Print - Ctrl + P
Select All - Ctrl + A
Copy - Ctrl + C
Paste - Ctrl + V

Line - L + Enter
Poly Line - PL + Enter
Special Line - SPL + Enter
Construction Line - XL + Enter
Ray Line - RAY + Enter
Circle - C + Enter
Rectangle - REC + Enter
Polygon - POL + Enter
Ellipse - EL + Enter
Arc - A + Enter
Hatch - H + Enter
Gradient - GD + Enter
Point - PO + Enter
Multiple - MULTIPLE + Enter
Divide - DIV + Enter
Measure - ME + Enter
Point Style - PTYPE +Enter

Boundary	-	BO + Enter
Region	-	REG + Enter
Wipeout	-	WIPEOUT + Enter
3D Polyline	-	3DPOLY + Enter
Helix	-	HELIX + Enter
Revision Cloud	-	REVCLOUD + Enter
Solid	-	SO + Enter
Fill	-	FILL + Enter
Donut	-	DO + Enter
Text	-	DT + Enter
Multi Text	-	MT + Enter
Block	-	B + Enter
Write Block	-	WB + Enter
Insert	-	I + Enter
Attribute	-	ATT + Enter
Move	-	M + Enter
Copy	-	CO + Enter
Stretch	-	S + Enter
Rotate	-	RO + Enter
Mirror	-	MI + Enter
Scale	-	SC + Enter
Trim	-	TR + Double Enter
Extend	-	EX + Double Enter
Fillet	-	F + Enter
Chamfer	-	CHA + Enter
Blend Curves	-	BLEND + Enter
Array	-	AR + Enter
Explode	-	X + Enter
Offset	-	O + Enter
Lengthen	-	LEN + Enter
Align	-	AL + Enter

Break - BR + Enter

Join - J + Enter

Delete Duplicate Object - OVERKILL + Enter

Draw Order - DRAWORDER + Enter

Poly Line Edit - PE + Enter

Special Line Edit - SPE + Enter

Hatch Edit - HE + Enter

Block Edit - BEDIT + Enter

Layer - LA + Enter

Purge - PU + Enter

Distance - DI + Enter

List - LI + Enter

Area - AA + Enter

Dimension - DIM + Enter

Dimension Style - D + Enter

Center Mark - CM + Enter

Table - TB + Enter

QLeader - LE + Enter

Leader - LEAD + Enter

Multi Leader - MLD + Enter

WHAT IS NEW IN AutoCAD 2022?

Every year AutoCAD new version is released with some new tools and feature as well as carrying previous feature.

AutoCAD 2022 is also released with some new and enhanced feature.

For ex.

- DWG Compare
- PDF import
- External file references
- Object selection

- Text to Mtext
- User interface
- Share design views
- High-resolution monitor support
- AutoCAD mobile app

WHAT IS WORKSPACE?

Workspace provides us a platform for carrying out our work with definite sets of Menus, toolbars, palettes, which are displayed according to the work space selected. A workspace may also display the ribbon toolbar; it is a distinct palette with task specific Control panels. One can easily switch between workspaces. We are aided with the following task-based Workspaces in AutoCAD 2022:

- 2D Drafting & Annotation
- 3D Modeling
- 3D Basic

Say for example, if we have to create 3D models, we can use the 3D modeling Workspace, which provides us only 3D-related toolbars, menus, and palettes. And hides the other interface items that we do not need for 3D modeling, thus maximizing the screen area available for our work. Depending upon our drawing requirement, we can modify a selected workspace with our choices of tools and pallets and save it as a new workspace with a different name for easy access in future.

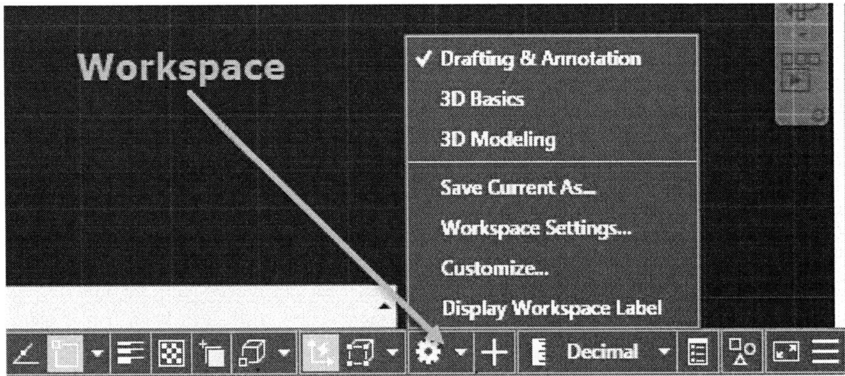

Figure 8 *Workspace*

2D Drafting & Annotation

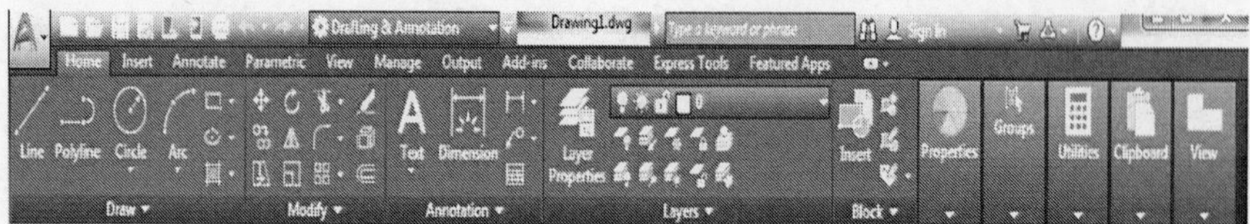

Figure 9 *2D Drafting & Annotation*

3D Modeling

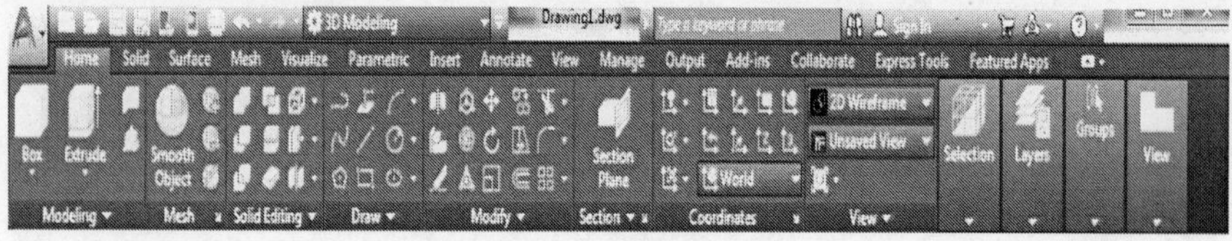

Figure 10 *3D Modeling*

3D Basic

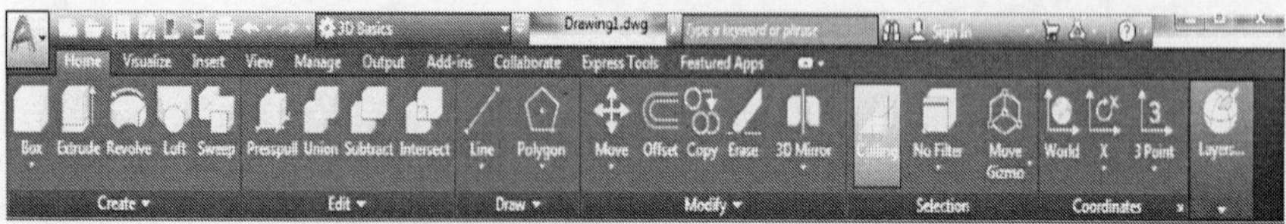

Figure 11 *3D Basic*

Chapter 2
Overview

WELCOME SCREEN

It is the first time that Autodesk AutoCAD has introduced a welcome screen in its version of 2022. In this version when we open the AutoCAD we get to see a welcome screen. The welcome screen provides easy learning, starting, and exploring AutoCAD. In this screen, we will get to see two different types of tab at the bottom namely LEARN and CREATE. In this version, we can add the number of new tab according to our requirement. When we choose to add a new tab, we get Create page by default.

What is NEW TAB CREATE?

In this tab, we will have three columns providing us options to proceed as per our Requirement. Three columns namely Get Started, Recent Documents and Get connected. The name of columns gives us a notion of its use. Let's begin with "GET STARTED" it is for starting a fresh new drawing page, or we can work upon our previously drawn file by browsing the folder. Next is "RECENT DOCUMENT" this column provides instant access to the file that we lastly worked upon in AutoCAD. And finally "GET CONNECTED" provides us web access to Autodesk 360 and also shows us notifications (if any) regarding AutoCAD.

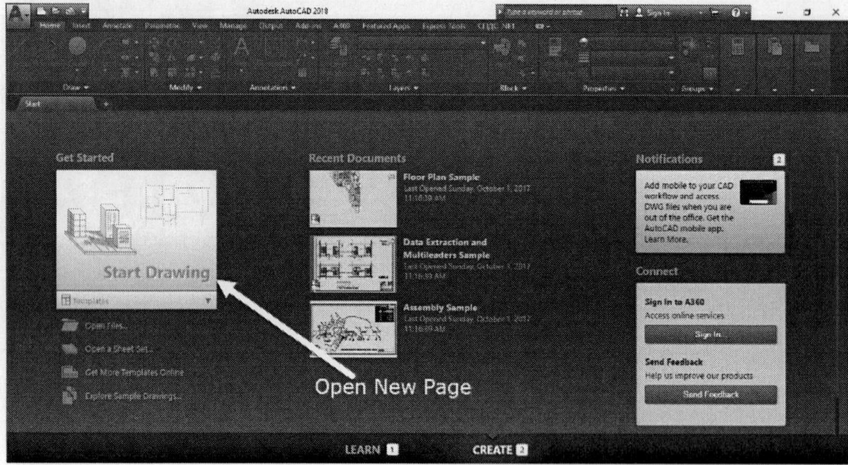

Figure 12 Create tab

What is NEW TAB LEARN?

Day by day increasing use of AutoCAD is attracting new users, Keeping this in mind AutoCAD 2022 comes with a learn tab providing its new users easy learning via its three columns namely:

What's new, Getting Started Videos and TIP/Online Resources.

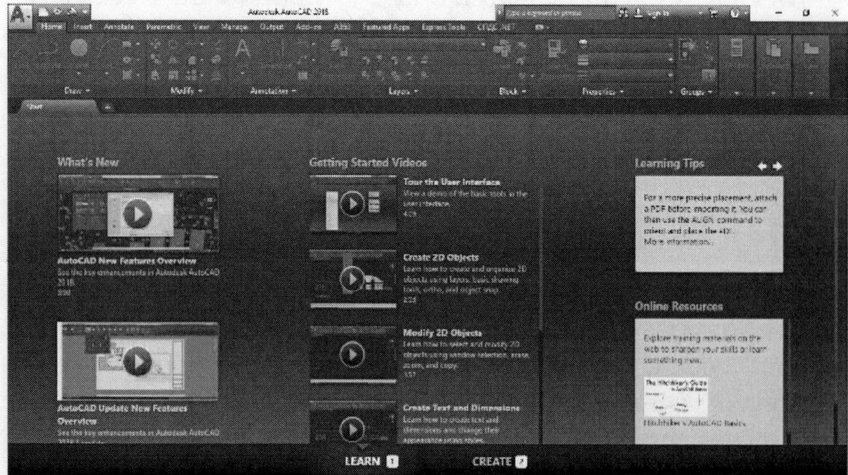

Figure 13 Learn tab

GUI (Graphical User Interface) Overview

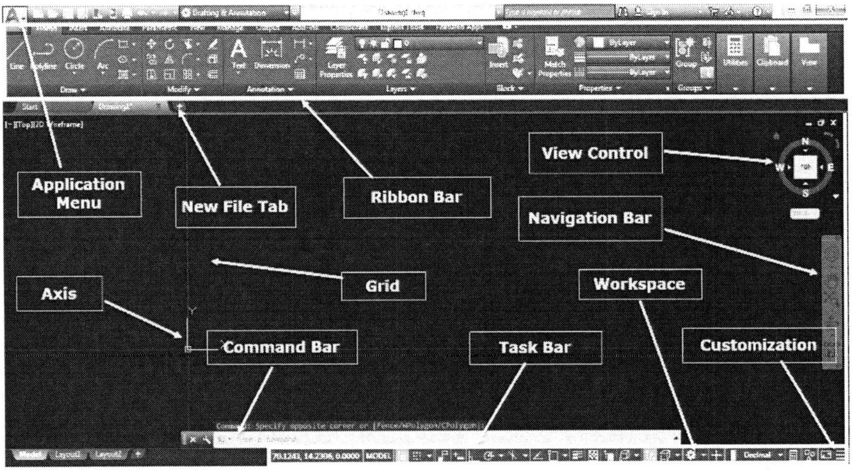

Figure 14 GUI

MOUSE USE

Left button of mouse is used to CLICK and Right button is used for ENTER. To move the AutoCAD page, press the scroll button and move the mouse. If you have to do zoom in and zoom out the page just revolve the scroll button.

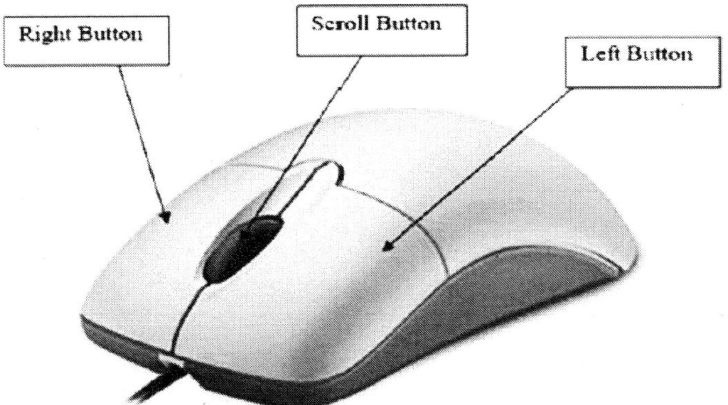

Figure 15 Mouse setting

DIFFERENCE BETWEEN COMMAND WORK & VISUAL WORK

AutoCAD provide two modes of operation, first is Command based work and another is visual work.

When you work using GUI (Graphical User Interface), consider an example of using tools icon this is visual work and when you do same thing using command that is visual work. For Example, if you have to draw line using command write L in command bar and press ENTER, and if you want to draw using visual click on line Icon.

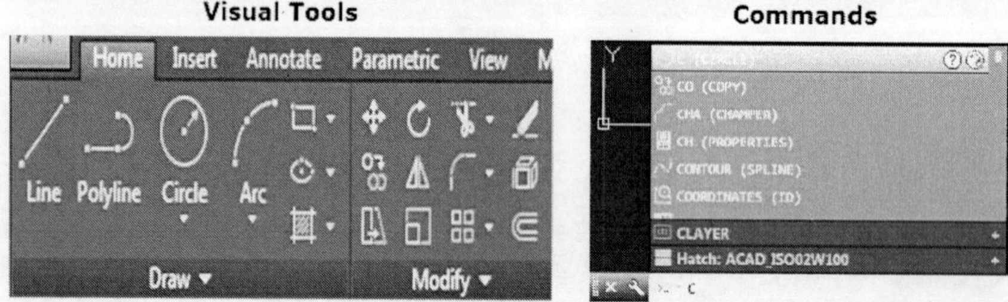

Figure 16 *Visual/Command*

COORDINATE SYSTEM WITH LINE COMMAND

Our AutoCAD page is based on graphical coordinate system that constitutes three axis viz. x, y, z. As we know these three axis starts from a point origin (0, 0, 0) one in the vertical direction, next horizontal and the last parallel to the page. Moving forward in any of the axes increases the value of the coordinate in that axis.

We can draw using any of the three coordinates system given below:

- Absolute Coordinate System (X, Y)

  We use absolute coordinate system when we know the precise distance of x coordinate and y coordinate from the origin.

  Step 1: Command: L Enter

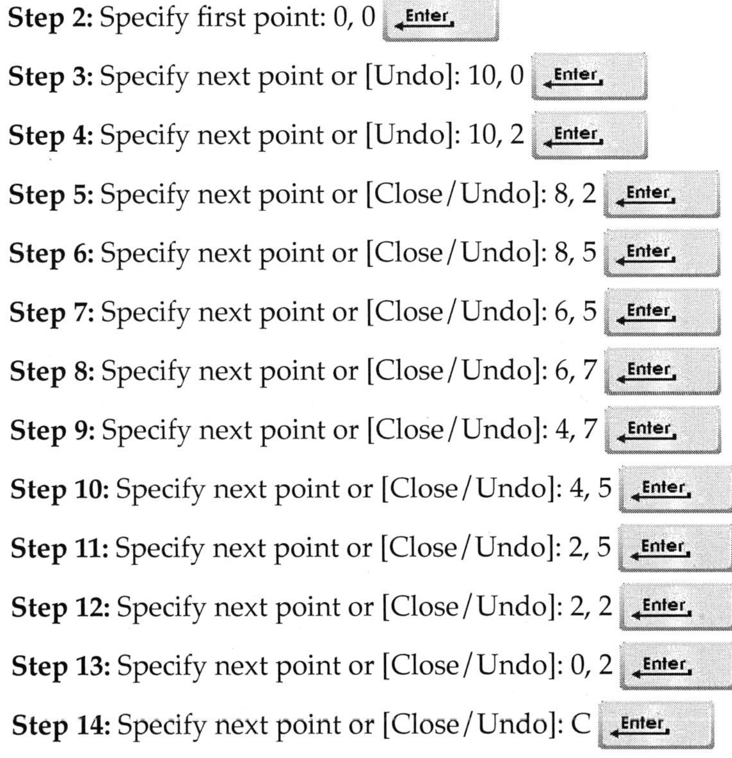

Step 2: Specify first point: 0, 0 Enter

Step 3: Specify next point or [Undo]: 10, 0 Enter

Step 4: Specify next point or [Undo]: 10, 2 Enter

Step 5: Specify next point or [Close/Undo]: 8, 2 Enter

Step 6: Specify next point or [Close/Undo]: 8, 5 Enter

Step 7: Specify next point or [Close/Undo]: 6, 5 Enter

Step 8: Specify next point or [Close/Undo]: 6, 7 Enter

Step 9: Specify next point or [Close/Undo]: 4, 7 Enter

Step 10: Specify next point or [Close/Undo]: 4, 5 Enter

Step 11: Specify next point or [Close/Undo]: 2, 5 Enter

Step 12: Specify next point or [Close/Undo]: 2, 2 Enter

Step 13: Specify next point or [Close/Undo]: 0, 2 Enter

Step 14: Specify next point or [Close/Undo]: C Enter

(*Note:* Enter command and then follow instructions.)

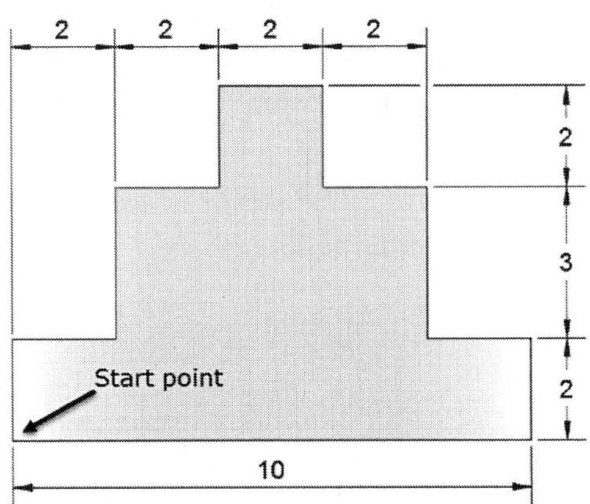

***Figure 17** Absolute coordinate system*

- Relative Rectangular Coordinate System (@X, Y)

  We use this coordinate system when we have a relative distance, i.e., distance of the next point with respect to previous drawn point.

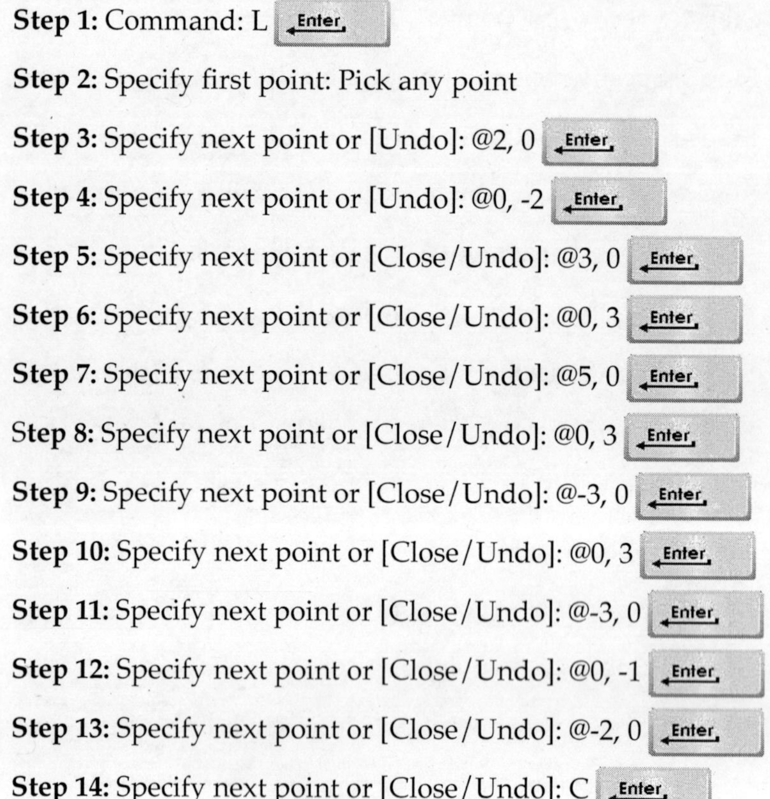

Step 1: Command: L Enter

Step 2: Specify first point: Pick any point

Step 3: Specify next point or [Undo]: @2, 0 Enter

Step 4: Specify next point or [Undo]: @0, -2 Enter

Step 5: Specify next point or [Close/Undo]: @3, 0 Enter

Step 6: Specify next point or [Close/Undo]: @0, 3 Enter

Step 7: Specify next point or [Close/Undo]: @5, 0 Enter

Step 8: Specify next point or [Close/Undo]: @0, 3 Enter

Step 9: Specify next point or [Close/Undo]: @-3, 0 Enter

Step 10: Specify next point or [Close/Undo]: @0, 3 Enter

Step 11: Specify next point or [Close/Undo]: @-3, 0 Enter

Step 12: Specify next point or [Close/Undo]: @0, -1 Enter

Step 13: Specify next point or [Close/Undo]: @-2, 0 Enter

Step 14: Specify next point or [Close/Undo]: C Enter

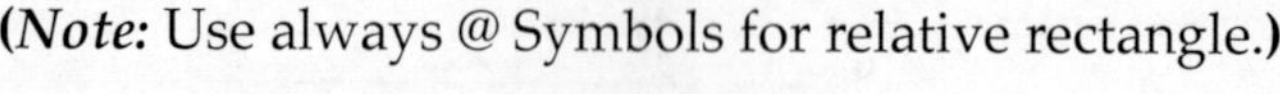

(*Note:* Use always @ Symbols for relative rectangle.**)**

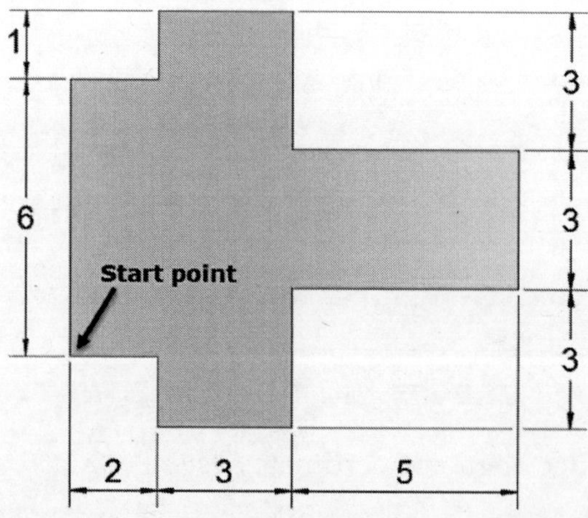

Figure 18 *Relative Rectangular Coordinate System*

- Relative Polar Coordinate System (@ distance < angle)

  We use relative polar coordinate system when we have a relative distance and angle of a point to draw with respect to the previous point. The use of angle is compulsory in this coordinate system which is measured in Anti clock direction, taking towards the right.

  Step 1: Command: L Enter

  Step 2: Specify first point: Pick any point

  Step 3: Specify next point or [Undo]: **@30<0** Enter

  Step 4: Specify next point or [Undo]: **@30<-60** Enter

  Step 5: Specify next point or [Undo]: **@30<60** Enter

  Step 6: Specify next point or [Close/Undo]: **@30<0** Enter

  Step 7: Specify next point or [Close/Undo]: **@30<120** Enter

  Step 8: Specify next point or [Close/Undo]: **@30<60** Enter

  Step 9: Specify next point or [Close/Undo]: **@30<180** Enter

  Step 10: Specify next point or [Close/Undo]: **@30<120** Enter

  Step 11: Specify next point or [Close/Undo]: **@30<240** Enter

  Step 12: Specify next point or [Close/Undo]: **@30<180** Enter

  Step 13: Specify next point or [Close/Undo]: **@30<-60** Enter

  Step 14: Specify next point or [Close/Undo]: C Enter

  (*Note:* Use always @ Symbols for relative and < for angle)

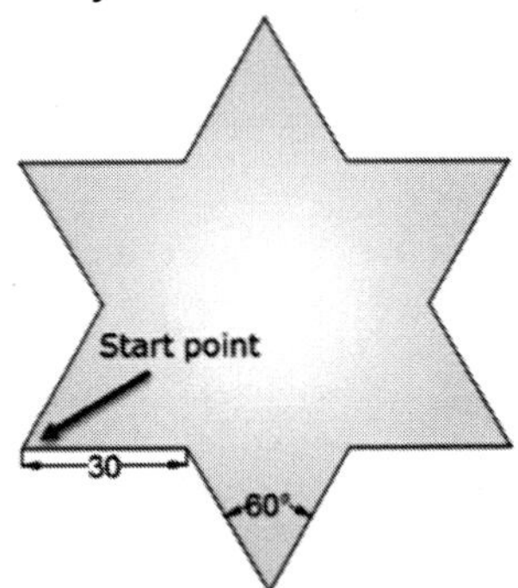

Figure 19 *Relative Polar Coordinate System*

ZOOM AND EXTENTS

Use the mouse scroll bar to ZOOM IN ZOOM OUT the drawing created on AutoCAD page, in case scroll does not support then type z in command bar and press enter to zoom.

If created drawing have unexpected size then zoom it and extend after.

Step 1: Command: Z Enter

Step 2: Zoom [All Center Dynamic Extents Previous Scale Window Object]: **E** Enter

Before Zoom command

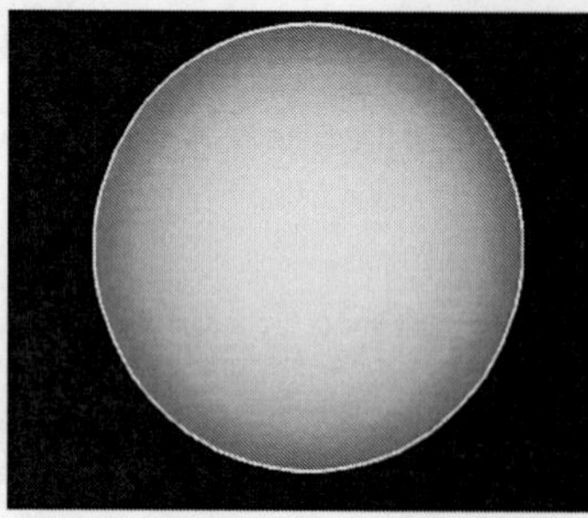

After Zoom command

Figure 20 Zoom

If you want to select an option like-

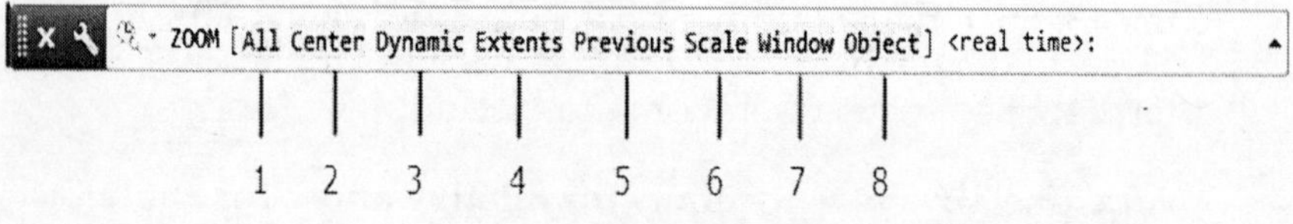

Figure 21 Zoom option

1. All

It is used to only for gird limits.

Step 1: Z Enter Then A Enter

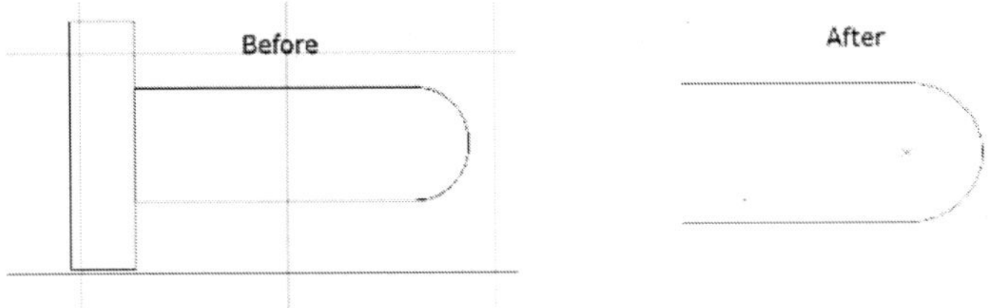

Figure 22 Zoom all

2. Center

It is used as s center point and a magnification value or a height.

Step 1: Z Enter Then C Enter

Step 2: Pick center point

Step 3: Specify height

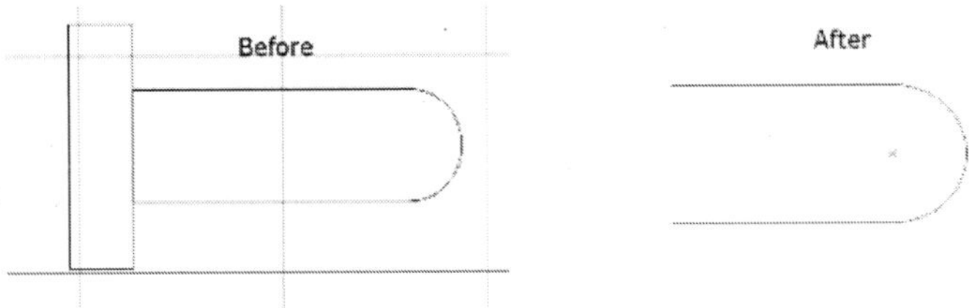

Figure 23 Zoom center

3. Dynamic

Pans and zooms using a rectangular view box. The view box represents your view, which you can shrink or enlarge and move around the drawing. Positioning and sizing the view box pans or zooms to fill the viewport with the view inside the view box. Not available in perspective projection.

Step 1: Z Enter Then D Enter

Step 2: Specify the area again Enter

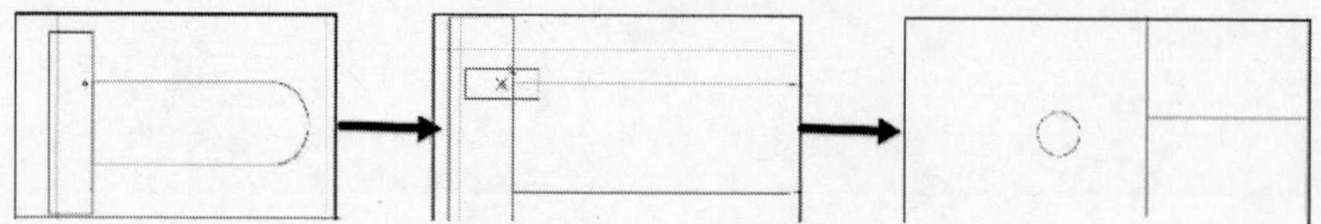

Figure 24 Zoom dynamic

4. Extents

It is used to zoom all objects.

Step 1: Z Enter Then E Enter

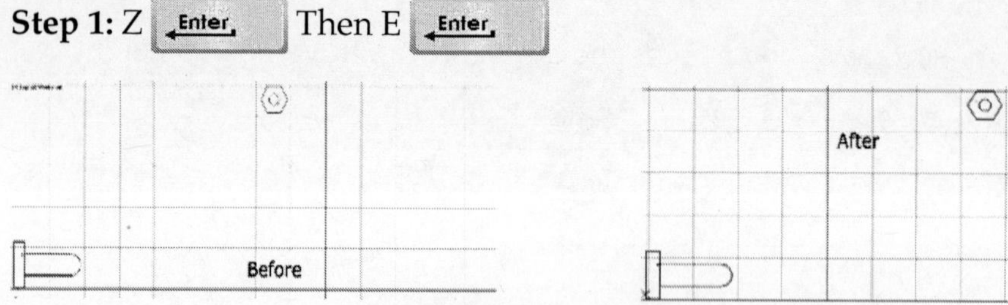

Figure 25 Zoom extents

5. Previous

Zooms to display the previous view. You can restore up to 10 previous views.

Step 1: Z Enter Then P Enter

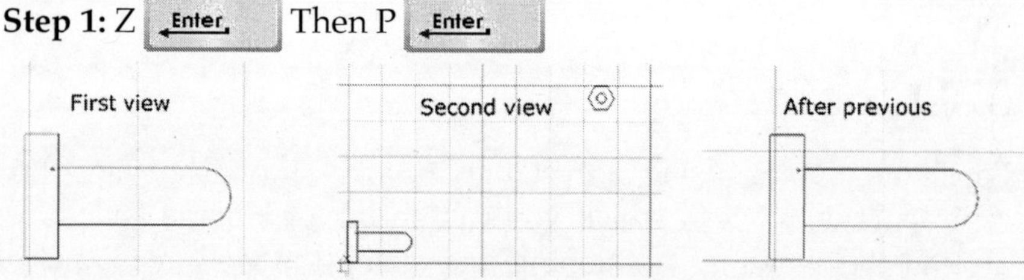

Figure 26 Zoom previous

6. Scale

It is used to zoom scale like 2 times, 3 times.

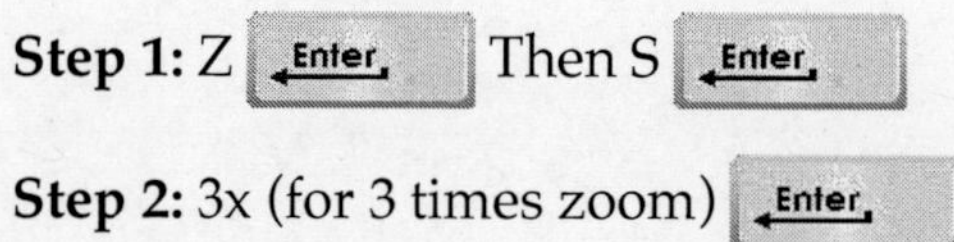

Step 1: Z Enter Then S Enter

Step 2: 3x (for 3 times zoom) Enter

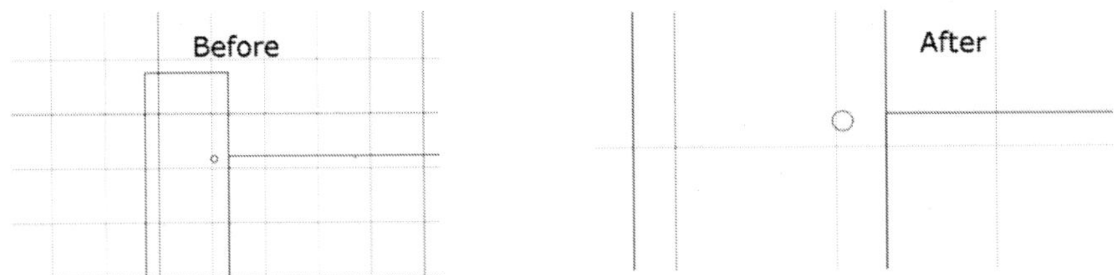

Figure 27 Zoom Scale

7. Window

Zooms to display an area by rectangle window.

Step 1: Z Enter Then W Enter

Step 2: Select window area corner to corner.

Figure 28 Zoom window

8. Object

It is used to zoom select object.

Step 1: Z Enter Then O Enter

Step 2: Select object

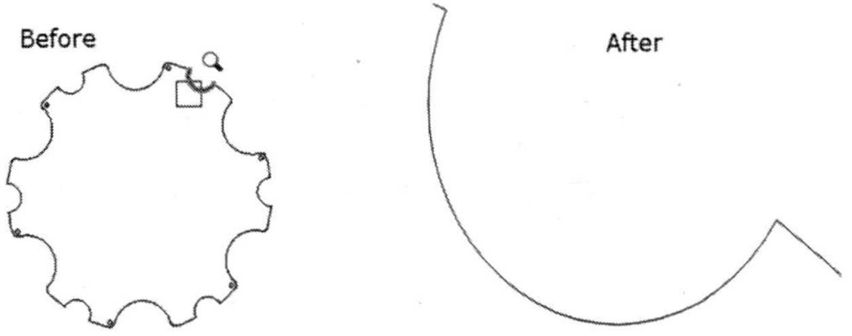

Figure 29 Zoom object

REGEN

Usually and mostly during zoom in and zoom out of AutoCAD pages, it's not working properly, Or when you move the page it refrain to move, Or when you create circle and want to view by zoom in it appear like polygon. So, to resolve these problem use the REGAN command to overcome such type of problem.

Step 1: Re

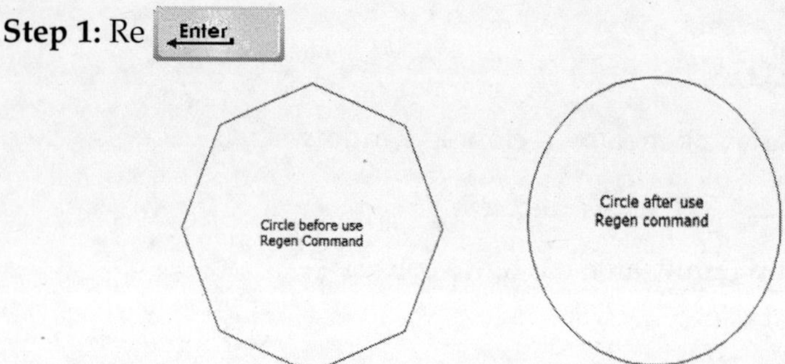

Figure 30 *Regen command*

CHAPTER 3
Draw Tools

What do you mean by LINE?

Line command is straight continuous joining points without any curve and infinite if we do not mention its start point and end point.

Step 1: Ribbon: Home tab ➢ Draw panel ➢ Line

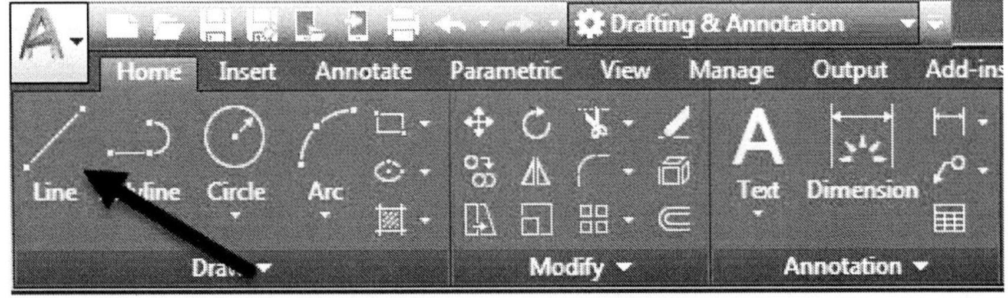

Figure 31 *Line tool icon*

OR

Command: L Enter

Step 2: Specify first point: Pick any point

Step 3: Specify next point: 4 Enter

(Give Direction then specify distance)

Step 4: Specify next point or [Undo]: 1.5 Enter

Step 5: Specify next point or [Close/Undo]: 4 Enter

Step 6: Specify next point or [Close/Undo]: 3 Enter

Step 7: Specify next point or [Close/Undo]: 1 Enter

Step 8: Specify next point or [Close/Undo]: 2 Enter

Step 9: Specify next point or [Close/Undo]: 3 Enter

Step 10: Specify next point or [Close/Undo]: 3 Enter

Step 11: Specify next point or [Close/Undo]: 4 Enter

Step 12: Specify next point or [Close/Undo]: 3 Enter

Step 13: Specify next point or [Close/Undo]: 2.5 Enter

Step 14: Specify next point or [Close/Undo]: 1.5 Enter

Step 15: Specify next point or [Close/Undo]: 2.5 Enter

Step 16: Specify next point or [Close/Undo]: 1 Enter

(*Note:* Use again Enter or Esc for finish line command)

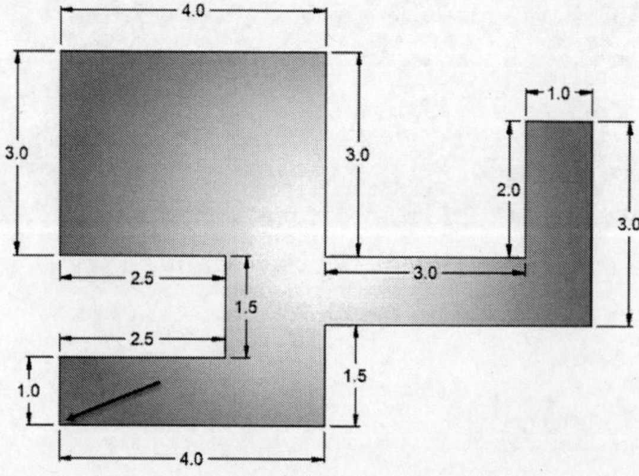

Figure 32 *Line drawing*

What do you mean by PLINE?

Command Pline stands for polyline and is same as line and created in the same way as line is created but it requires 1st and 2nd endpoints. It is an object but may have different segments. In polyline, each segment can be given required width and can be also given different width to the start and end of the polyline.

Step 1: Ribbon: Home tab ➤ Draw panel ➤ Pline (polyline)

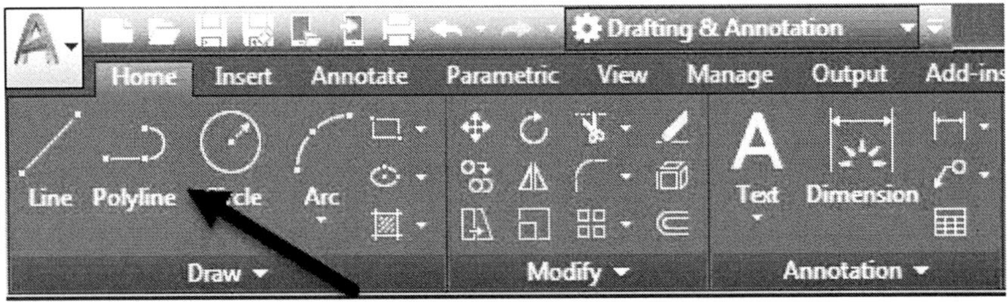

Figure 33 Pline tool icon

OR

Command: PL

Step 2: Specify first point: 1, 1 Enter

Step 3: PLINE Specify next point or [Arc Halfwidth Length Undo Width]:2, 2

Step 4: PLINE Specify next point or [Arc Halfwidth Length Undo Width]:3 Enter (give right side direction then enter value)

Step 5: PLINE Specify next point or [Arc Close Halfwidth Length Undo Width]: 1 Enter (give down side direction then enter value)

Step 6: PLINE Specify next point or [Arc Close Halfwidth Length Undo Width]: 2 Enter (give right side direction then enter value)

Step 7: PLINE Specify next point or [Arc Close Halfwidth Length Undo Width]: @2<45

Step 8: PLINE Specify next point or [Arc Close Halfwidth Length Undo Width]: 3 Enter (give up side direction then enter value)

Step 9: PLINE Specify next point or [Arc Close Halfwidth Length Undo Width]: 1 Enter (give left side direction then enter value)

Step 10: PLINE Specify next point or [Arc Close Halfwidth Length Undo Width]: 1 Enter (give up side direction then enter value)

Step 11: PLINE Specify next point or [Arc Close Halfwidth Length Undo Width]: 3 Enter (give left side direction then enter value)

Step 12: PLINE Specify next point or [Arc Close Halfwidth Length Undo Width]: 1.4 Enter (give down side direction then enter value)

Step 13: PLINE Specify next point or [Arc Close Halfwidth Length Undo Width]: 2.6 Enter (give left side direction then enter value)

Step 14: PLINE Specify next point or [Arc Close Halfwidth Length Undo Width]: C Enter (C for close line)

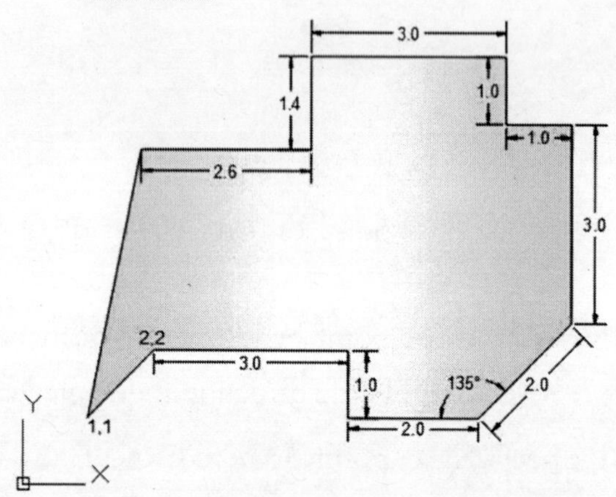

Figure 34 Pline drawing

If you want to select an option like-

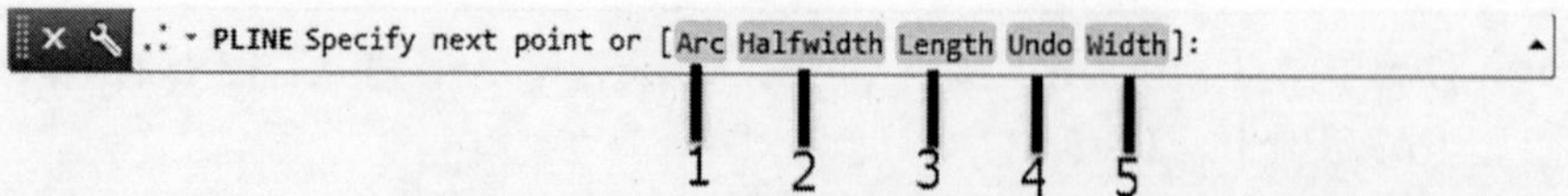

Figure 35 Pline command option

1. Arc

It is used to create Arc. Arc is a part of circle.

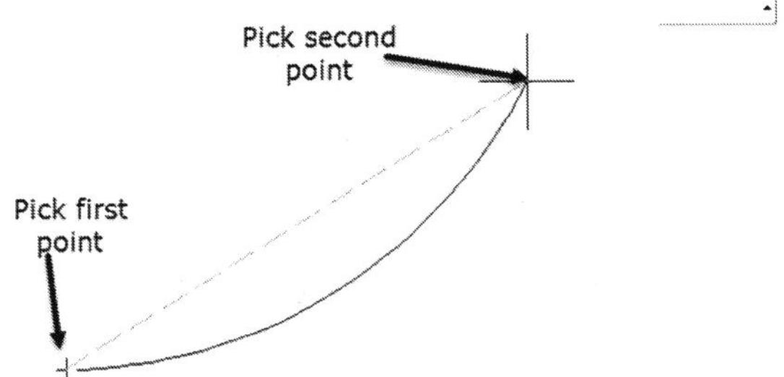

Figure 36 Pline arc option

2. Halfwidth

It is used to change the line width. But it is two directional.

Figure 37 Pline halfwidth option

3. Length

It is used to create a line with same direction.

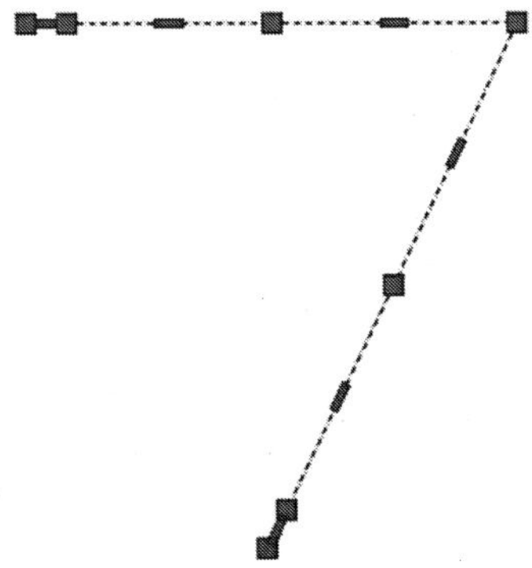

Figure 38 Pline length option

4. Undo

It is used to reverse step.

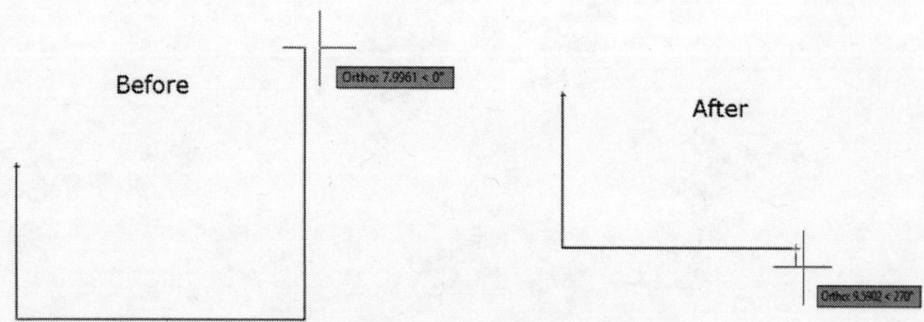

Figure 39 Pline undo option

5. Width

It is used to Change the line width.

Figure 40 Pline width option

What do you mean by XLINE?

It is a command which is infinite and used to create construction line, reference line and for trimming boundaries.

Step 1: Ribbon: Home tab ➢ Draw panel ➢ Xline

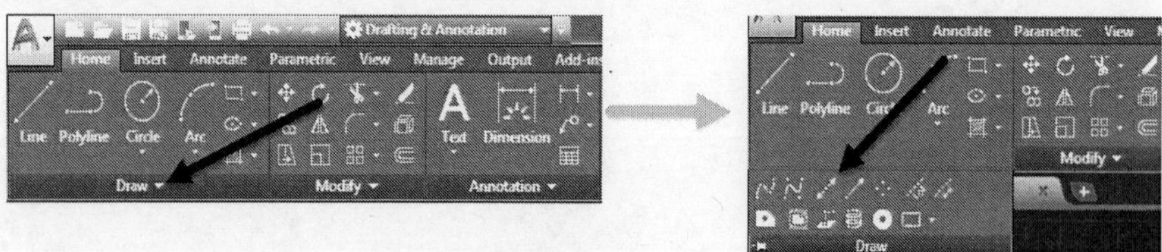

Figure 41 Xline tool icon

OR

Command: XL Enter

Step 2: Specify a point or [Hor Ver Ang Bisect Offset]: **Use one of the points fixing methods or enter an option**

Step 3: Specify through point: **Pick through point**

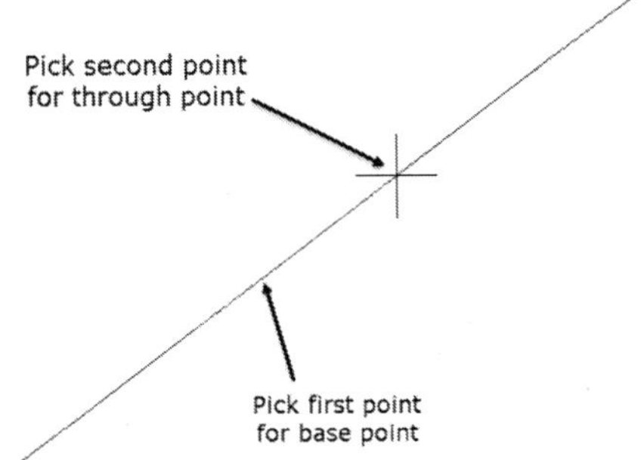

Figure 42 *use of xline*

If you want to select an option like-

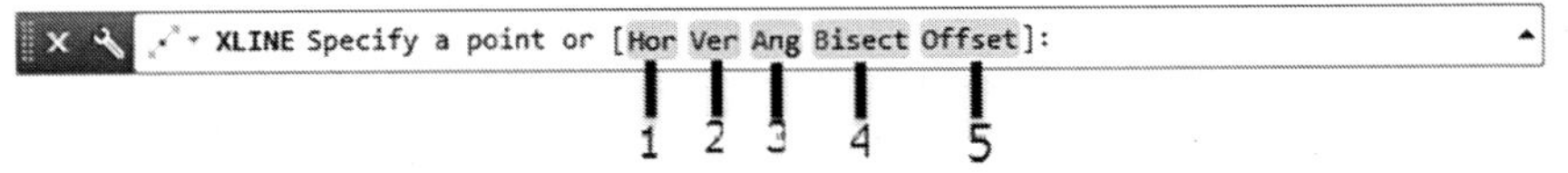

Figure 43 *xline option*

1. Hor

Creates a horizontal xline passing through a selected point.

Figure 44 *Xline hor*

2. Ver

Creates a Vertical xline passing through a selected point.

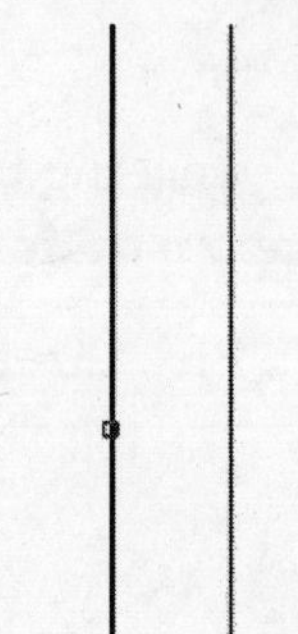

Figure 45 xline ver

3. Ang

Creates a xline at a specified angle.

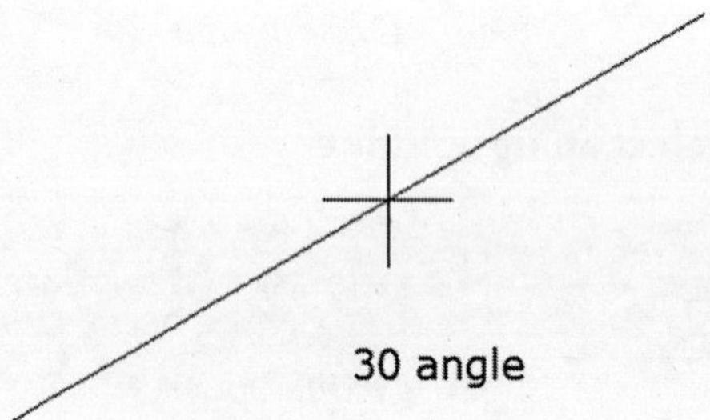

Figure 46 xline angle

4. Bisect

It creates a xline that passes through a selected angle vertex and bisects the angle between first and second line.

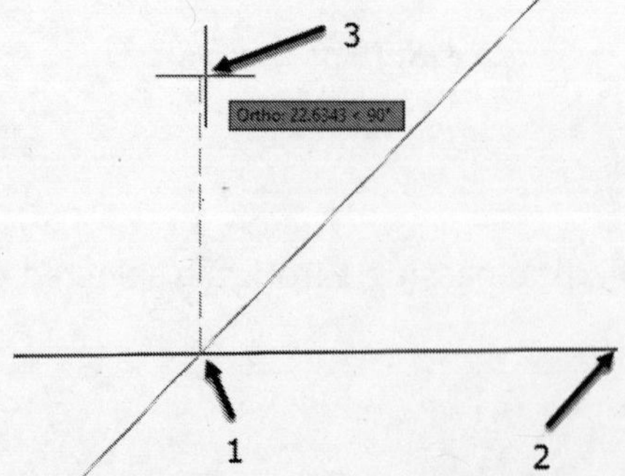

Figure 47 xline bisect

5. Offset Distance

Specifies the distance the xline is offset from the selected object.

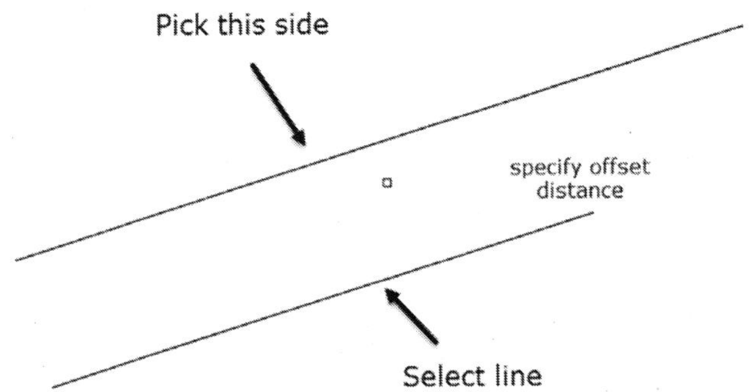

***Figure 48** xline offset distance*

What do you mean by SPLINE?

It is a command for making smooth curves and can be constructed along specific points.

Step 1: Ribbon: Home tab ➢ Draw panel ➢ Spline

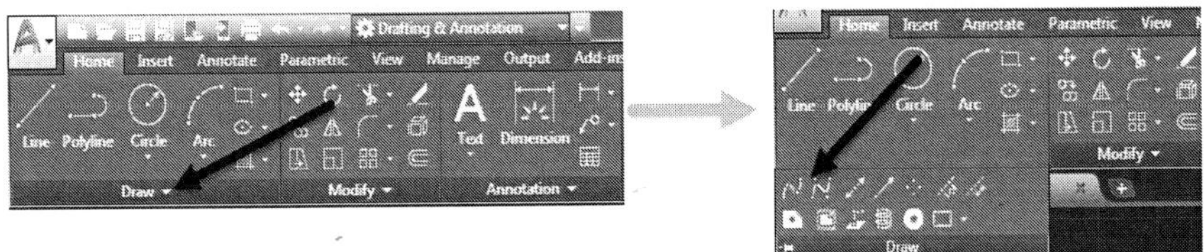

***Figure 49** spline tool icon*

OR

Command: SPL Enter

Step 2: SPLINE Specify first point or [Method Knots Object]: pick point 1

Step 3: Specify Enter next point or [start Tangency toLerance]: pick point 2

Step 4: Specify Enter next point or [end Tangency toLerance Undo]: pick point 3

Step 5: Specify Enter next point or [end Tangency toLerance Undo Close]: pick point 4

Step 6: Specify Enter next point or [end Tangency toLerance Undo Close]: pick point 5

Step 7: Specify Enter next point or [end Tangency toLerance Undo Close]: pick point 6

Step 8: Specify Enter next point or [end Tangency toLerance Undo Close]: pick point 7

Step 9: Specify Enter next point or [end Tangency toLerance Undo Close]: pick point 8

Step 10: Specify Enter next point or [end Tangency toLerance Undo Close]: pick point 9

Step 11: Specify Enter next point or [end Tangency toLerance Undo Close]: pick point 10

Step 12: Specify Enter next point or [end Tangency toLerance Undo Close]: C Enter

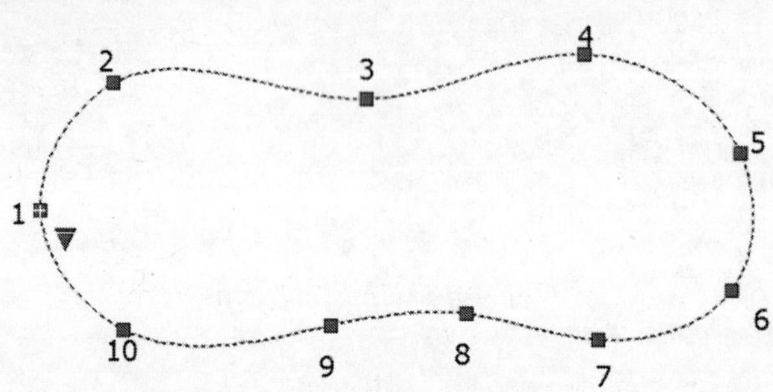

Figure 50 *spline drawing*

If you want to select an option like-

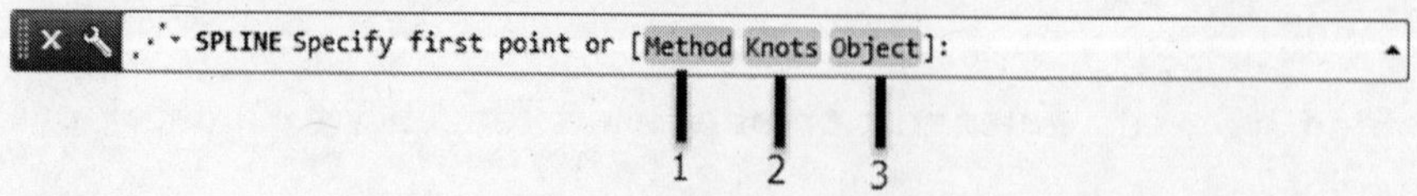

Figure 51 *spline option*

1. Method

It is used to create Fit and CV spline.

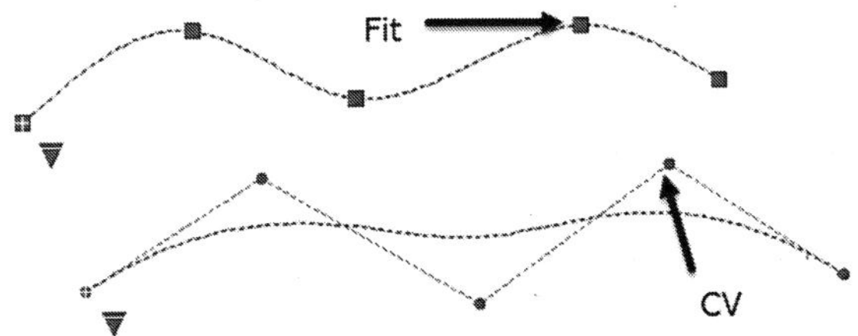

***Figure 52** spline method*

2. Knots

It is used to create knots.

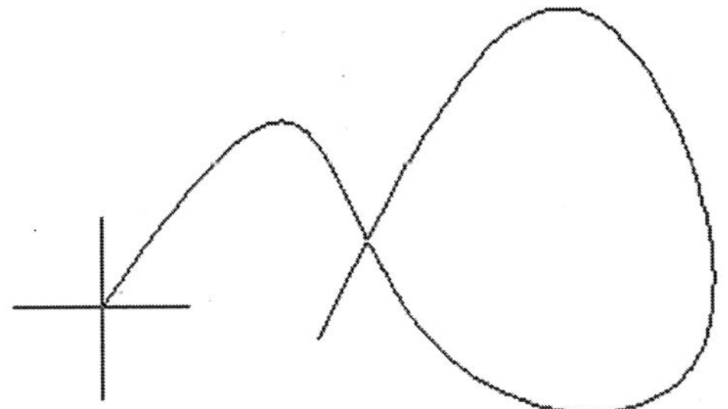

***Figure 53** spline knots*

3. Method

It is used to create Fit and CV spline.

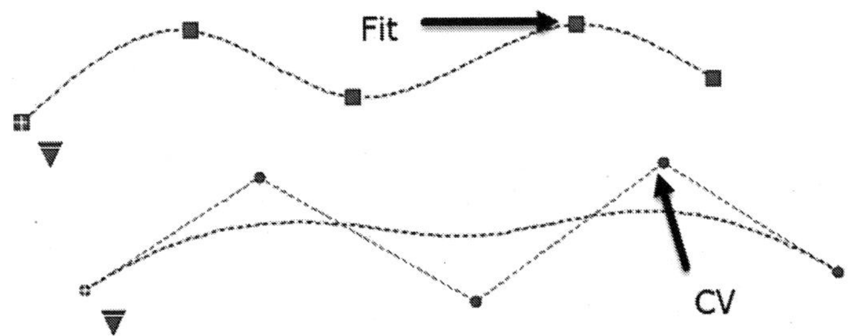

***Figure 54** wrong*

What do you mean by CIRCLE?

It is a command by which we can make a curved line joined in the end having equal distance from the center point. Circle help us to create two-way normal. But in AutoCAD there are three ways to create Circle. One is by specifying the radius and second by specifying Diameter. Besides this 2point, 3point, and tan tan radius. Here we have five ways to create Circle.

Step 1: Ribbon: Home tab ➢ Draw panel ➢ Circle

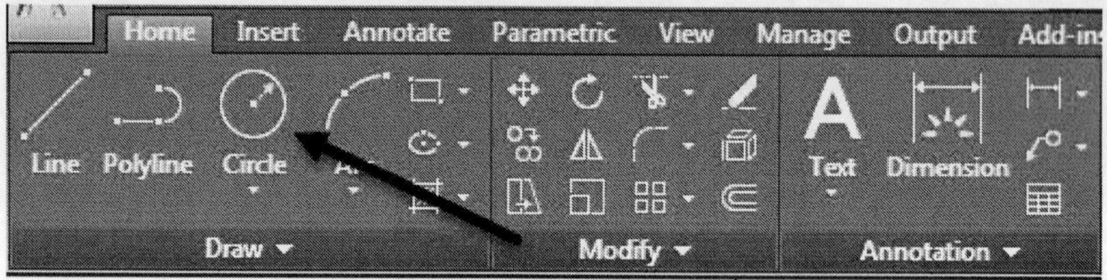

Figure 55 circle tool icon

OR

Command: C

Step 2: Specify center point for circle or [3P / 2P / Ttr (tan tan radius)]: **Pick a point**

Step 3: Specify radius of circle or [Diameter]: **10** Enter

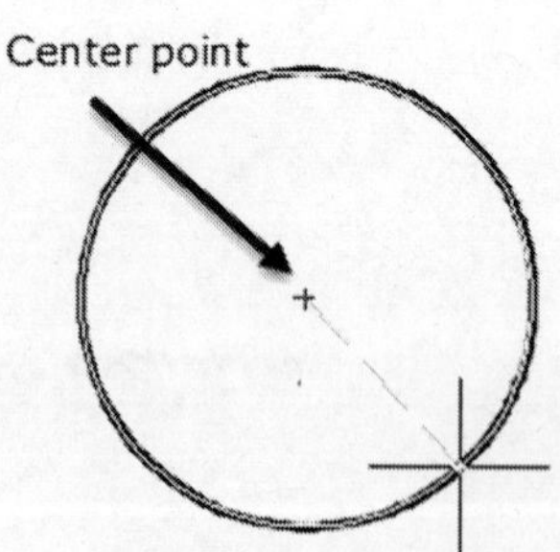

Figure 56 circle radius

Circle diameter

Command: C

Step 1: Specify center point for circle or [3P/ 2P/ Ttr (tan tan radius)]: **Specify a point**

Step 2: Specify radius of circle or [Diameter]: **D** Enter

Step 3: Specify diameter of circle: **20** Enter

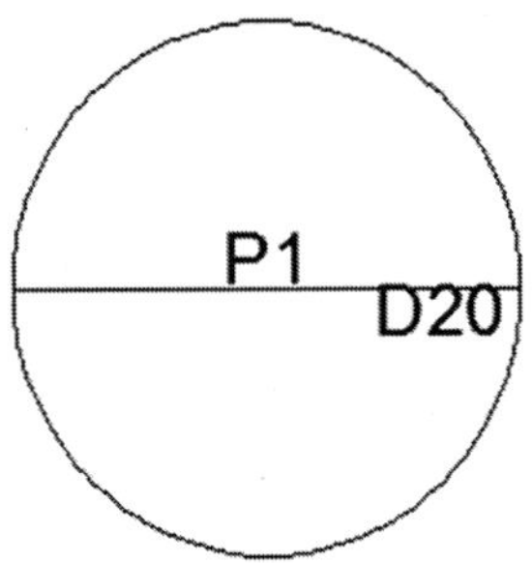

Figure 57 *circle diameter*

3P (Three point)

Draws a circle based on three points on the circumference.

Command: C Enter

Step 1: Specify center point for circle or [3P/ 2P/ Ttr (tan tan radius)]: **3P** Enter

Step 2: Specify first point on circle: **Specify a point (1)**

Step 3: Specify second point on circle: **Specify a point (2)**

Step 4: Specify third point on circle: **Specify a point (3)**

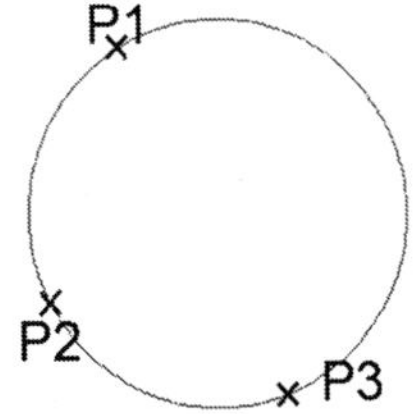

Figure 58 *circle 3point*

2P (Two point)

Draws a circle based on two endpoints of the diameter.

Command: C Enter

Step 1: Specify center point for circle or [3P/ 2P/ Ttr (tan tan radius)]:2P Enter

Step 2: Specify fxirst endpoint of circle's diameter: **Specify a point**

Step 3: Specify second endpoint of circle's diameter: **Specify a point**

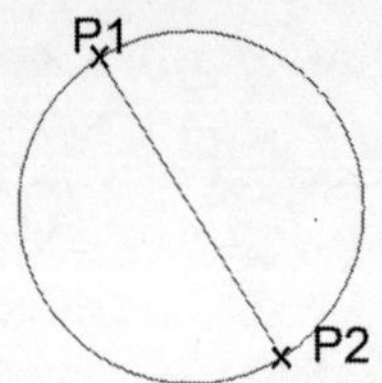

Figure 59 circle 2point

TTR (Tangent, Tangent, Radius)

Draws a circle with a specified radius tangent to two objects.

Command: C

Step 1: Specify center point for circle or [3P/ 2P/ Ttr (tan tan radius)]:

T Enter

Step 2: Specify point on object for first tangent of circle: **Select a line**

Step 3: Specify point on object for second tangent of circle: **Select a line**

Step 4: Specify radius of circle < *current*>: **Enter radius**

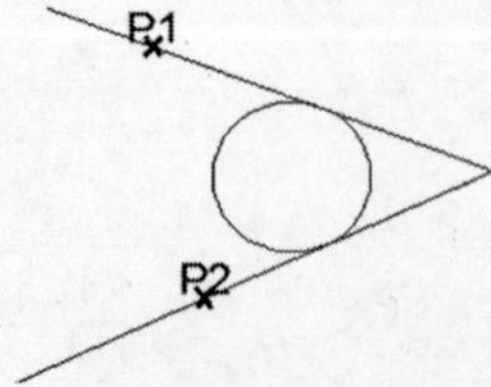

Figure 60 circle ttr

What do you mean by ARC?

It is a command by which we can create a circle segment (part of a circle) or part of the curve. An arc can be a 2-point or 3-point. In case of 3-point Arc, we can specify the angle, endpoint, start point, combination of centers, chord length, direction values and radius.

Step 1: Ribbon: Home tab ➢ Draw panel ➢ Arc

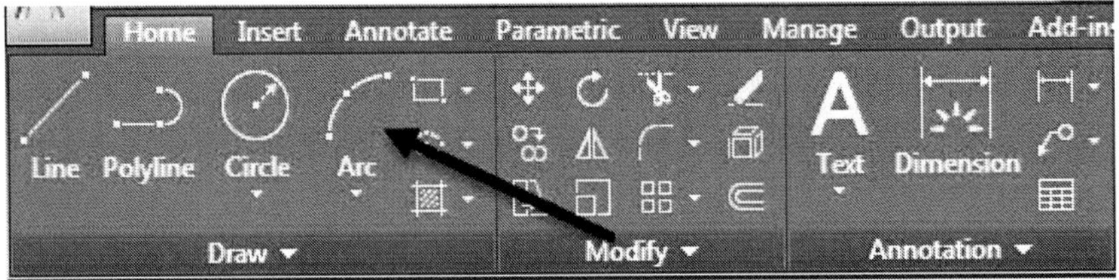

Figure 61 arc tool icon

OR

Command: A Enter

Step 2: Specify start point of arc or [Center]: **Pick 1 point**

Step 3: Specify second point of arc or [Center/End]: **Pick 2 point**

Step 4: Specify end point of arc: **Pick 3 point**

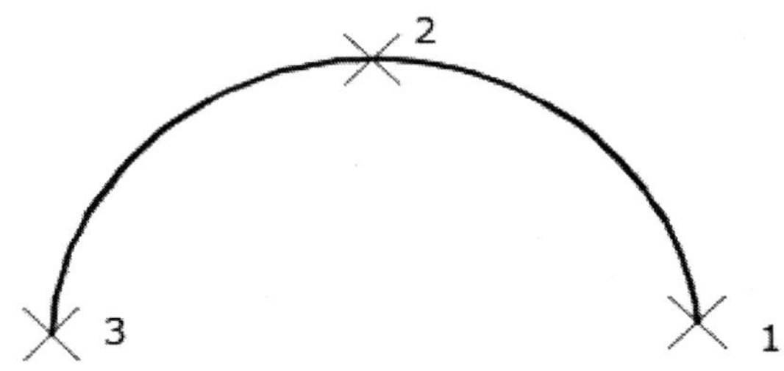

Figure 62 Arc drawing

Eleventh types of Arc-

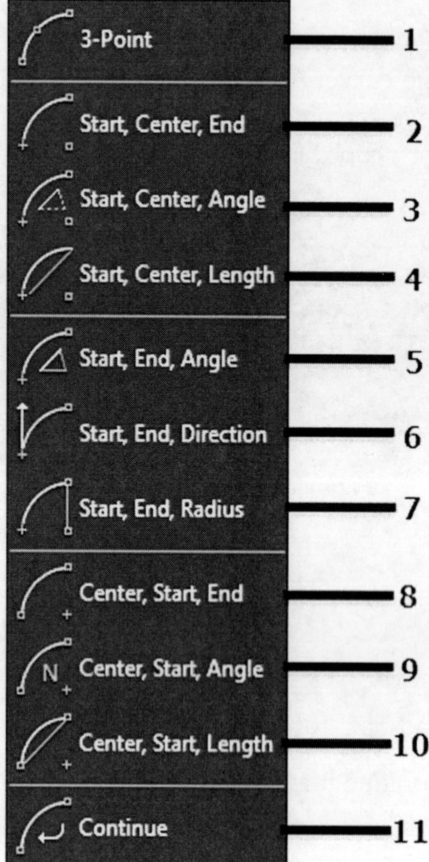

Figure 63 arc types

1. 3-point

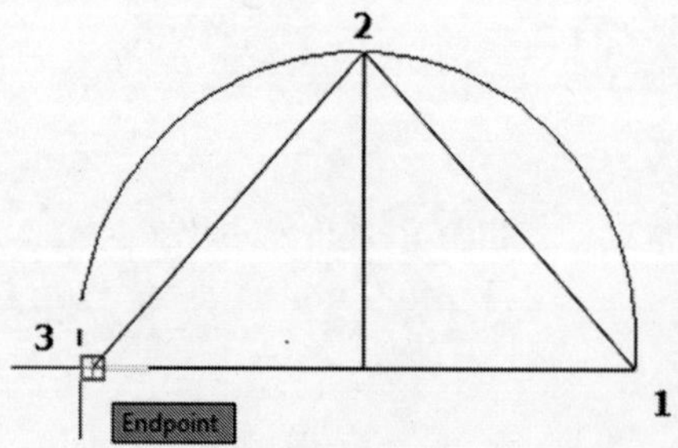

Figure 64 arc 3 point

2. Start, Center, End

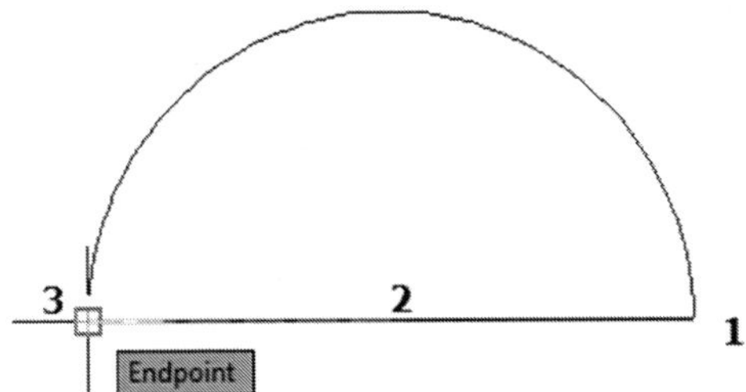

Figure 65 arc Start, Center, End

3. Start, Center, Angle

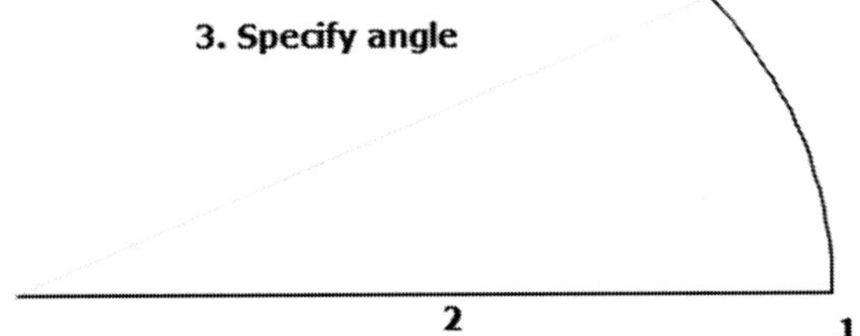

Figure 66 arc Start, Center, Angle

4. Start, Center, Length

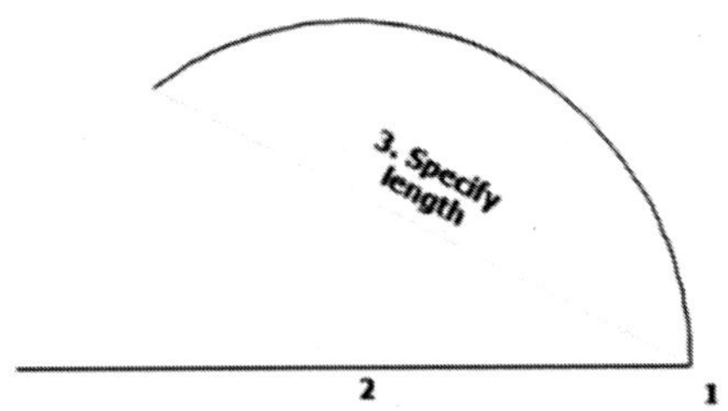

Figure 67 arc Start, Center, Length

5. Start, End, Angle

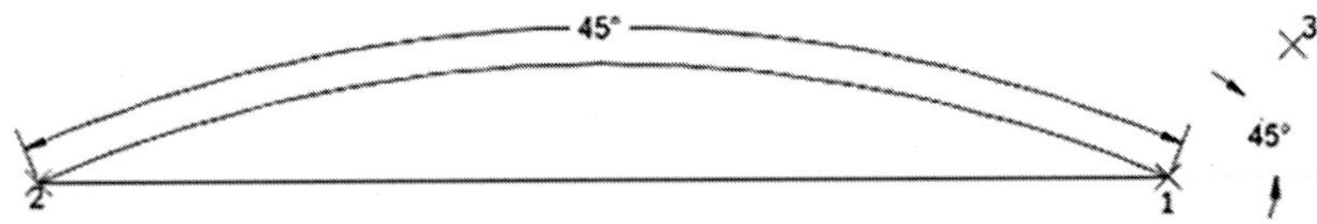

Figure 68 arc Start, End, Angle

6. Start, End, Direction

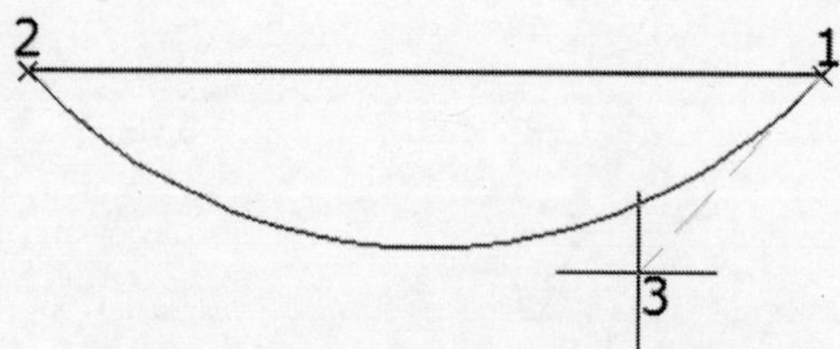

Figure 69 arc Start, End, Direction

7. Start, End, Radius

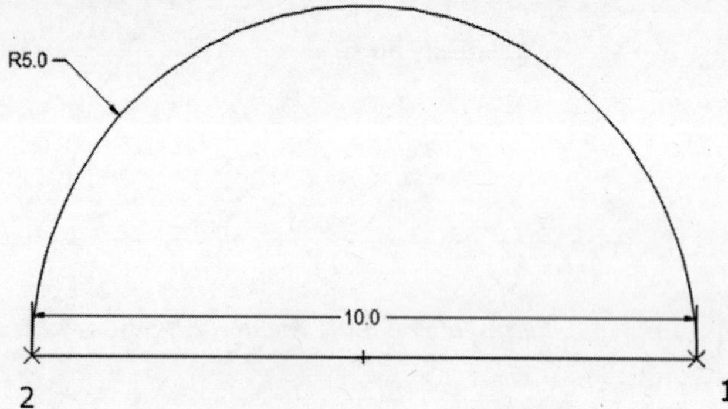

Figure 70 arc Start, End, Radius

8. Center, Start, End

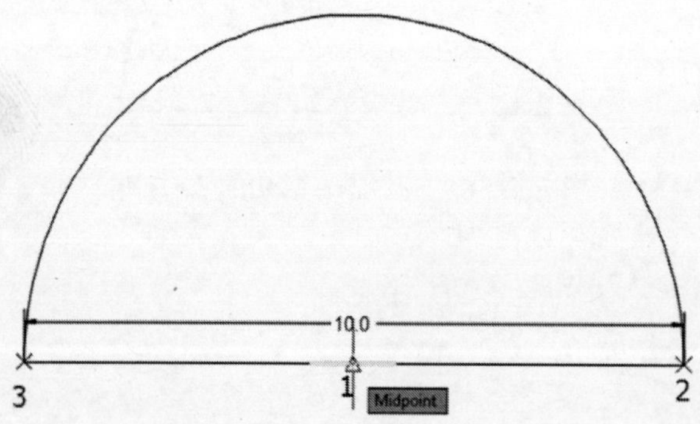

Figure 71 arc Center, Start, End

9. Center, Start, Angle

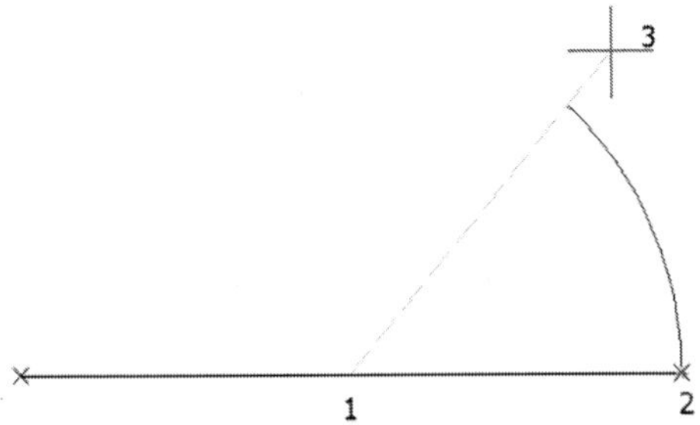

Figure 72 arc Center, Start, Angle

10. Start, Center, Length

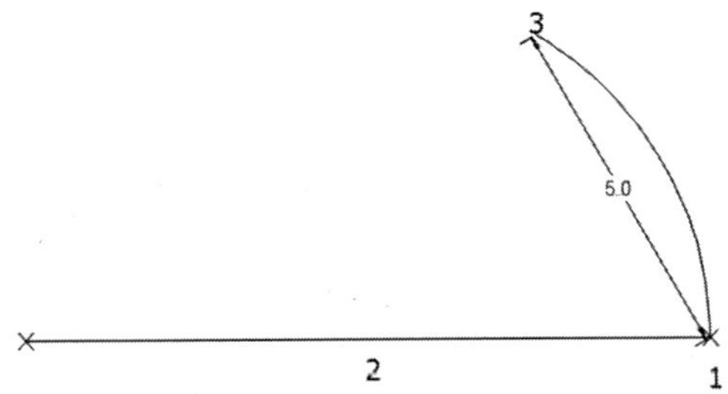

Figure 73 arc Start, Center, Length

11. Continue

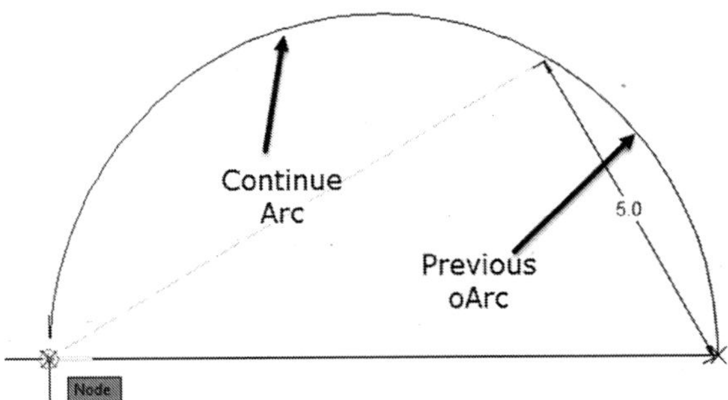

Figure 74 arc Continue

What do you mean by RECTANGLE?

It is a command by which we can make a rectangle having similar right angles and two sides are also similar.

Step 1: Ribbon: Home tab ➢ Draw panel Ø Rectangle

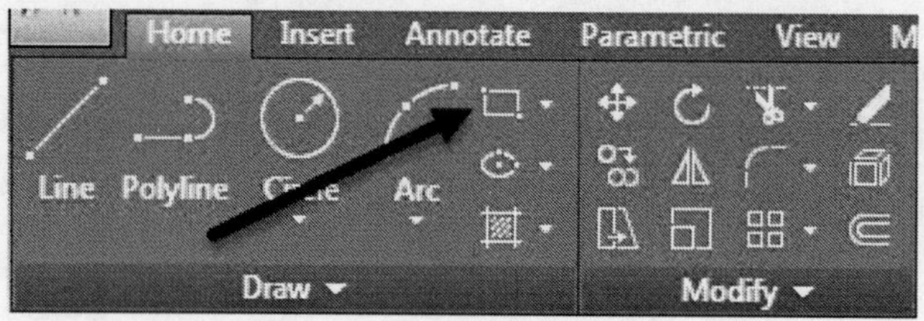

Figure 75 rectangle tool icon

OR

Command: REC Enter

Step 2: Specify first corner point or [Chamfer/ Elevation/ Fillet/ Thickness/ Width]: **Pick 1 point**

Step 3: Specify other corner point or [Area/Dimensions/Rotation]: **Pick 2 point**

Figure 76 rectangle

If you want to select an option like-

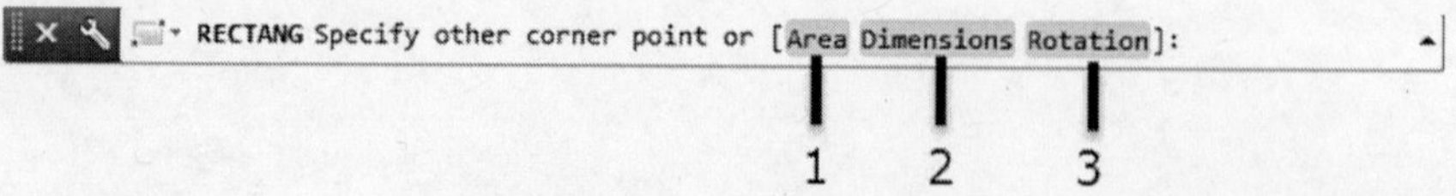

Figure 77 rectangle option

1. Area

It can be explained as the region inside the boundary of any 2D

Step 1: Command: **REC** Enter

Step 2: Specify first corner point or [Chamfer/ Elevation/ Fillet/ Thickness/ Width]: **Pick 1 point**

Step 3: Specify other corner point or [Area/Dimensions/Rotation]: **A** Enter

Step 4: Enter area of rectangle in current units: 500 Enter

Step 5: Calculate rectangle dimensions based on [Length/Width]: **L** Enter

Step 6: Enter rectangle length: **50** Enter

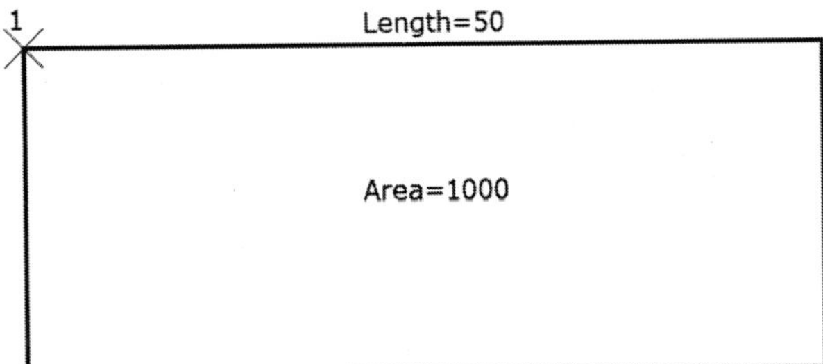

Figure 78 rectangle area

2. Dimensions

Creates a rectangle by using length and width values:

Step 1: Command: REC Enter

Step 2: Specify first corner point or [Chamfer/ Elevation/ Fillet/ Thickness/ Width]: **Pick 1 point**

Step 3: Specify other corner point or [Area/Dimensions/Rotation]: **D** Enter

Step 4: Specify length for rectangles: **50** Enter

Step 5: Specify width for rectangles: **10** Enter

Step 6: Specify other corner point or [Area/Dimensions/Rotation]: **Pick 2 point**

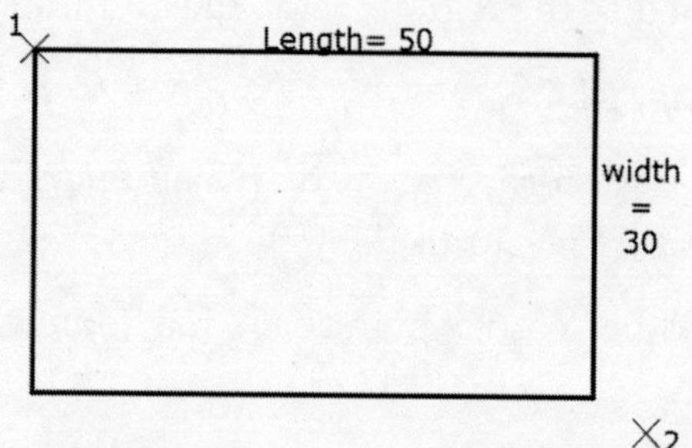

Figure 79 rectangle dimensions

3. Rotation

Creates a rectangle at a specified rotation angle.

Step 1: Command: REC Enter

Step 2: Specify other corner point or [Area/Dimensions/Rotation]: R Enter

Step 3: Specify rotation angle or [Pick point]: **45** Enter

Step 4: Specify other corner point or [Area/Dimensions/Rotation]: D Enter

Step 5: Specify length for rectangles: **50** Enter

Step 6: Specify width for rectangles: **10** Enter

Step 7: Specify other corner point or [Area/Dimensions/Rotation]: **Pick 2 point**

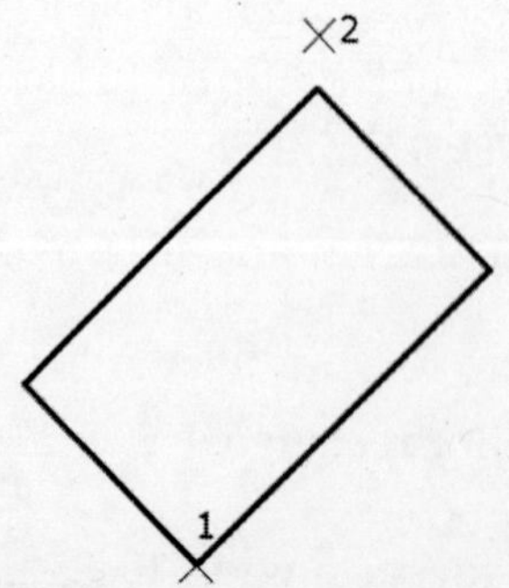

Figure 80 rectangle rotation

What do you mean by POLYGON?

It is a command by which we can create a plane figure having at least three straight sides and angles. Triangle, rectangle and pentagon can be created through this command. In AutoCAD we can construct a polygon object that has a minimum of three closed sides and maximum of 1024 sides. There are two type Polygon. First inscribed in the circle and second circumscribed about circle.

Step 1: Ribbon: Home tab ➤ Draw panelØPolygon

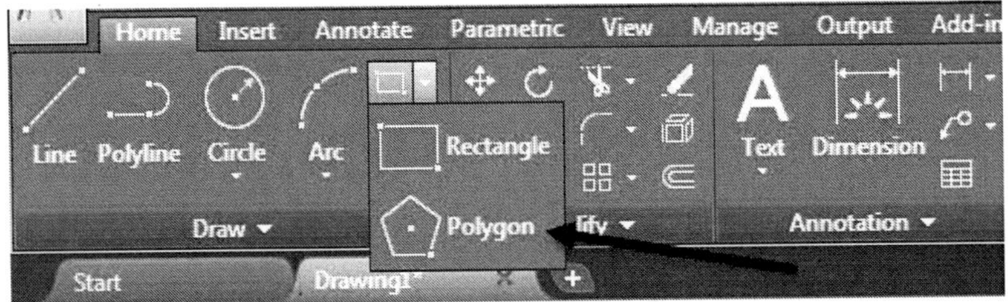

***Figure 81** polygon tool icon*

Command: POL Enter

Inscribed in the Circle

In this, the polygon lies inside the circle with its vertices on the circumference.

Step 2: Polygon enter number of sides: **8** Enter

Step 3: Specify center of polygon or [Edge]: **Specify a center point**

Step 4: Enter an option [Inscribed in circle/Circumscribed about circle]: **I** Enter

Step 5: Specify radius of circle: **12** Enter

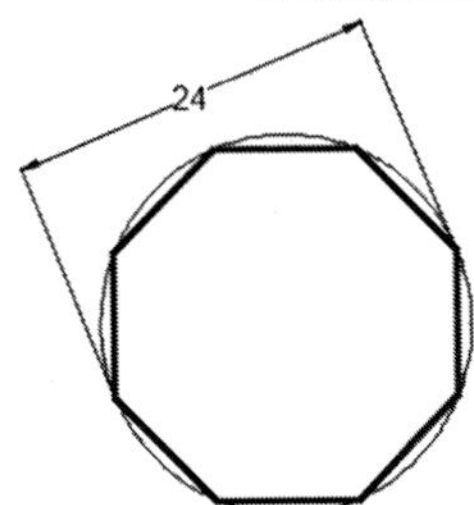

***Figure 82** Inscribed in the Circle*

Circumscribed about Circle

It is a polygon constructed such that circles lies within it and its circumference crosses through the mid-points of the vertices of polygon.

Step 1: Command: **POL** Enter

Step 2: Polygon enter number of sides: **8** Enter

Step 3: Specify center of polygon or [Edge]: **Specify a center point**

Step 3: Enter an option [Inscribed in circle/Circumscribed about circle]: **C** Enter

Step 4: Specify radius of circle: **10** Enter

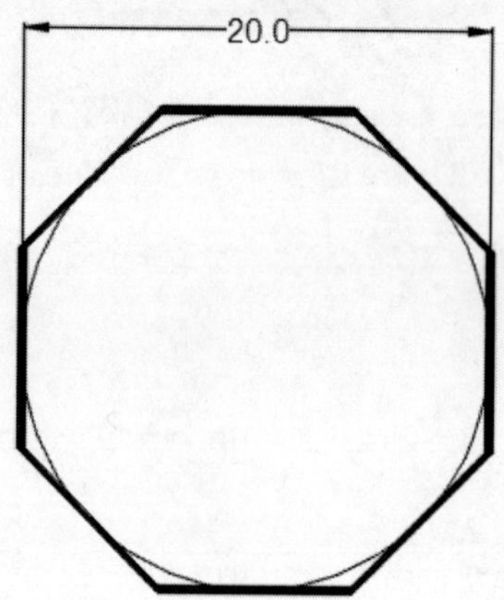

Figure 83 Circumscribed about Circle

What do you mean by ELLIPSE?

It is a command to create an Elliptical type arc. The first two points determine the location and length of the first axis whereas the third point fixes the distance from the center of the ellipse to the end point of the second axis.

Step 1: Ribbon: Home tab ➤ Draw panel ➤ ELLIPSE

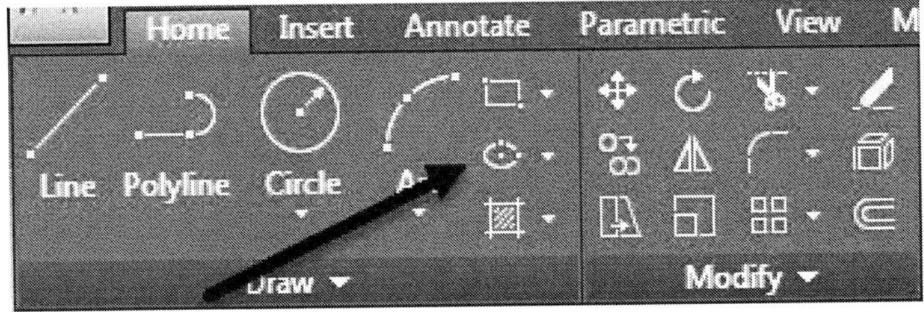

Figure 84 ellipse tool icon

OR

Command: EL Enter

Step 2: Specify axis endpoint of ellipse or [Arc/Center]: **Pick 1 point**

Step 3: Specify another endpoint of the axis: **10** Enter **(Give direction then enter value)**

Step 4: Specify the distance to other axis or [Rotation]: **10** Enter

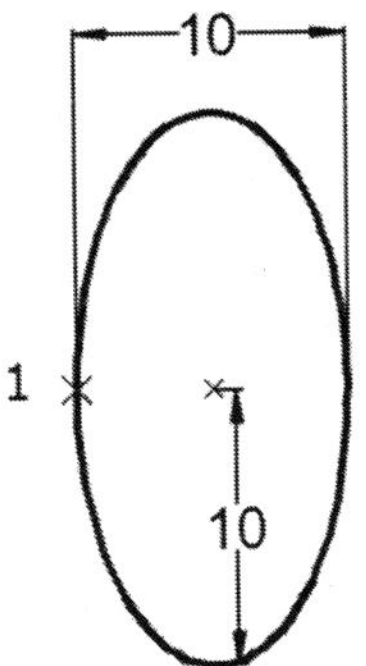

Figure 85 ellipse

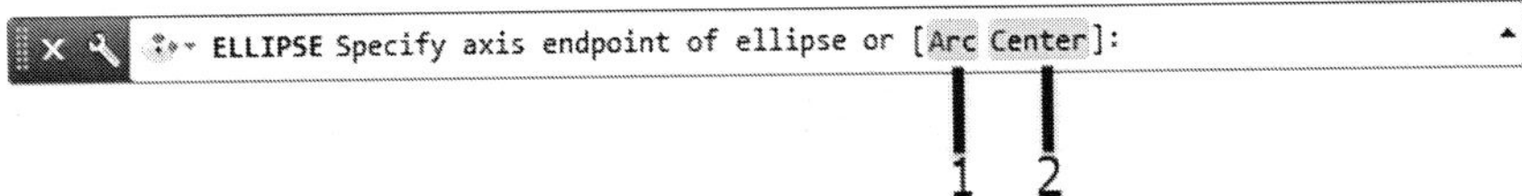

Figure 86 ellipse option

1. Arc

First of all. Specify first axis dimension then specify second axis dimension. Then specify start angle and end angle.

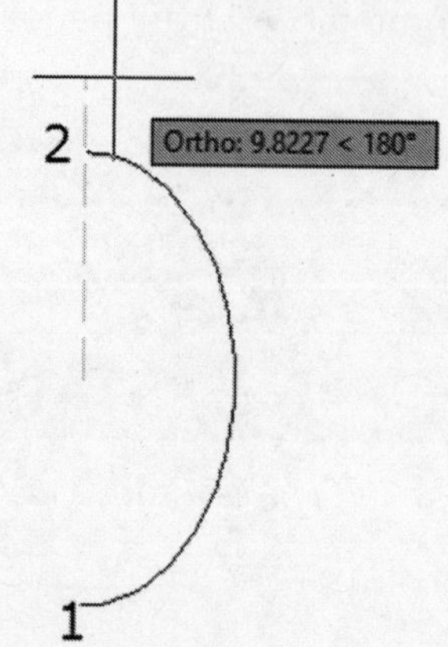

Figure 87 ellipse arc

2. Center

Specify center point of ellipse.

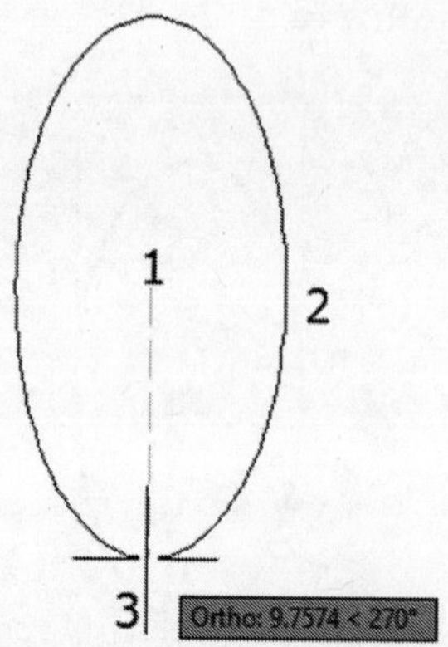

Figure 88 ellipse center

What do you mean by HATCH?

It is a command to create lines for section viewing and filling of an area of an object so that it is distinguished from other objects.

Step 1: Ribbon: Home tab ➢ Draw panel ➢ Hatch

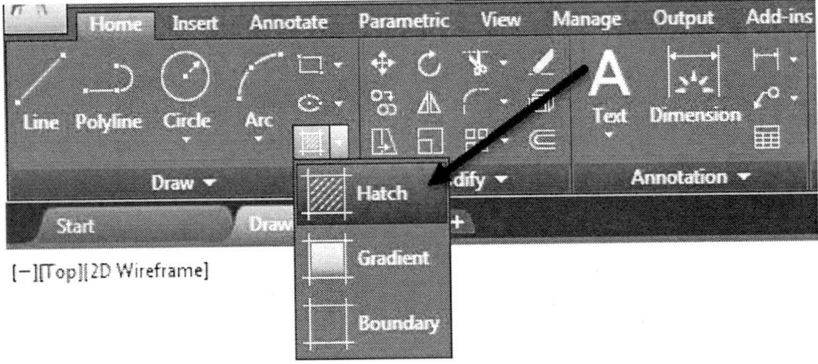

***Figure 89** hatch tool icon*

OR

Step 2: H Enter

Step 3: Give the command 'H' enter, a ribbon toolbar will appear.

Step 4: Click "Hatch Pattern" and select the type of pattern.

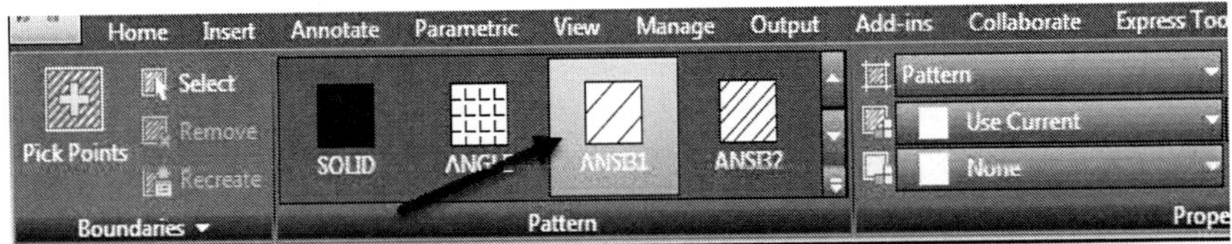

***Figure 90** hatching pattern*

Step 5: Click on pick points and select an area that is required to be hatched. (Remember only a closed area can be hatched)

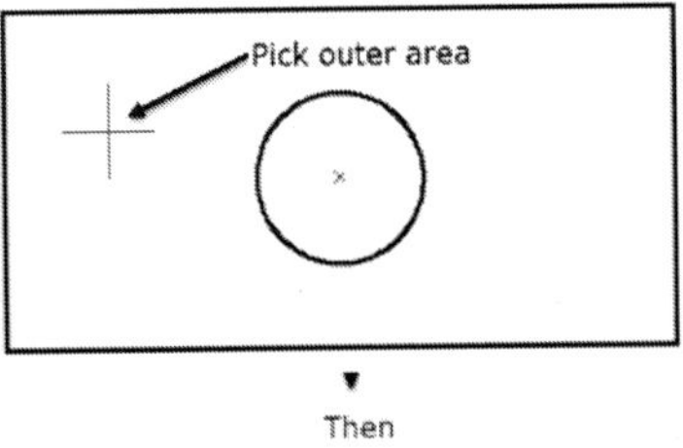

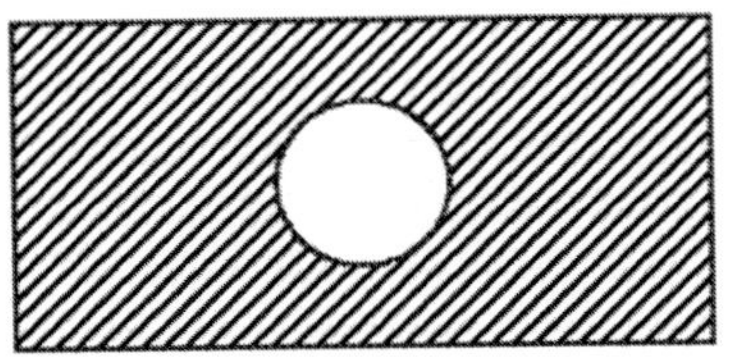

***Figure 91** use of hatch*

Step 6: In the ribbon toolbar, give the scale of the pattern and properties like color and background color.

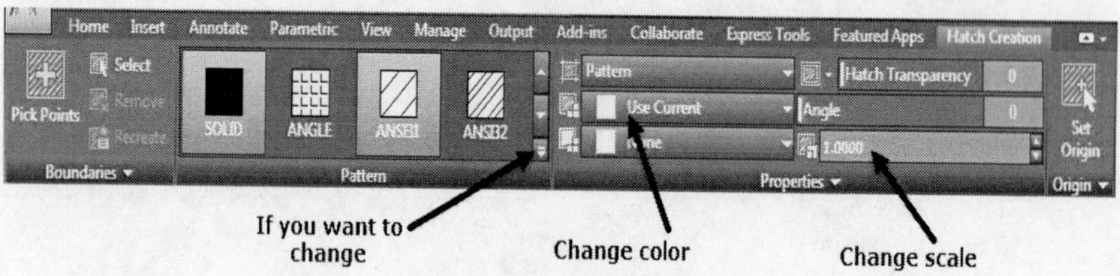

Figure 92 hatching setting

Figure 93 after hatching editing

What do you mean by GRADIENT?

Gradient command is used to create a gradient type of fill which means "two color types of filling." This two color types of filling is "transition filling."

Step 1: Ribbon: Home tab ➢ Draw panel ➢ Gradient

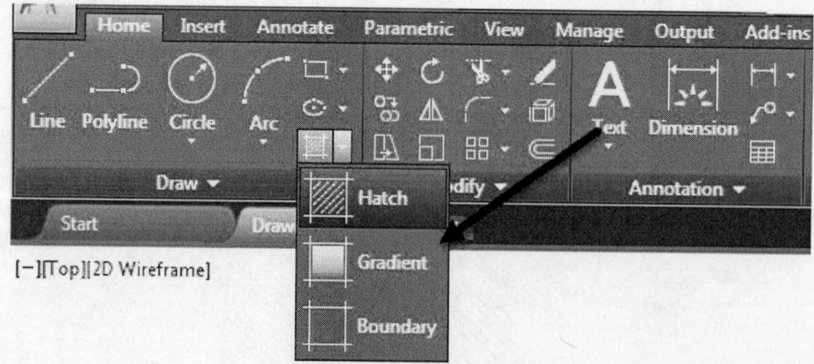

Figure 94 gradient tool icon

OR

Command: GD Enter

Step 2: Give the command 'GD' and press enter. A ribbon toolbar will appear.

Step 3: Select the gradient pattern from 'Hatch Pattern' option.

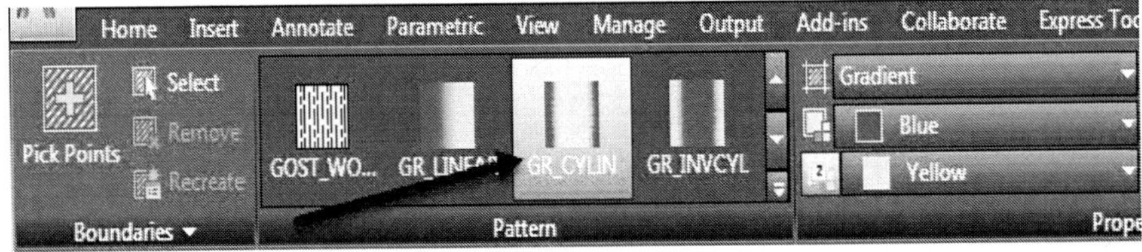

Figure 95 gradient pattern

Step 4: Give the required color, such as a single or a pair of two color.

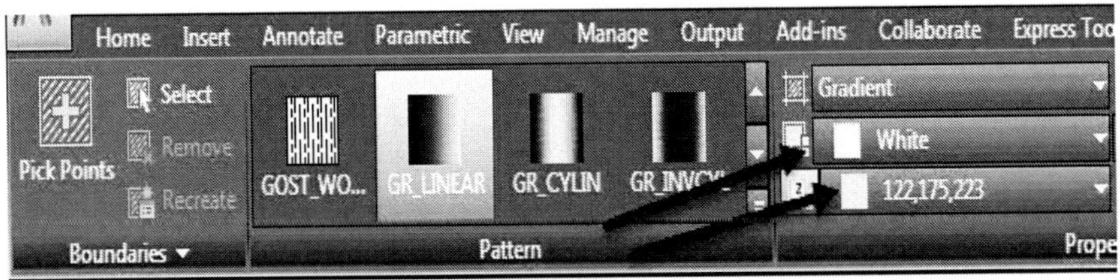

Figure 96 gradient color

Step 5: Click 'Pick Point' to select a point in a closed area.

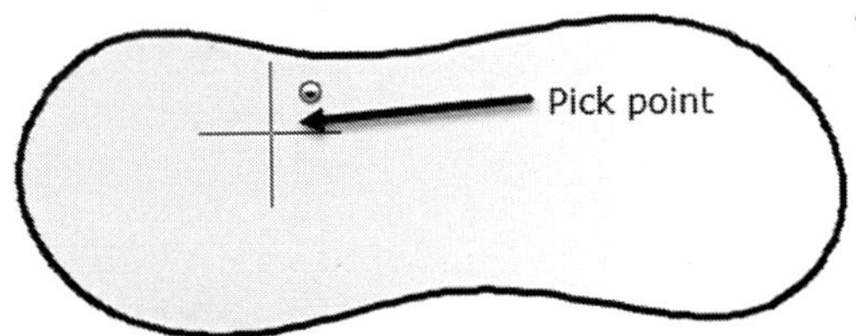

Figure 97 use of gradient

What do you mean by BOUNDARY?

Boundary command is used to create a region in an enclosed area.

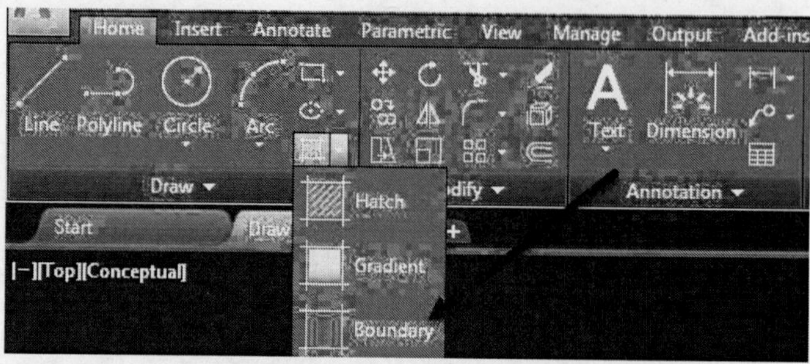

Figure 98 boundary tool icon

OR

Command: BO Enter

Step 2: On giving command 'BO' enter, a boundary creation tab appears.

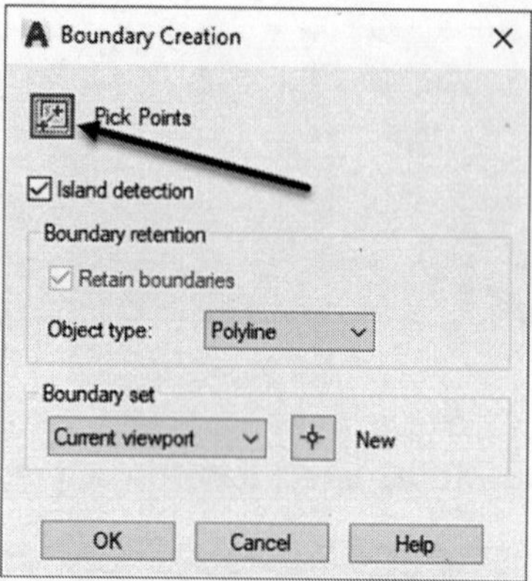

Figure 99 Boundary creation

Step 2: Click the option of 'pick points,' then select an enclosed point in an enclosed area that you need to make a boundary.

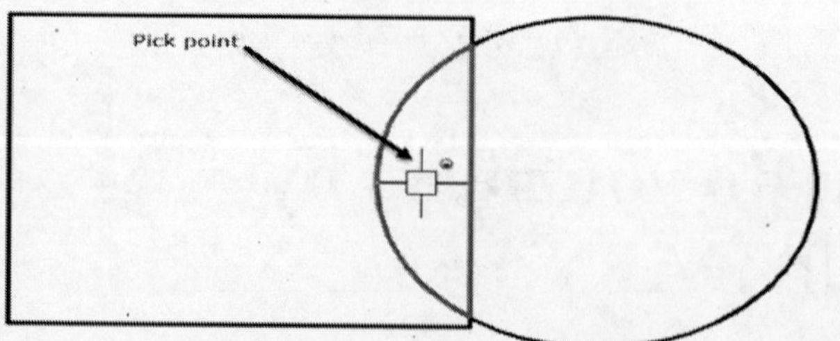

Figure 100 use of boundary tool

Step 3: Then enter.

What do you mean by RAY?

It is a command to create a line starting from a point to infinity in one direction. It can be used as a reference for creating other objects.

Step 1: Ribbon: Home tab ➢ Draw panel Ø Ray

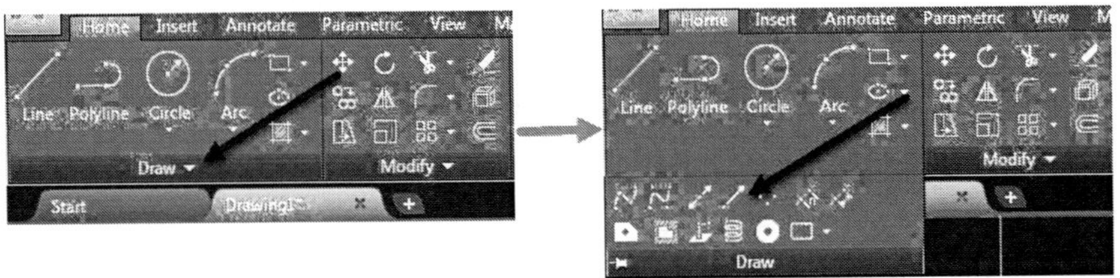

Figure 101 ray tool icon

OR

Command: RAY Enter

Step 2: Pick Start Point.

Step 3: Pick through point.

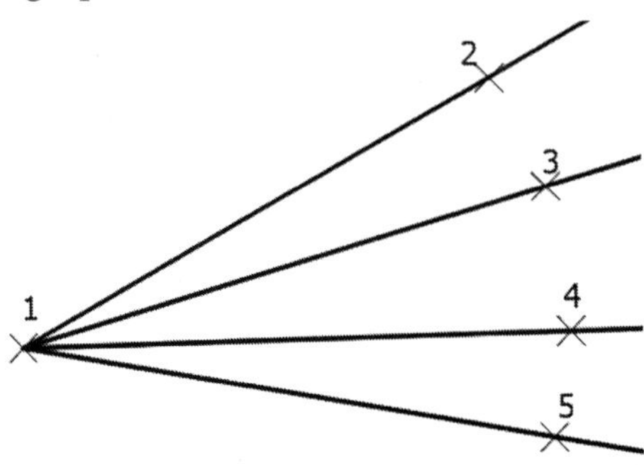

Figure 102 use of ray

What do you mean by POINT?

We used point to create point objects. With the help of this command, we specify the 3d location for a point, can snap objects, view current elevation (if we neglect the z axis.)

Step 1: Ribbon: Home tab ➢ Draw panel ➢ Multiple points

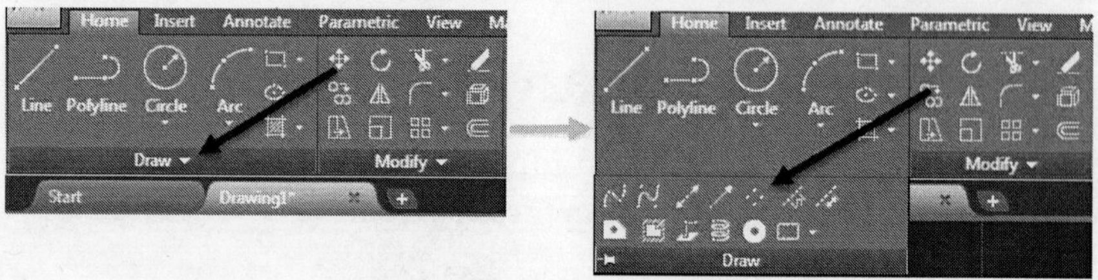

Figure 103 point tool icon

OR

Command: PO Enter

Step 2: Pick point.

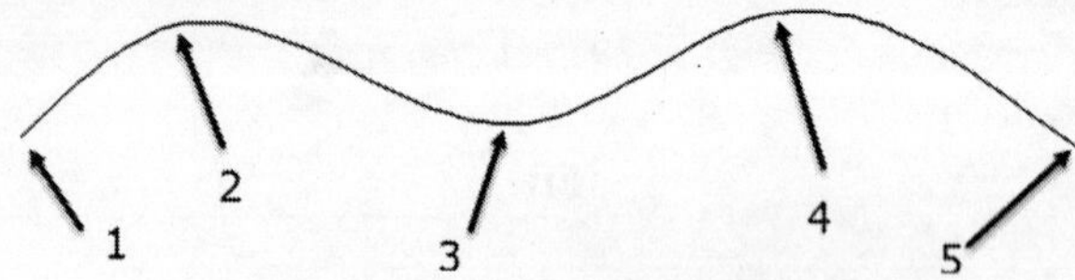

Figure 104 pick point

Step 3: Command: DDPTYPE (for point style).

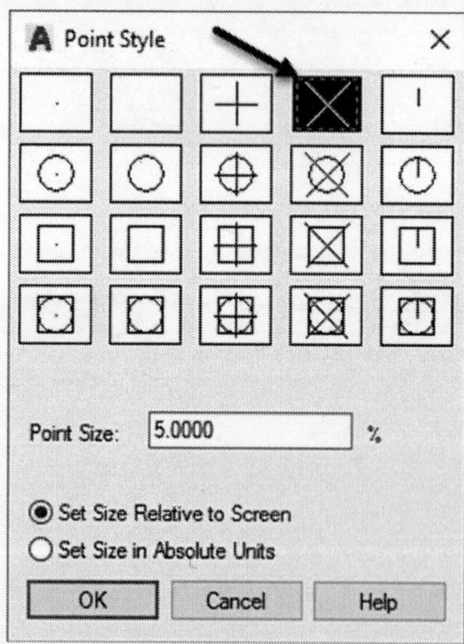

Figure 105 point style

Step 3: Select point style then ok.

Figure 106 point style result

What do we mean by DIVIDE?

When we use the command divide, it places a point along the line, arc, circle, polyline dividing it into the required number of segments.

Step 1: Ribbon: Home tab ➢ Draw panel ➢ Divide

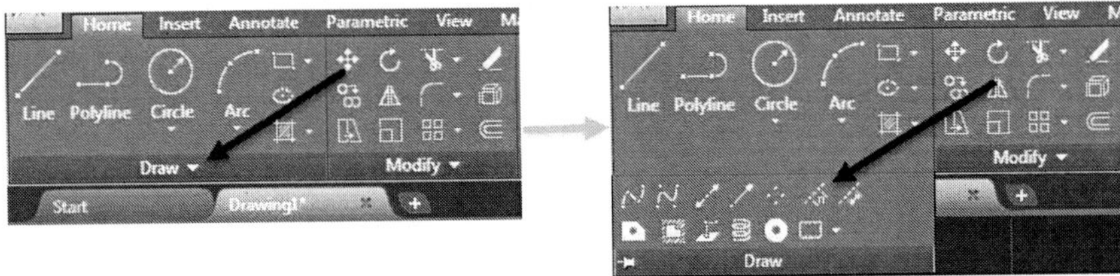

Figure 107 divide tool icon

OR

Command: DIV Enter

Step 2: Select object to divide: **Select object**

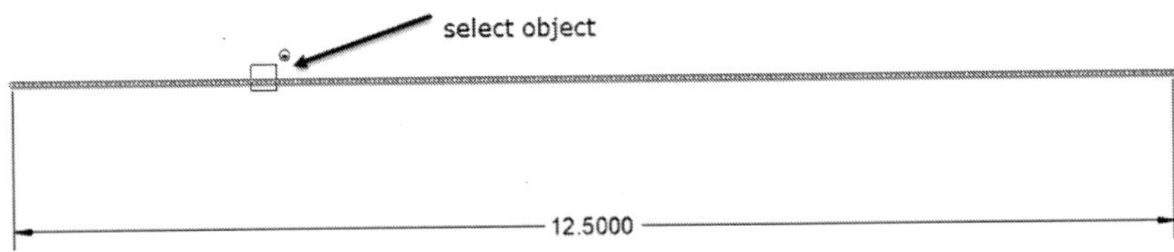

Figure 108 use of divide tool

Step 3: Enter the number of segments or [Blocks]: **5**

Step 4: Command: PTYPE Enter **(Select any point style and OK)**

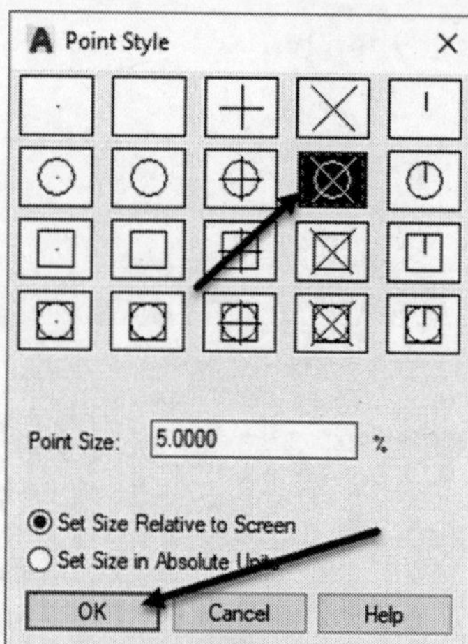

Figure 109 point style

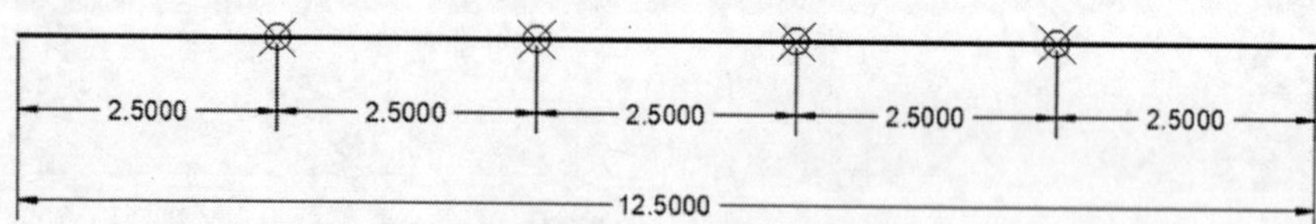

Figure 110 use of divide

When do we use MEASURE?

When we need to place points at specific required intervals along the line, polyline, arc or circle we use the command measure.

Step 1: Ribbon: Home tab ➢ Draw panel ➢ Measure

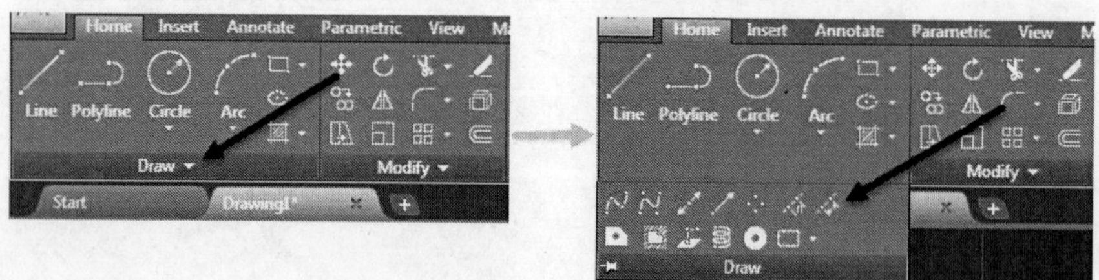

Figure 111 Measure tool icon

Command: ME Enter

Step 2: Select object to measure: Select object

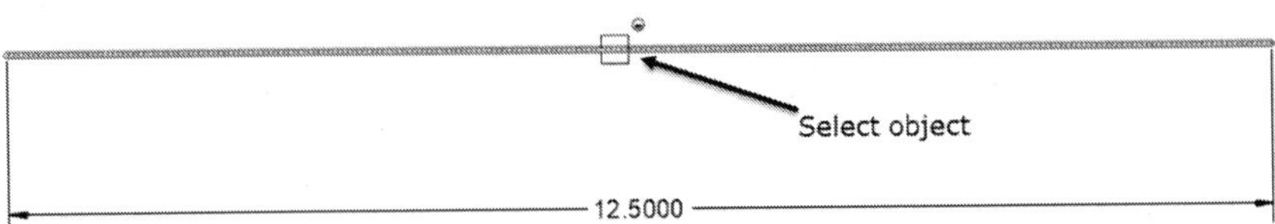

Figure 112 Select line

Step 3: Specify length of segment or [Block]: **3** Enter

Step 4: Command: PTYPE Enter **(Select any point style and OK)**

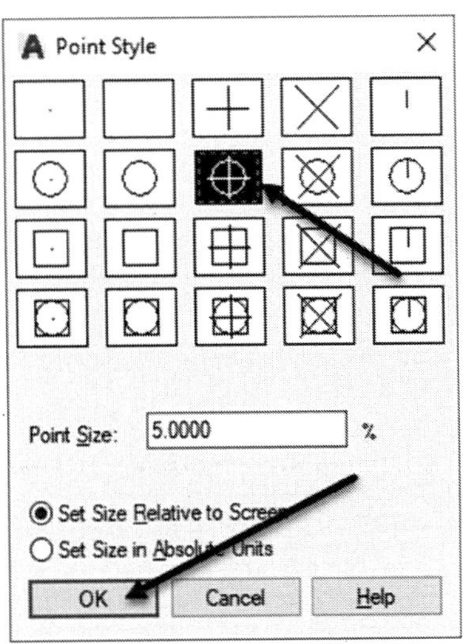

Figure 113 point style option

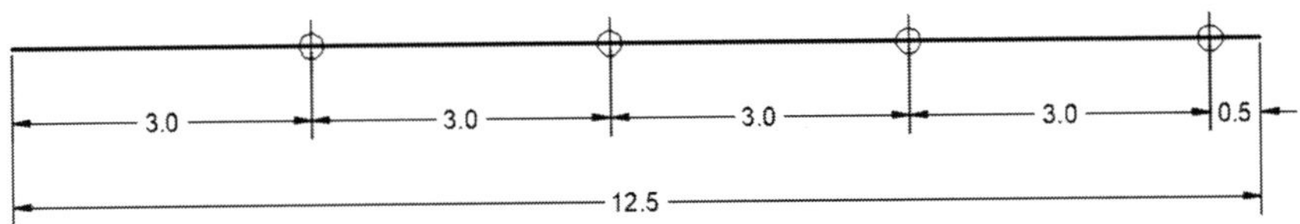

Figure 114 use of measure

What do you mean by REGION?

By using the command region, it converts a set of objects into a region object. Region is a 2D area made by different objects like arc, circle or line. It is used to convert 2d to 3d object.

Step 1: Ribbon: Home tab ➤ Draw panel Ø Region

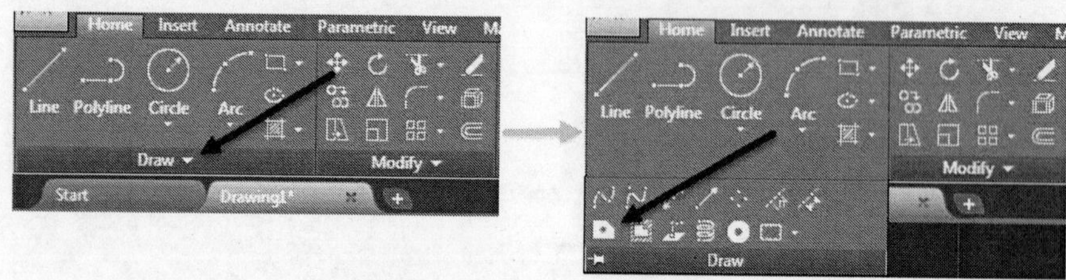

Figure 115 region tool icon

OR

Command: REG Enter

Step 2: Select object: select first object and second object then Enter

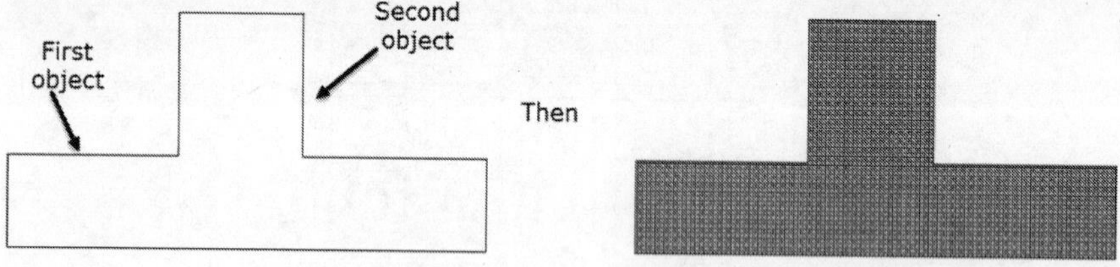

Figure 116 use of region

What do you mean by WIPEOUT?

It is used to hideout an object whenever needed. It can be of any cross-section area made by bounded sides such as polygon, rectangle, etc. The wipe-out area can be TURN ON for editing and TURNOFF for plotting.

Step 1: Ribbon: Home tab ➢ Draw panelØWipeout

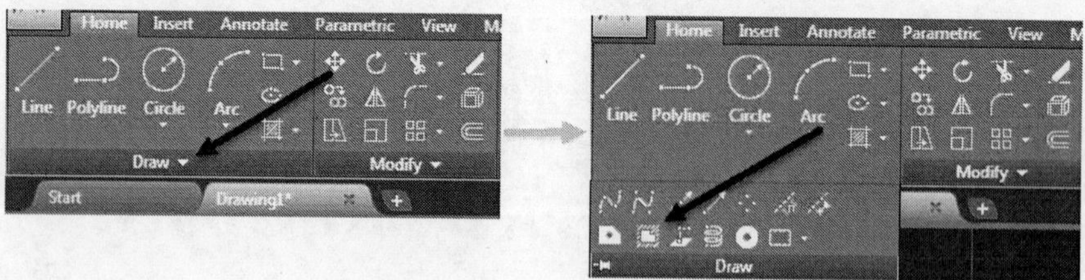

Figure 117 wipeout tool icon

OR

Command: WIP Enter

Step 2: Specify first point or [Frames/Polyline]: **Pick 1 point**

Step 3: Specify next point: **Pick 2 point**

Step 4: Specify next point or [Undo]: **Pick 3 point**

Step 5: Specify next point or [Undo/Close]: **Pick 4 point**

Step 6: Specify next point or [Undo/Close]: **C** Enter

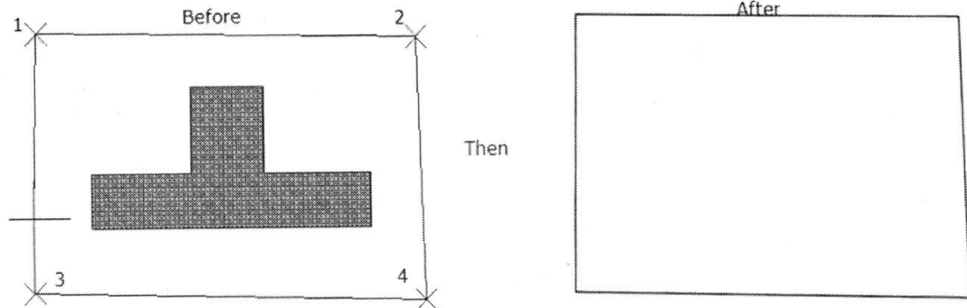

Figure 118 use of wipeout

What do you mean by 3D POLYLINE?

A 3D polyline is a connected sequence of straight line segments created as a single object. 3D polylines can be non-coplanar; however, they cannot include arc segments.

Step 1: Ribbon: Home tab ➢ Draw panelØ3D polyline

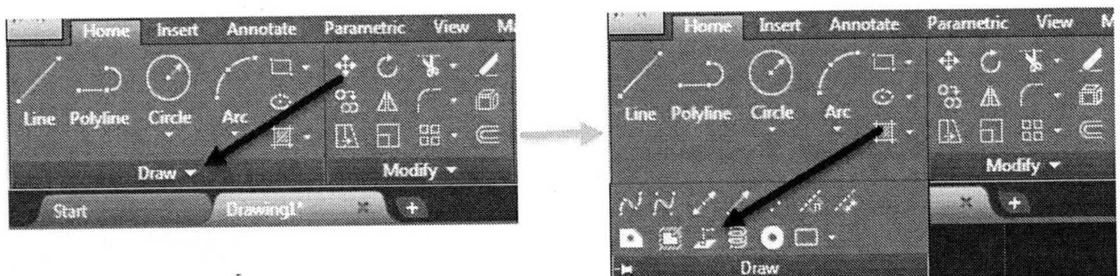

Figure 119 3d polyline tool icon

OR

Command: 3DPOLY Enter

Step 2: Specify start point of polyline: **Pick 1 point**

Step 3: Specify end point of line or [Undo]: **Pick 2 point**

Step 4: Specify end point of line or [Undo]: **Pick 3 point**

Step 5: Specify end point of line or [Close Undo]: **Pick 4 point** Enter

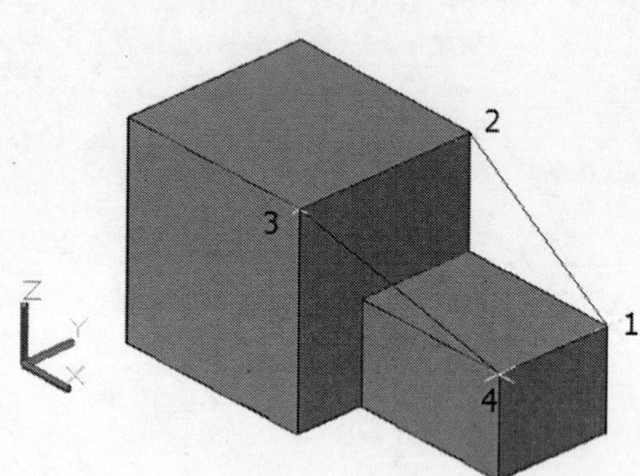

***Figure 120** use of 3D polyline*

What do you mean by HELIX?

Helix command creates a spring. Firstly give base radius, top radius and height as well as turns to the use of helix.

Step 1: Ribbon: Home tab ➢ Draw panel ➢ Helix

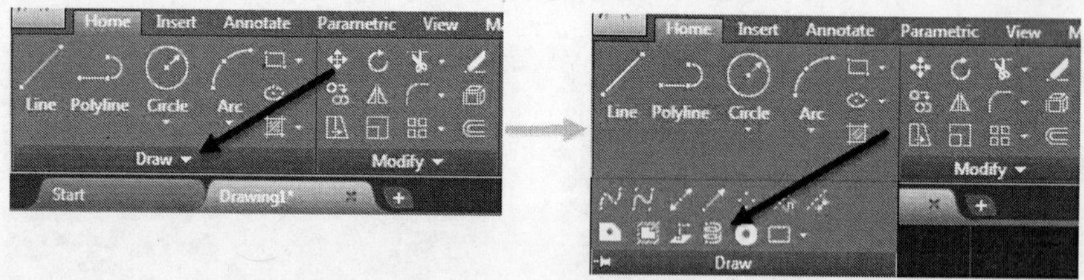

***Figure 121** helix tool icon*

OR

Command: HELIX Enter

Step 2: Specify center point of base: **Pick 1 point**

Step 3: Specify base radius or [Diameter]: **20** Enter

Step 4: Specify top radius or [Diameter]: **10** Enter

Step 4: Specify helix height or [Axis endpoint Turns Turn height tWist]: **T** Enter **(T for turns)**

Step 4: Enter the number of turns: **10** Enter

Step 4: Specify helix height or [Axis endpoint Turns Turn height tWist]: **15** Enter

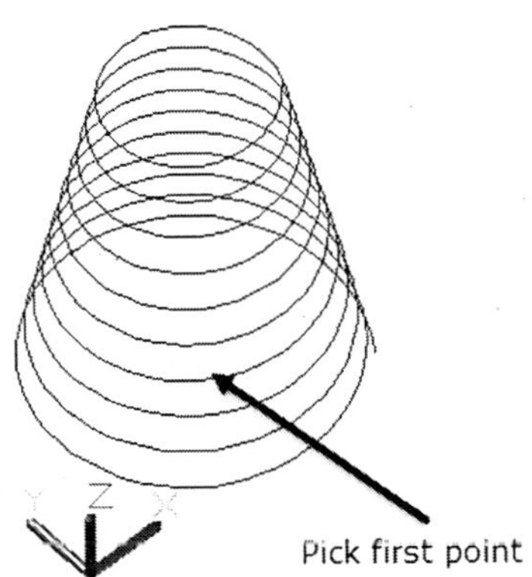

***Figure 122** use of helix*

What do you mean by REVISION CLOUD?

It is a command to highlight the area of the revision cloud. It is a series of arc formed to create a revision cloud.

Step 1: Ribbon: Home tab ➢ Draw panelØRevision Cloud

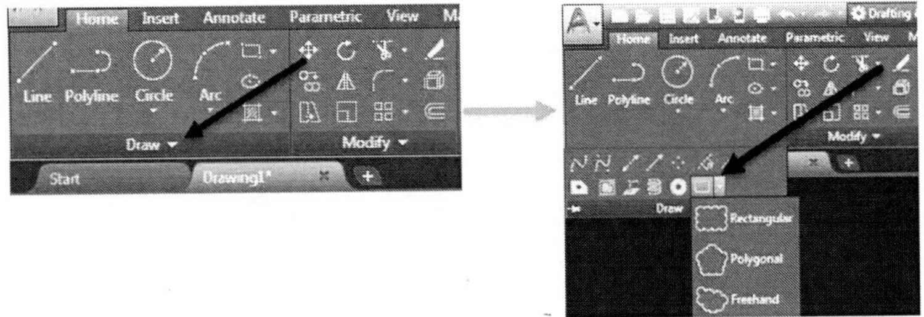

***Figure 123** revision cloud tool icon*

OR

Command: REVCLOUD Enter

Step 2: F Enter for freehand option.

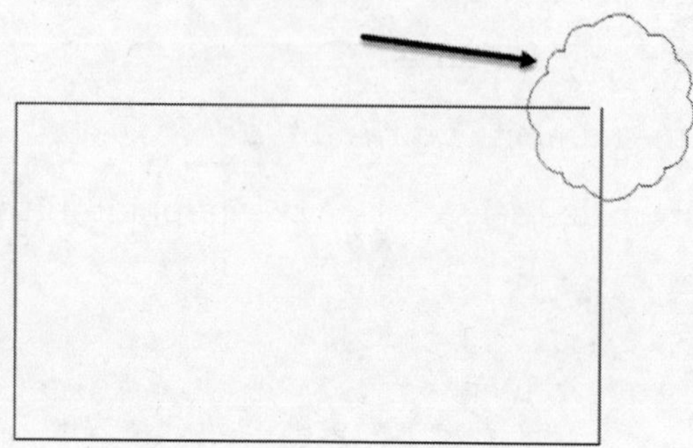

Figure 124 use of revision cloud

What do you mean by SOLID?

It is a command to create 2d filled polygons.

Step 1: Command: **SO** Enter

Step 2: Specify first point: **Specify a point (1)**

Step 3: Specify second point: **Specify a point (2)**

Step 4: Specify third point: **Specify a point (3)**

Step 5: Specify fourth point or <exit>: **Specify a point (1)**

Step 6: Specify third point: **Specify a point (4)**

Step 7: Specify fourth point or <exit>: **Specify a point (3)** Enter

Figure 125 use of solid

What do you mean by Fill?

It is used to control the filling of an object such as in the hatch, 2d solid and wide polylines. Then we need to use regenerate command to refresh the object. It is a "mode" command by which we can view the filling through on and no filling of objects through off mode.

Command: FILL Enter

FILL enter mode [ON/OFF]: Enter option

ON

By turning the fill mode on, the complete solid object is displayed. For the filling of a 3D object to be visible, its extrusion direction must be parallel to the current viewing direction, and hidden lines must not be suppressed.

Figure 126 fill on

OFF

By turning the fill mode off, only the outlines of objects are displayed. Changing Fill mode affects existing objects after the drawing is regenerated. The display of line weights is not affected by the Fill mode setting.

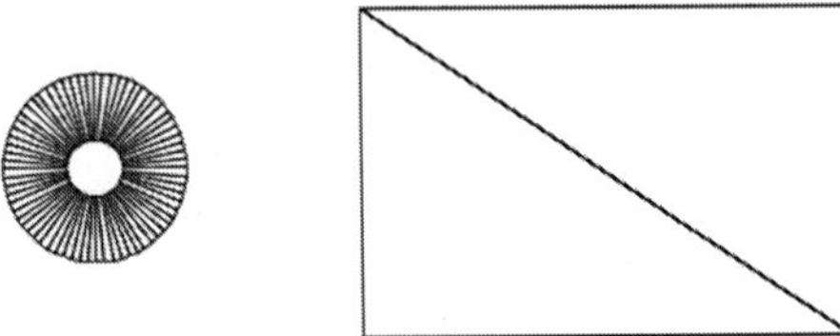

Figure 127 fill off

CHAPTER 4
Modify Tools

What do you mean by MOVE?

By using move we select an object, then select its base point and move it to the required position and direction.

Step 1: Ribbon: Home tab ➢ Modify panel ➢ Move

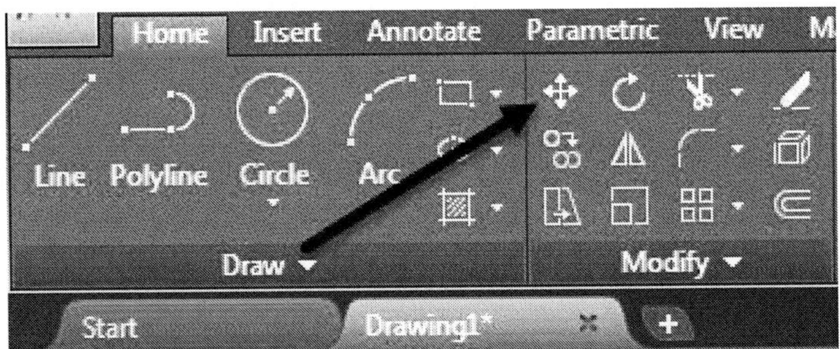

Figure 128 move tool icon

OR

Command: M Enter

Step 2: Select object

Step 3: Specify base point or [Displacement]: Pick base point

Step 4: Specify second point or <use the first point as displacement>:

Give direction then 50 Enter

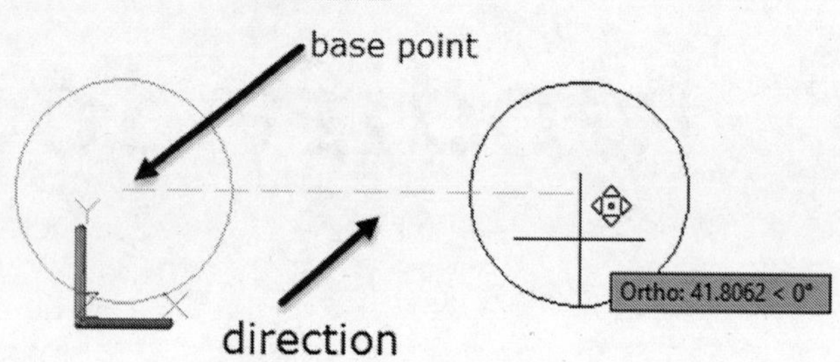

Figure 129 *use of move tool*

What do you mean by COPY?

When we need the same object at more than one place, we draw an object once and then use the command 'copy' to use the same object at other places.

Step 1: Ribbon: Home tab ➢ Modify panel ➢ Copy

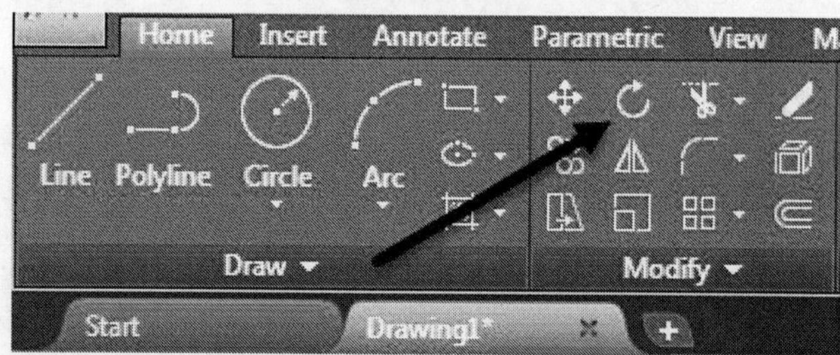

Figure 130 *copy tool icon*

OR

Command: CO Enter

Step 2: Select object Enter

Step 3: Specify base point or [Displacement/mOde]: Specify a base

Step 4: Specify second point or [Array]: **Pick first point**

Step 5: Specify second point or [Array]: **Pick second point**

Step 6: Specify second point or [Array]: **Give direction then 50** Enter

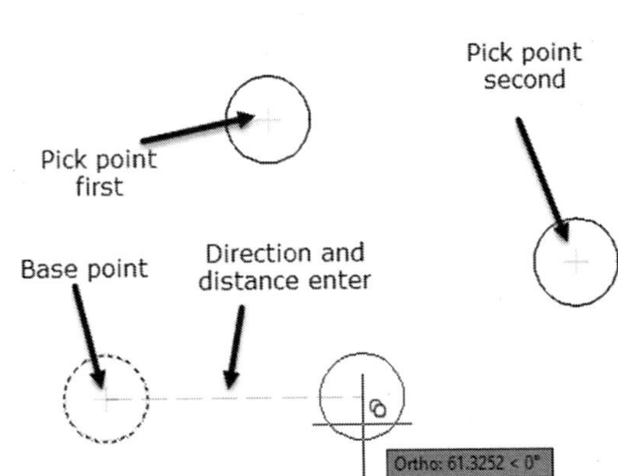

***Figure 131** use of copy tool*

What do you mean by STRETCH?

Command stretch allows us to move a portion of a drawing without distorting their connections with other parts of the drawing. But we cannot stretch Blocks, Hatch patterns, or Text entities.

Step 1: Ribbon: Home tab ➢ Modify panel Ø Stretch

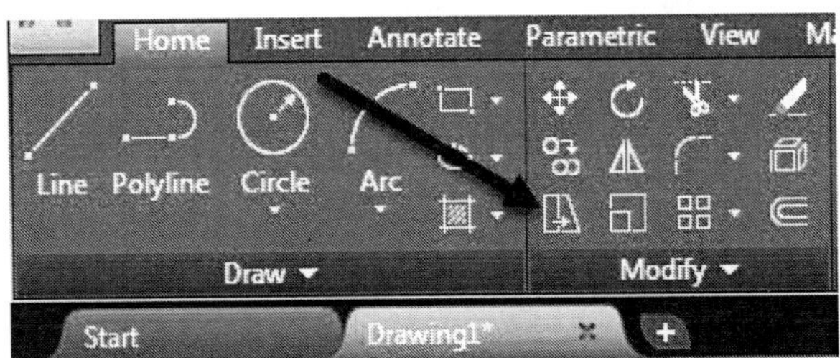

***Figure 132** stretch tool icon*

OR

Command: S Enter

Step 2: Select object then Enter

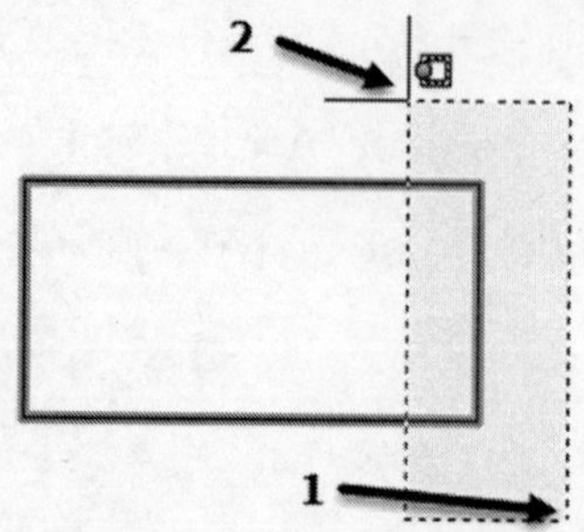

Figure 133 use of stretch

Step 3: Specify base point or [Displacement]: **Pick first point**

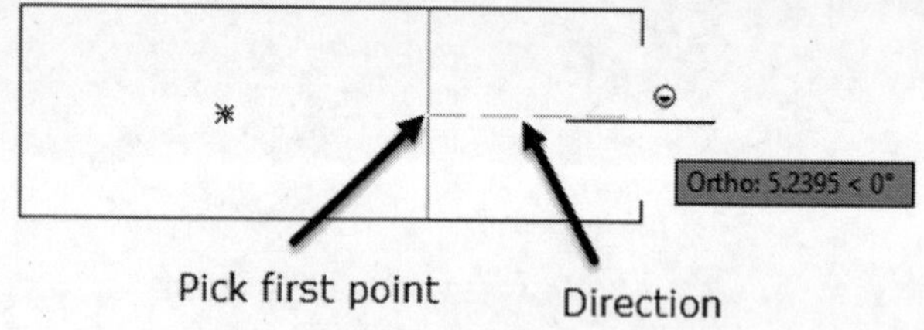

Figure 134 Stretch

What do you mean by ROTATE?

By using the command rotate, we can give inclination to an object from an axis.

Step 1: Ribbon: Home tab ➤ Modify panelØRotate

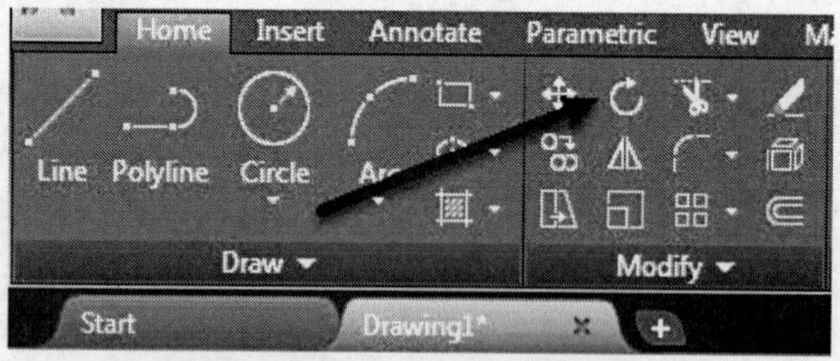

Figure 135 rotate tool icon

OR

Command: RO Enter

Step 2: Select object then Enter

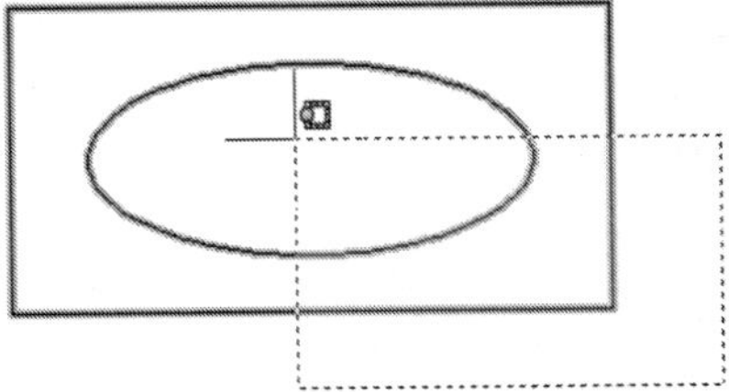

Figure 136 select object for rotate

Step 2: Specify base point: Pick point

Step 3: Specify rotation angle or [Copy/Reference]: **90** Enter

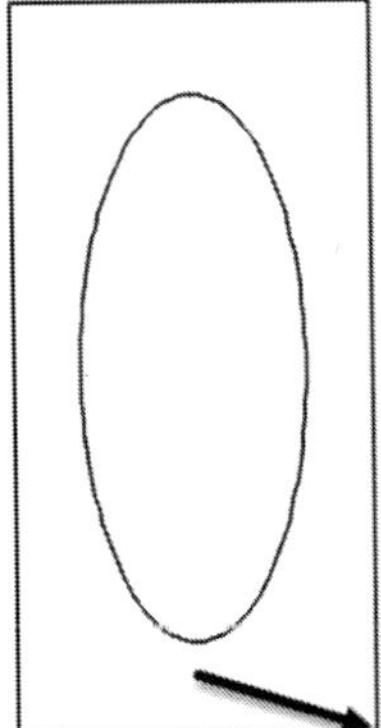

Figure 137 use of rotate

What do you mean by MIRROR?

We use the mirror command to create a reflection of a designated objected about a specified axis.

Step 1: Ribbon: Home tab ➢ Modify panel ➢ Mirror

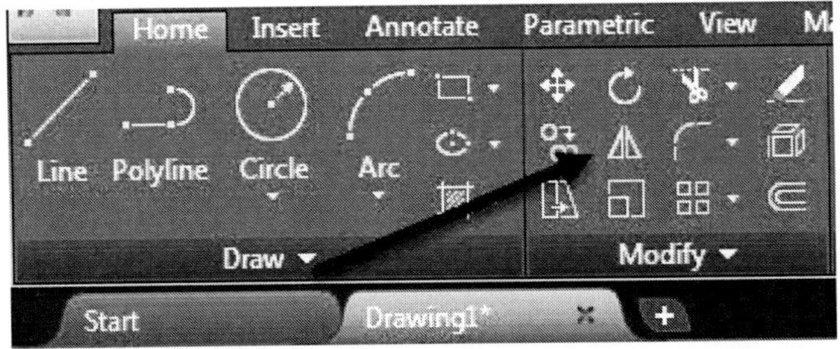

Figure 138 mirror tool icon

OR

Command: MI Enter

Step 2: Select object then Enter

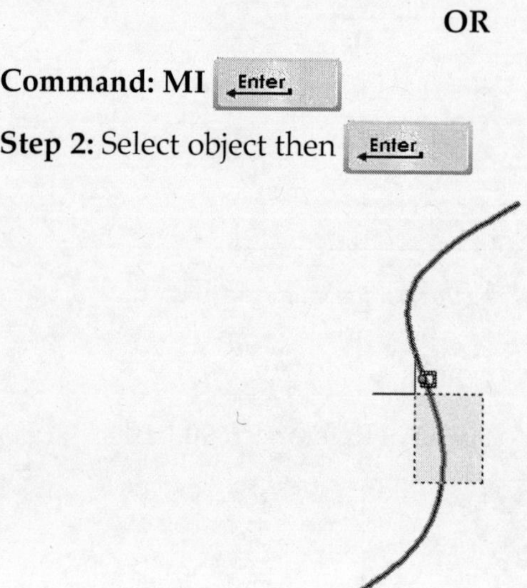

*Figure **139** select object*

Step 3: Specify first point of mirror line: **Pick first point**

Step 4: Specify second point of mirror line: **Pick second point**

Step 4: Erase source objects? [Yes/No]: **N** Enter

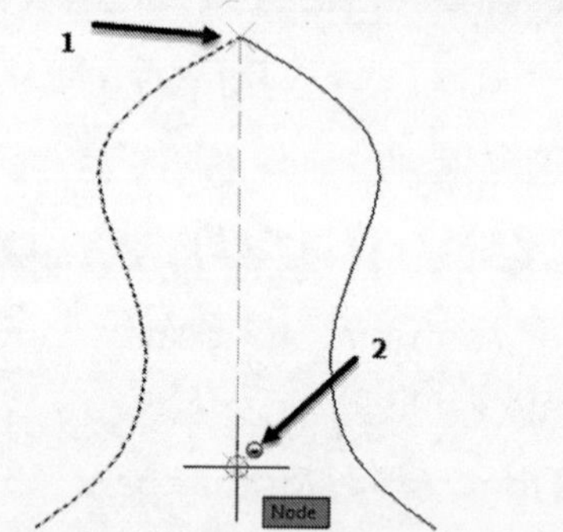

*Figure **140** mirror axis point*

What do you mean by SCALE?

By using command scale, we can alter the size of an object proportionally.

Step 1: Ribbon: Home tab ➢ Modify panel Ø Scale

Figure 141 scale tool icon

OR

Command: SC Enter

Step 2: Select object then

Step 3: Specify base point: **Pick base point**

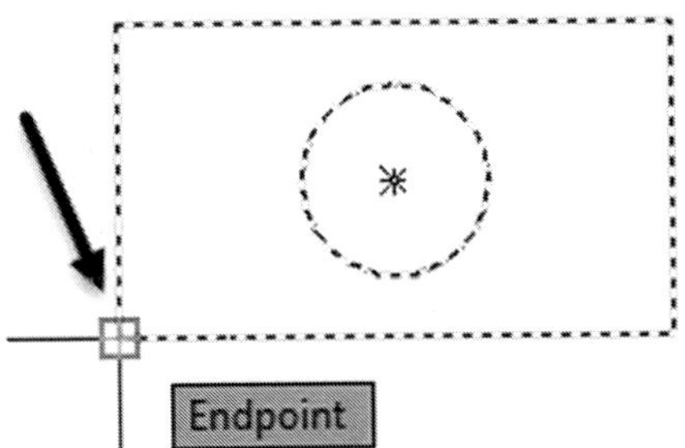

Figure 142 pick point

Step 4: Specify scale factor or [Copy/Reference]: R Enter **(R enter for reference)**

Step 5: Specify reference length: **1** Enter

Step 6: Specify new length or [Point]: **2** Enter

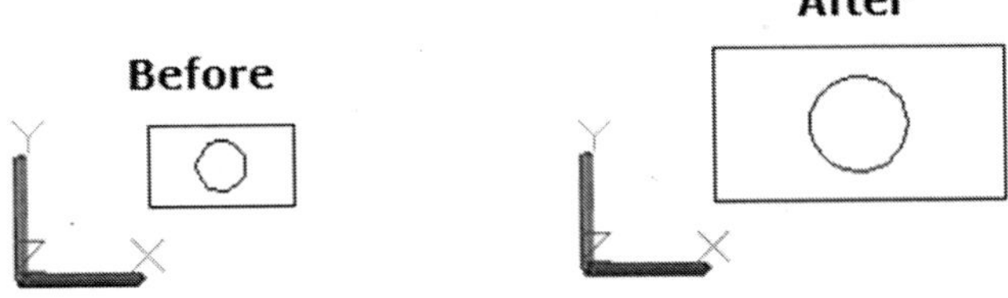

Figure 143 use of scale

What do you mean by TRIM?

We use command trim to erase a portion of the selected object that crosses a specified edge. In other words, we can use command trim on an object to meet edges of another object.

Step 1: Ribbon: Home tab ➢ Modify panelØTrim

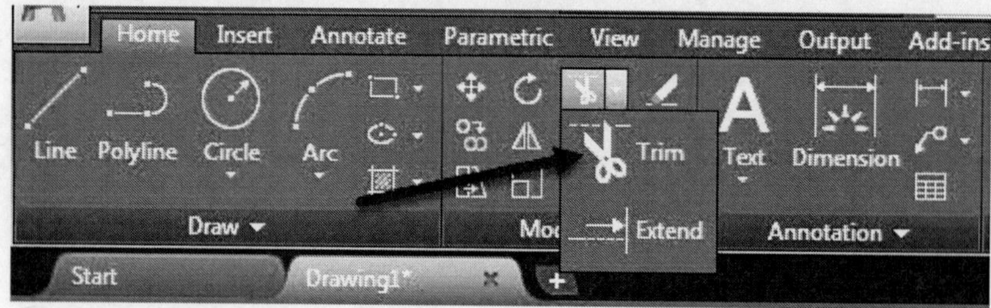

Figure 144 trim tool icon

OR

Command: TR Enter

Step 2: Select object or <select all>: **Select reference object then** Enter

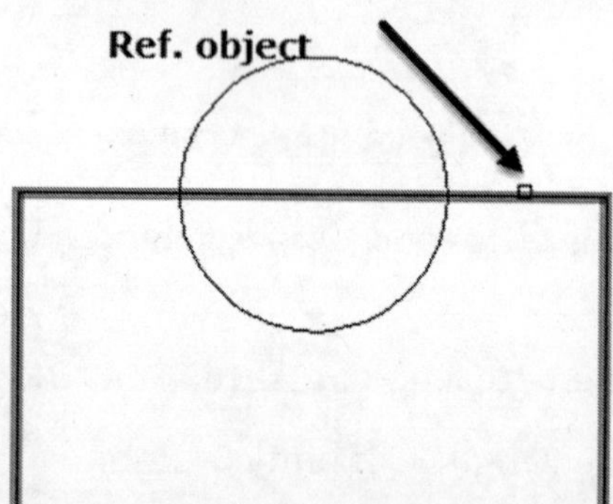

Figure 145 select ref. object

Step 3: Trim [Fence/Crossing/Project/eRase/Edge/Undo]: **Select trim object**

Figure 146 after trim

What do you mean by EXTEND?

By using the command extend, we can elongate or say lengthen a line, arc or polyline to meet a specified boundary edge.

Step 1: Ribbon: Home tab ➢ Modify panel ➢ Extend

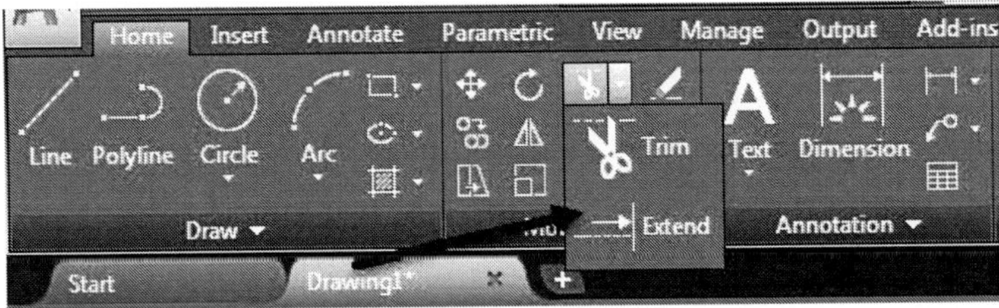

Figure 147 extend tool icon

OR

Command: EX Enter

Step 2: Select object or <select all>: **Select reference object then** Enter

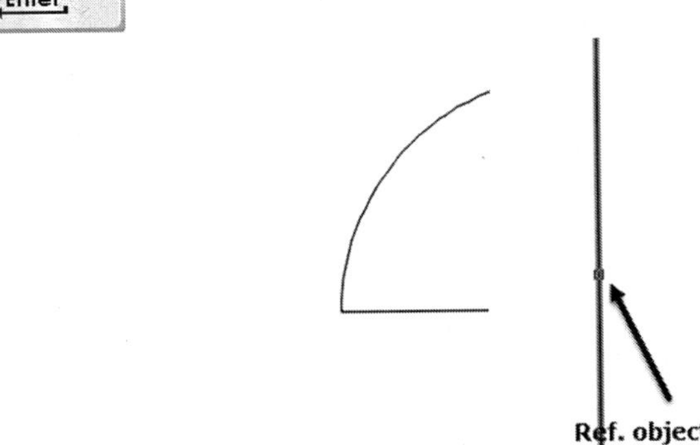

Figure 148 select ref. object

Step 3: Extend [Fence/Crossing/Project/Edge/Undo]: **Select Extend object**

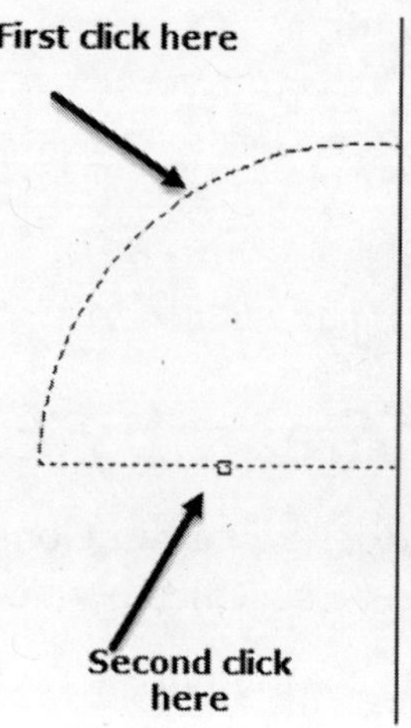

Figure 149 after extend

What do you mean by FILLET?

We use the command fillet when need to construct an arc of specified radius between two lines, arcs, circles or vertices of polylines.

Step 1: Ribbon: Home tab ➢ Modify panel ➢ Fillet

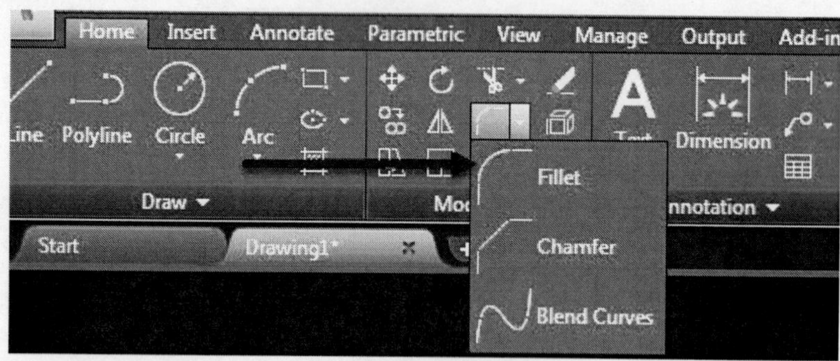

Figure 150 fillet tool icon

OR

Command: F Enter

Step 2: Select first object or [Undo/Polyline/Radius/Trim/Multiple]: **R** Enter **(R for fillet radius)**

Step 3: Specify fillet radius: **5** Enter

Step 4: Select first object or [Undo/Polyline/Radius/Trim/Multiple]: **Select first object**

Step 5: Select second object or shift-select to apply corner or [Radius]: **Select second object**

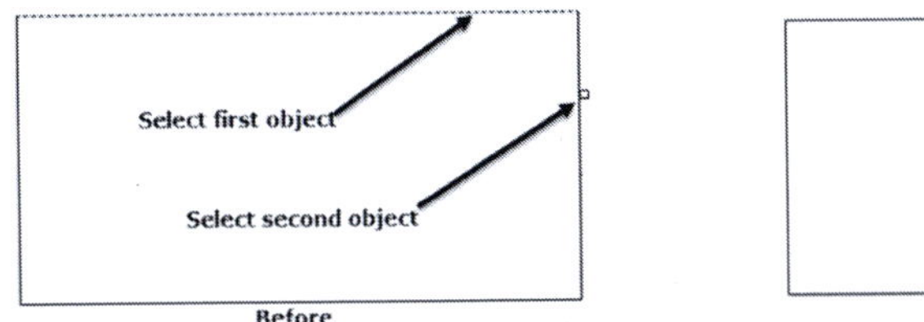

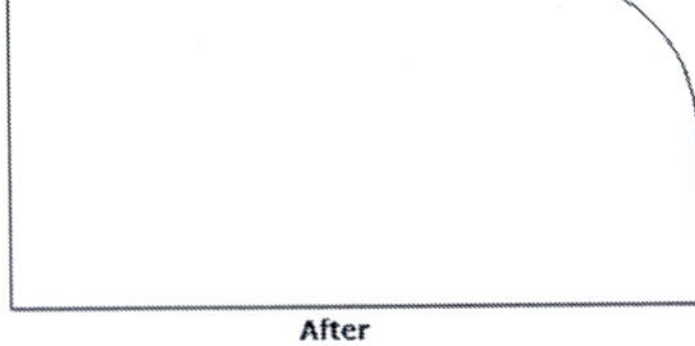

Figure 151 after fillet

What do you mean by CHAMFER?

A chamfer is an angled line connection, by using command chamfer we create an angled connection at the intersection of two lines.

Step 1: Ribbon: Home tab ➤ Modify panel ➤ Chamfer

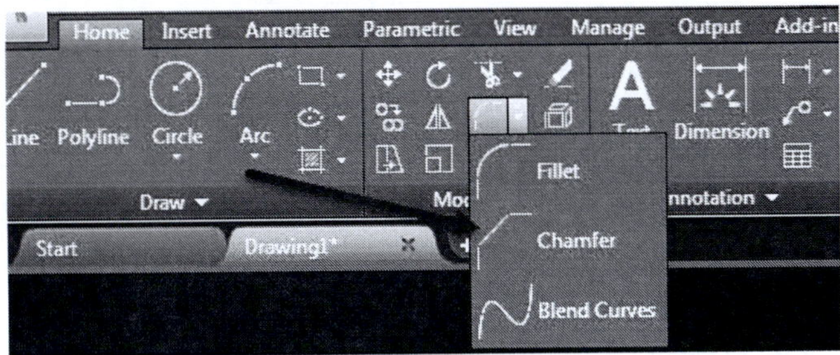

Figure 152 chamfer tool icon

OR

Command: CHA Enter

Step 2: Select first line or [Undo/Polyline/Distance/Angle/Trim/mEthod/Multiple]: **D** Enter **(D enter for Distance)**

Step 3: Specify chamfer length on the first line: **5** Enter

Step 4: Specify chamfer length on the first line: **10** Enter

Step 5: Select first line or [Undo/Polyline/Distance/Angle/Trim/mEthod/Multiple]: **Select first object**

Step 6: Select second line or shift-select to apply corner or [Distance/Angle/Method]: **Select second object**

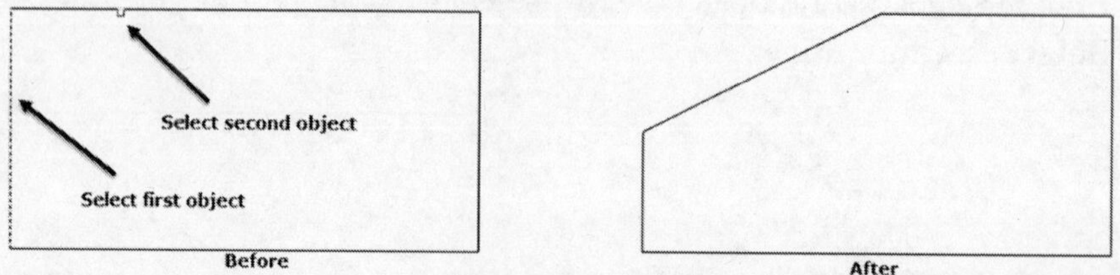

***Figure 153** after chamfer*

When do we use BLEND CURVES?

When we need to join two lines or curves, we use blend curves. It creates a spline between the selected object, shape of the spline depends upon specified points while the length of the selected object remains unchanged.

Step 1: Ribbon: Home tab ➤ Modify panel ➤ Chamfer

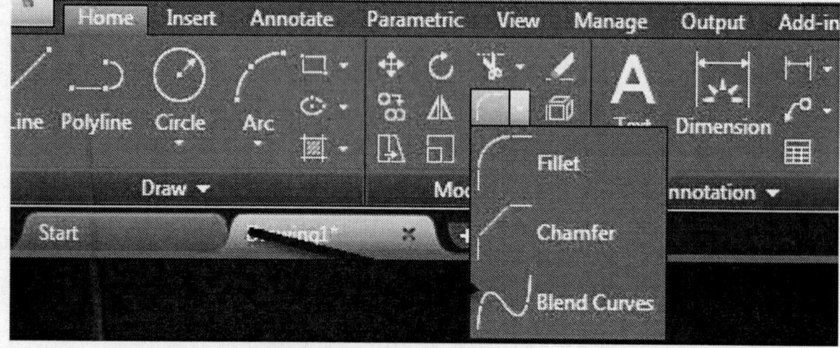

***Figure 154** blend tool icon*

OR

Command: BLEND Enter

Step 2: Select first object or [CONtinuity]: **Select first object**

Step 3: Select second object: **Select second object**

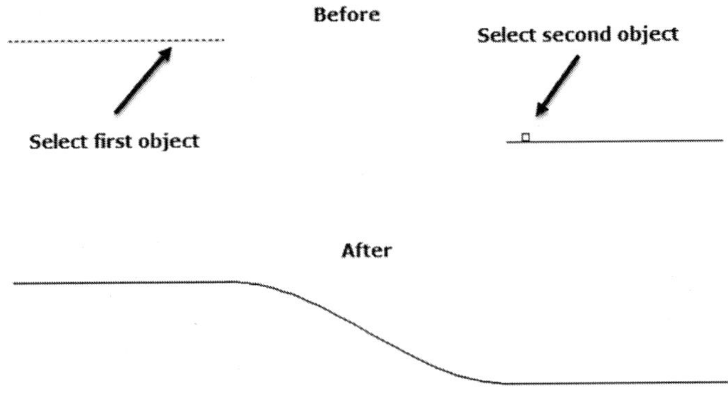

Figure 155 use of blend

What do you mean by ARRAY?

We use command array for creating a series of object in a continuous manner and the required number of rectangular, polar (circular) or any selected path.

Ribbon: Home tab ➢ Modify panel ➢ Array

Figure 156 array tool icon

Rectangular

Rectangular Array can be copied to multiple objects. Rectangular Array object is a copy of the row and column where we can give the distance between rows and columns.

Step 1: Command: AR Enter

Step 2: Select object: **Select rectangle** Enter

Step 3: Enter array type [Rectangular/PAth/POlar]: **R** Enter

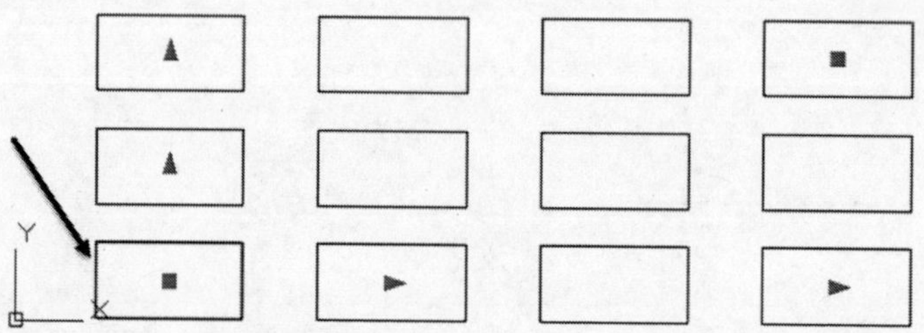

Figure 157 use of rectangle array

If you want to change the column distance and row distance or number

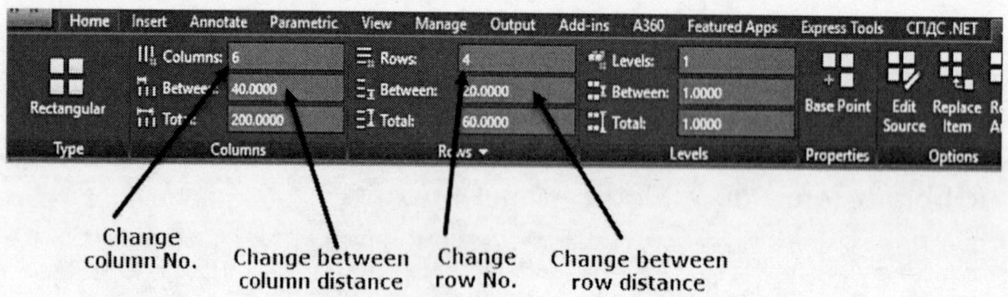

Figure 158 rectangle array setting

Then

Figure 159 after editing

Path

Polar Array of objects in multiple copies can be made in a circular pattern. Polor Array by the center point and the number and angle of the object copy is given to the use of Polor Array. Copy of which may be circular object.

Step 1: Command: AR Enter

Step 2: Select object: **Select object** Enter

Step 3: Enter array type [Rectangular/PAth/POlar]: **PA** Enter

Step 4: Select curve path**: Select path**

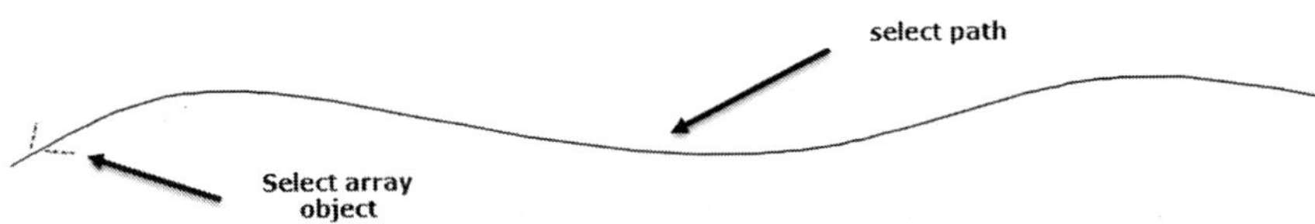

Figure 160 use of path array

If you want to change the distance or number

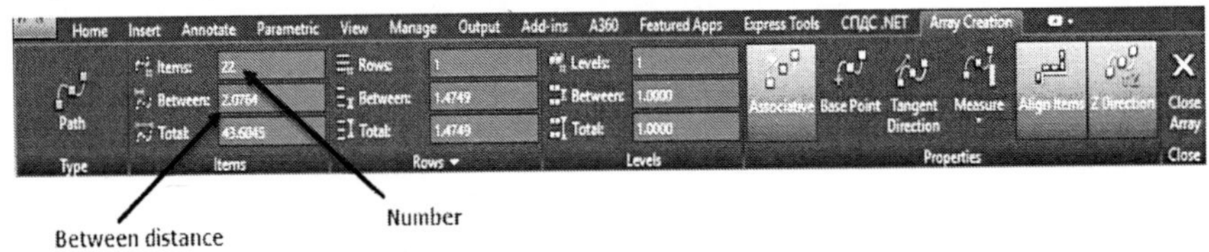

Figure 161 path array setting

Then

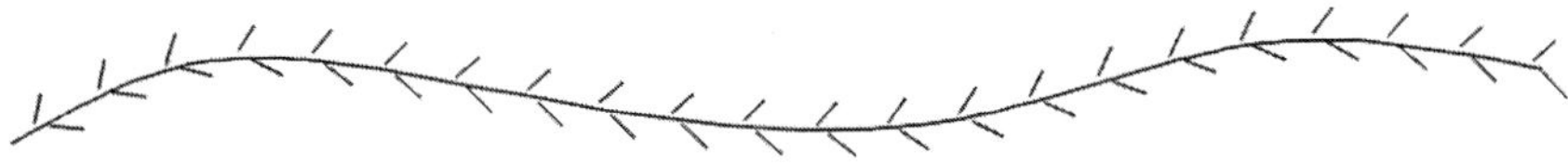

Figure 162 use of path array

Polar

Array path, the path of an object like any other object copies. The second object path which does work. The Curve is the path.

Step 1: Command: AR Enter

Step 2: Select object: **Select object** Enter

Step 3: Enter array type [Rectangular/PAth/POlar]: **PO** Enter

Step 4: Specify center point of array [Base point Axis of rotation]: **Pick center point**

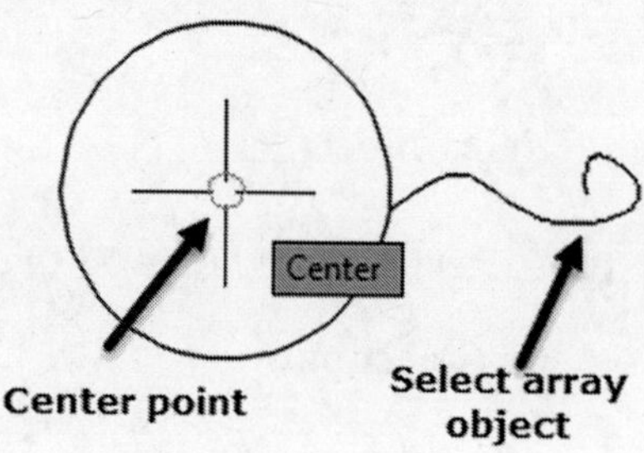

Figure 163 *use of polar array*

If you want change Angle or number

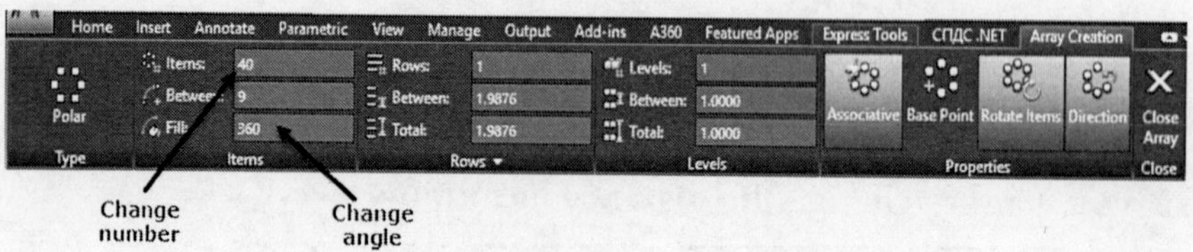

Figure 164 *polar array setting*

Then

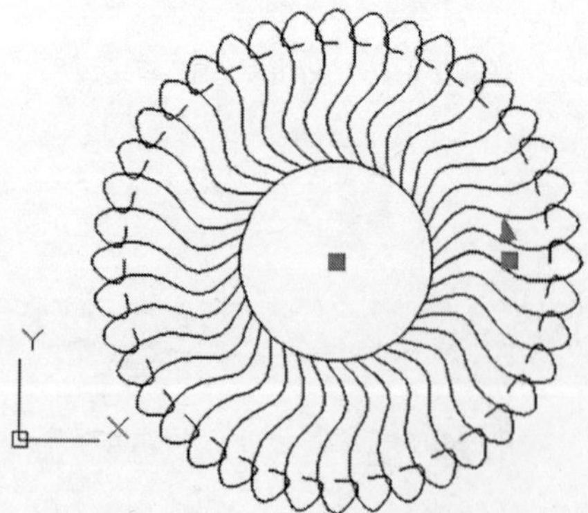

Figure 165 *after polar array editing*

What do you mean by EXPLODE?

Command Explode breaks a block, hatch pattern or dimension into its constituent entities and polyline into a series of straight lines. By using explode, we can also modify the properties of a particular object in block, etc.

Step 1: Ribbon: Home tab ➢ Modify panel ➢ Explode

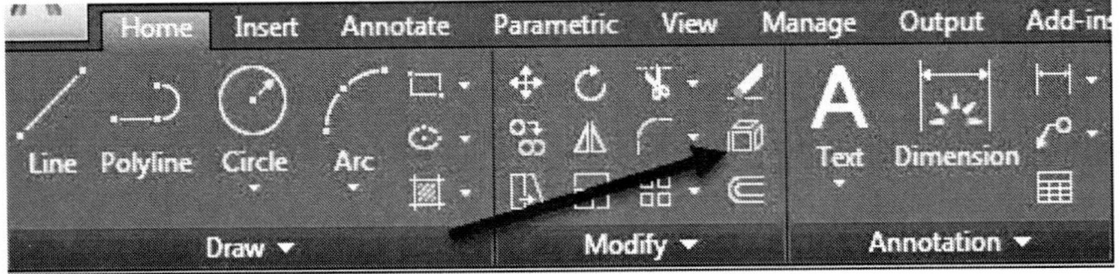

Figure 166 explode tool icon

OR

Command: X Enter

Step 2: Select object then Enter

Before

After

Figure 167 after explode

What do you mean by OFFSET?

By using the command offset, we can create a new line, polyline, and arc or circle parallel to the object and at a specified distance from it.

Step 1: Ribbon: Home tab ➢ Modify panel Ø Offset

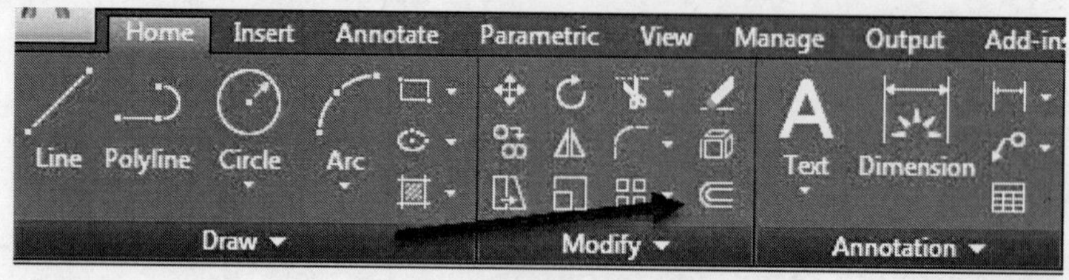

Figure 168 offset tool icon

OR

Command: O Enter

Step 2: Specify offset distance or [Through/Erase/Layer]: **1** Enter

Step 3: Select object to offset or [Exit/Undo]: **Select object**

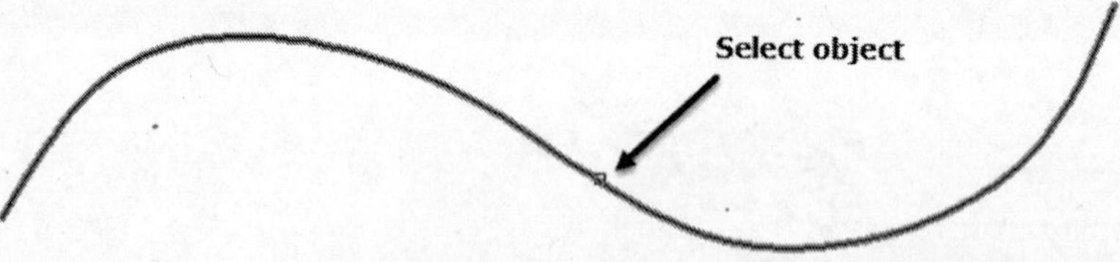

Figure 169 select object

Step 4: Specify point on side to offset or [Exit/Multiple/Undo]: **Pick a side**

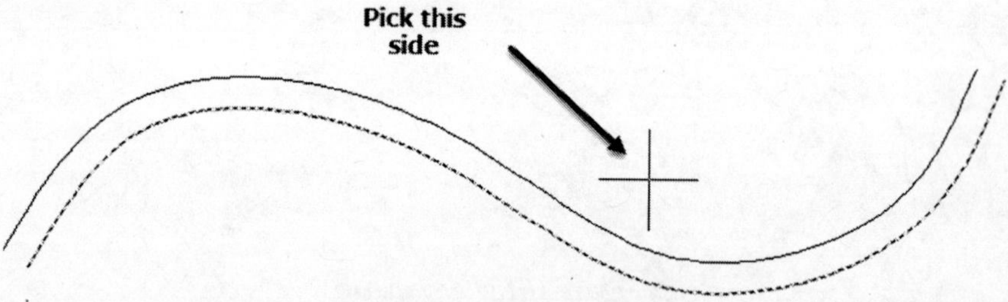

Figure 170 specify side

What do you mean by LENGTHEN?

Command LENGTHEN Changes the length of an object and the included angle of arcs. We can specify changes as the final length, an increment or angle. LENGTHEN can be used as an alternative tool instead off TRIM or EXTEND.

Step 1: Ribbon: Home tab ➢ Modify panel ➢ Lengthen

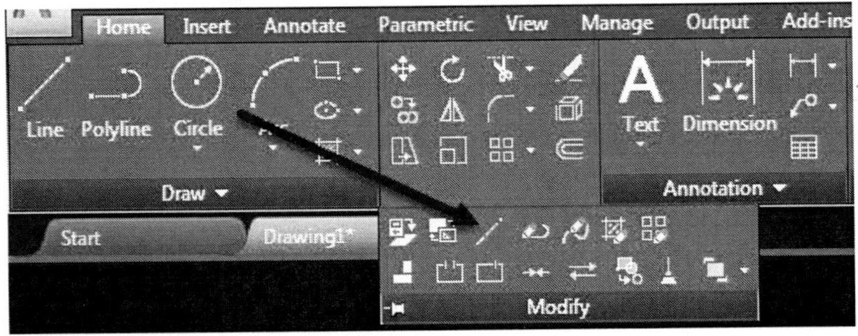

Figure 171 *Lengthen tool icon*

OR

Command: LEN Enter

Step 2: Select an object to measure or [DElta Percent Total DYnamic]:

select object then P Enter

Step 3: Enter percentage length: **150** Enter

Select object

50

25

Figure 172 *use of lengthen*

What do you mean by ALIGN

We use command Align when we need to keep an object in scale with another object i.e. it usexd for aligning one or more point of an object called source point with the points of other object called definition point.

Step 1: Ribbon: Home tab ➢ Modify Ø panelAlign

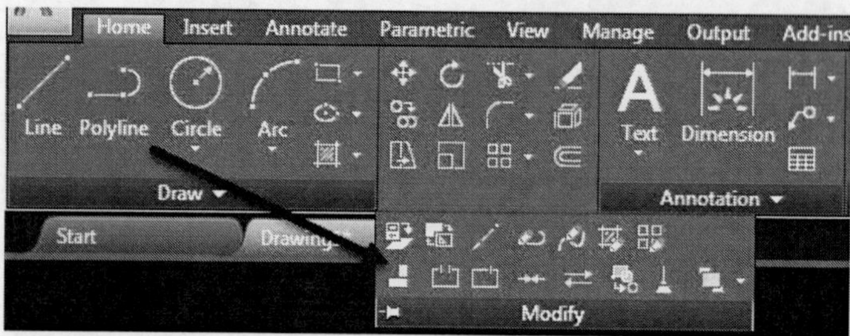

***Figure 173** align tool icon*

OR

Command: AL Enter

Step 2: Select object: **Select source object**

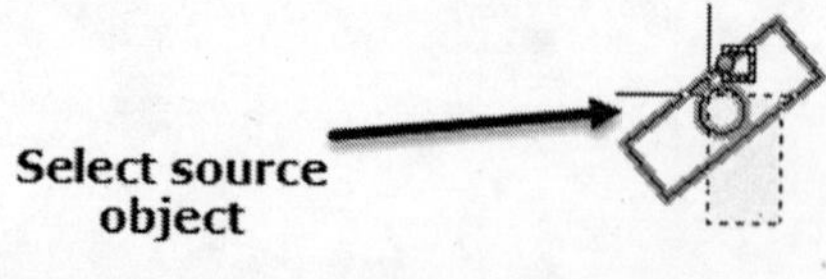

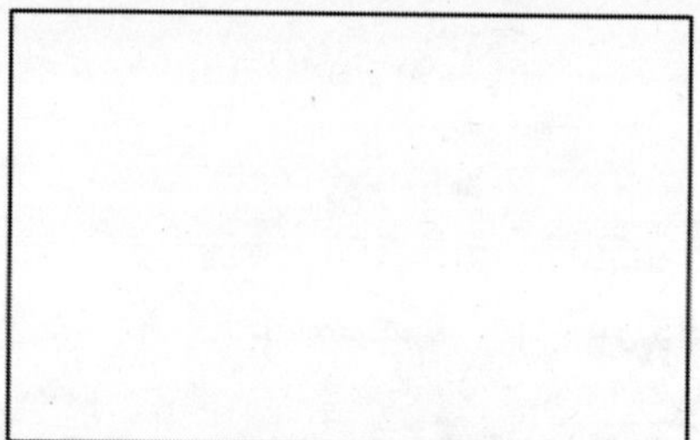

***Figure 174** Select source object*

Step 3: Specify first source point: **Pick first point**

Step 4: Specify first destination point: **Pick second point**

Step 5: Specify second source point: **Pick third point**

Step 6: Specify second destination point: **Pick fourth point**

Step 7: Specify third destination point or <continue>: Enter

Step 8: Scale objects based on alignment point? [Yes/No]: **Y** Enter

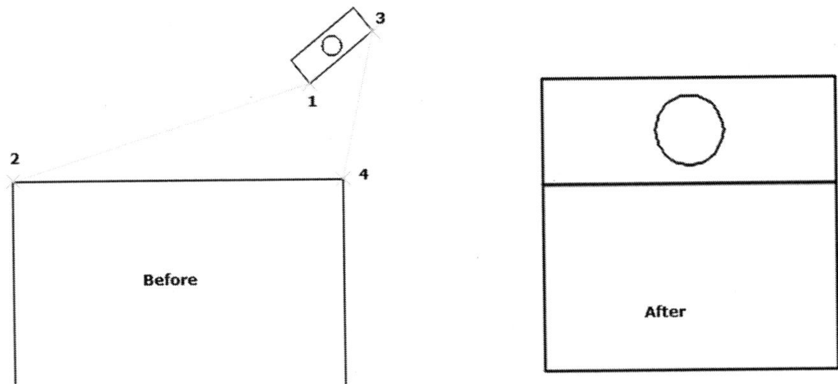

Figure 175 Use of align

What do you mean by BREAK?

By using command break, we can erase part of the line, arc or a circle or used to split it into two lines or arc. Generally, we use it for creating a gap between lines for writing text.

Step 1: Ribbon: Home tab ➢ Modify panel ➢ Break

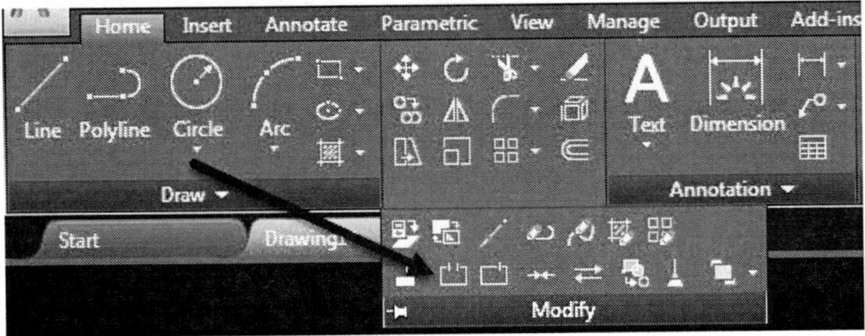

Figure 176 break tool icon

OR

Command: BR Enter

Step 2: Select object

Step 3: Specify second break point or [First point]: **F** Enter

Step 4: Specify first break point: **Pick first point**

Step 5: Specify second break point: **Pick second point**

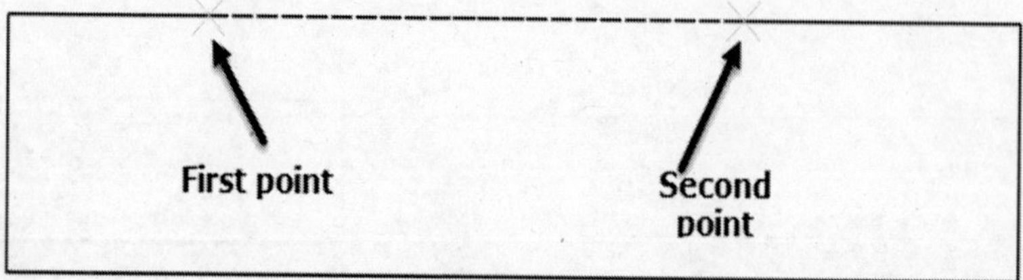

Figure 177 use of break

What do you mean by JOIN?

By using Command join, we can attach two objects lying in the same plane.

Step 1: Ribbon: Home tab ➢ Modify panel ➢ Join

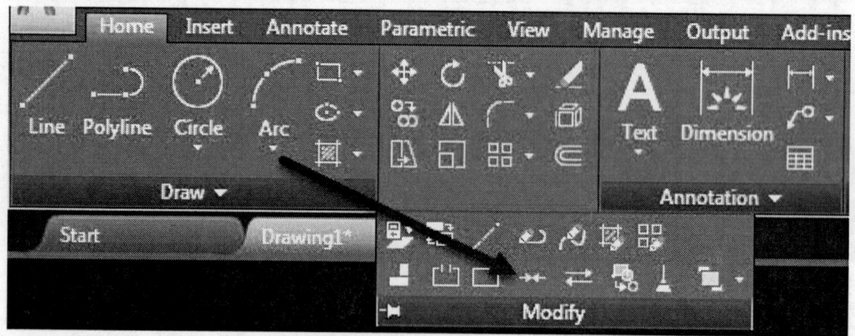

Figure 178 join tool icon

OR

Command: J Enter

Step 2: Select source object or multiple objects to join at once: **Select first line**

Step 3: Select objects to join: **Select second line then** Enter

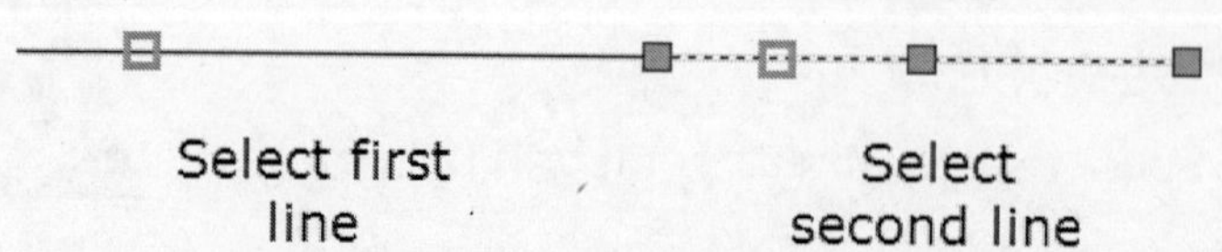

Figure 179 use of join

What do you mean by DELETE DUPLICATE OBJECT?

This command removes duplicate or overlapping lines, arcs, and polylines. Also, combines partially overlapping or contiguous ones.

Step 1: Ribbon: Home tab ➢ Modify panel ➢ Delete duplicate object

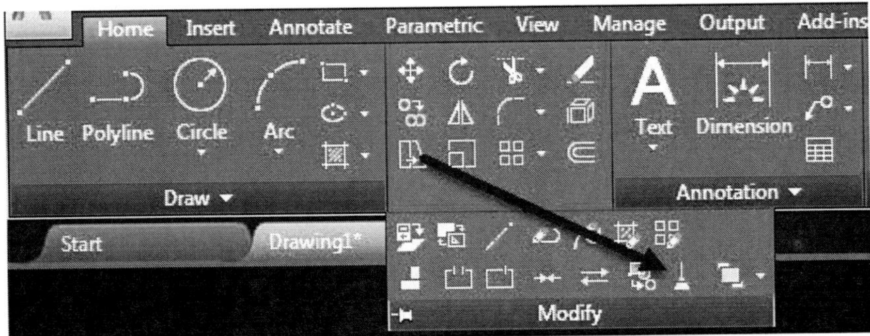

Figure 180 delete duplicate object tool icon

OR

Command: OVERKILL Enter

Step 2: Select object then Enter

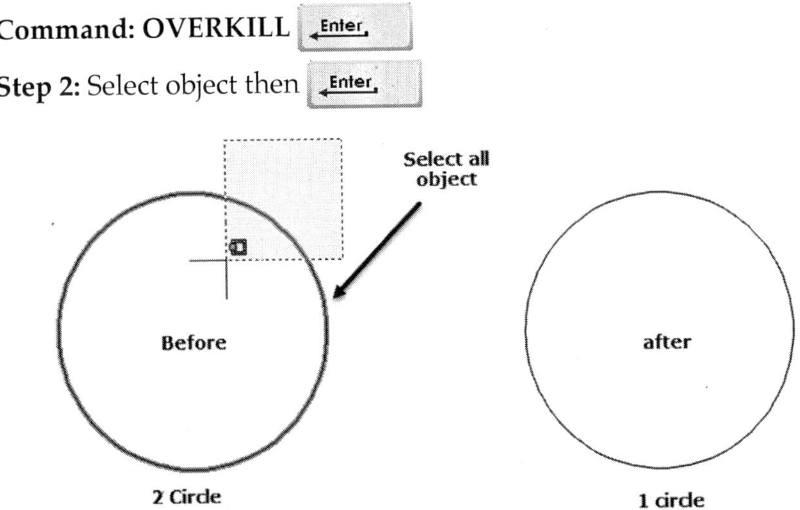

Figure 181 use of overkill command

Step 3: Select all Radio Button and click Ok

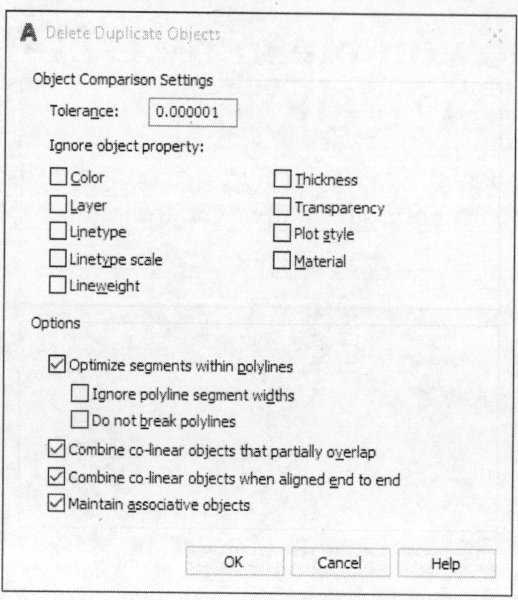

Figure 182 option

What do you mean by DRAW ORDER?

Several options are available that control the order in which overlapping objects are displayed. In addition to the DRAWORDER command, the TEXTTOFRONT command brings all text, dimensions, or leaders in a drawing in front of other objects, and the HATCHTOBACK command sends all hatch objects behind other objects.

Select Objects

Specifies the objects for which you want to change the draw order. For the above and under options, an additional prompt displays in which you select the reference objects that the originally selected objects should be above or under.

Above Objects

Moves the selected object above the specified reference objects.

Under Objects

Moves the selected objects below the specified reference objects.

Front

Moves the selected objects to the top of the order of objects in the drawing.

Back

Moves the selected objects to the bottom of the order of objects in the drawing.

Step 1: Ribbon: Home tab ➤ Modify panel ➤ Draw order

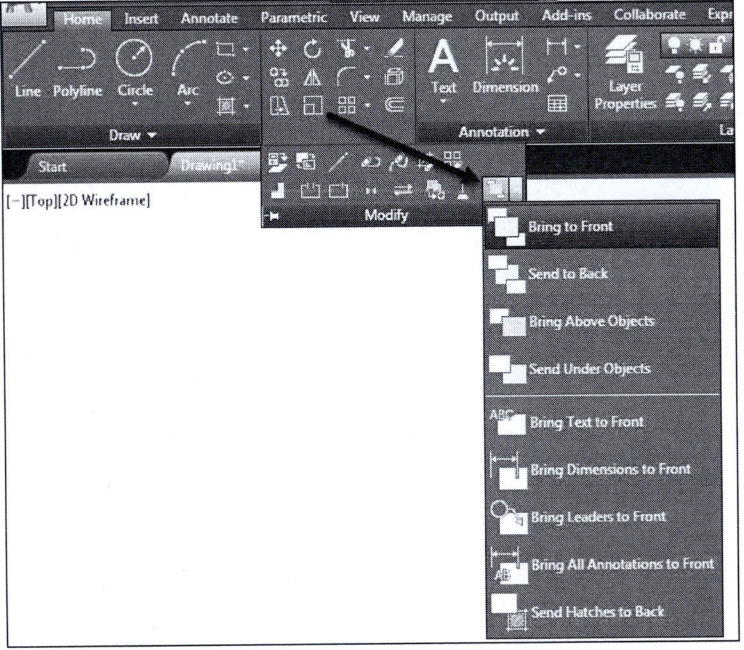

Figure 183 draw order tool icon

OR

Command: DR Enter

Step 2: Select object then Enter

Step 3: Enter object ordering option [Above objects Under objects Front Back]: **B** Enter

Figure 184 *use of draw order*

What do you mean by BLOCKS?

It is used to create a block by selecting that object and giving it an insertion point and then save it by the name of itself. These blocks are saved in the design centre toolbar and the tool palettes.

Ribbon: Insert tab ➢ Block panel ➢ Create block

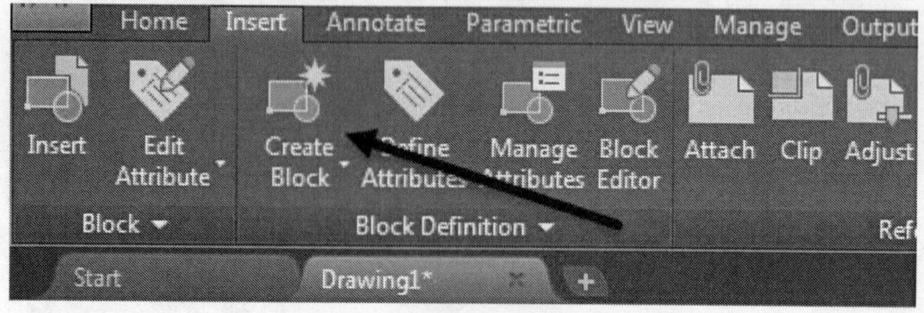

Figure 185 *block tool icon*

OR

Command: B Enter

Step 1: Give the command 'B' and press Enter, A block definition tab appears.

Step 2: Give a name to your block followed by selecting the option of "select object" and select the object you want to convert to blocks.

Step 3: Select the base point by clicking "pick points" and give the values of X, Y and Z coordinates.

Step 4: Click OK.

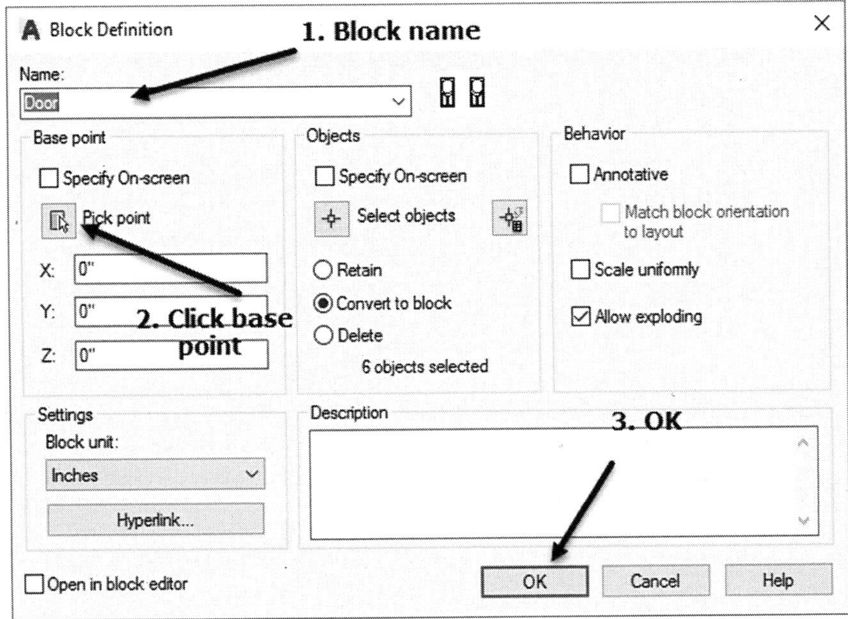

Figure 186 block setting tab

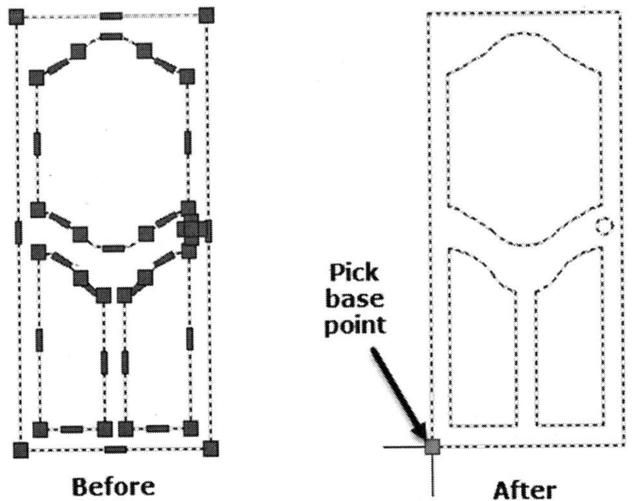

Figure 187 use of block

CHAPTER 5
Annotation

What do you mean by TEXT?

It is a command to create a single-line text object. It is sometimes used to define different line text objects which we can modify, relocate.

Step 1: Ribbon: Annotation tab ØText ØSingle line text

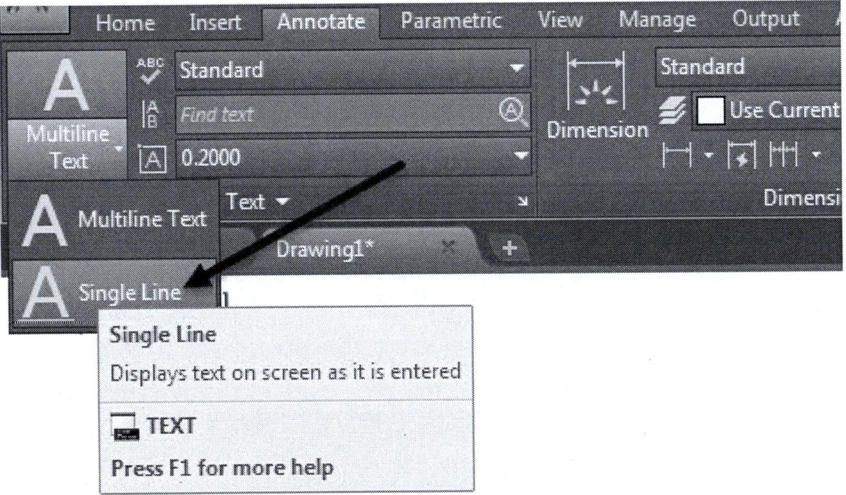

Figure 188 text tool icon

OR

Command: DT Enter

Step 2: Specify start point of text or [Justify/Style]: **Pick Start point**

Step 3: Specify the height: **2** Enter

Step 4: Specify rotation angle of the text: **30** Enter

Step 5: Type any text Ex: **AutoCAD 2022 By Linkan Sagar** then Enter Enter

AutoCAD 2022 By Linkan Sagar

Figure 189 text

What do you mean by MULTILINE TEXT?

It is a used to create multiline text objects such as paragraphs. It can also be modified, relocate. Using this command, we can format text appearance, boundaries and columns.

Step 1: Ribbon: Annotation tab ØText ➢ Multiline text

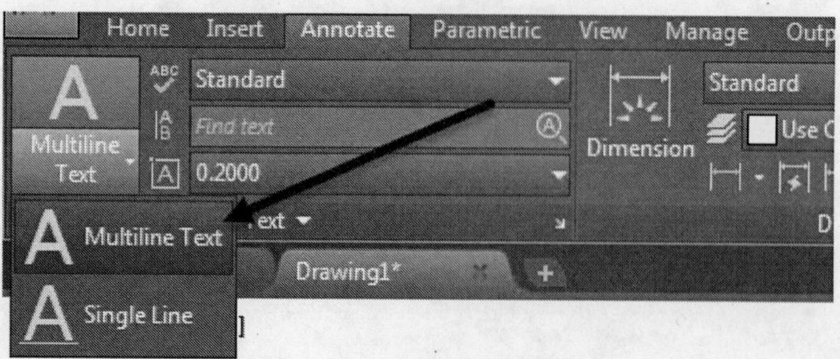

***Figure 190** mtext tool icon*

OR

Command: MT Enter

Step 2: Specify first corner: **Pick first corner**

Step 3: Specify opposite corner or [Height/Justify/Line spacing/ Rotation/Style/Width/Columns]: **Pick second corner**

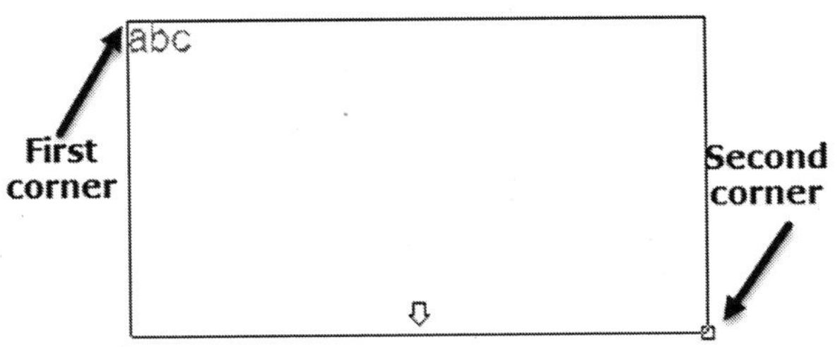

Figure 191 *pick corner*

Step 4: Type any text and text formatting, click Close **X**

	Name	Designation
1.	Linkan sagar	CAD Consultant
2.	Simranjit	CAD Consultant
3.	Vishal Gupta	coordinator
4.	Devesh singh	coordinator
5.	Jawed	system administrator
6.	Ritu gupta	Head counsellor
7.	Megha	counsellor
8.	Ginni	counsellor
9.	Aarushi	receptionist
10.	Deep singh	Java trainer
11.	Rajeev Shishodia	Java trainer
12.	Pankaj Singh	.NET & Python
13.	Kuldeep Shishodia	Networking
14.	Vivek jha	C/C++
15.	Punit katiyar	PHP
16.	Anuj Kumar	PHP & UI
17.	Nitesh Bhardwaj	Embedded system
18.	Shashank	Digital marketing

Figure 192 *mtext*

What do you mean by TEXT STYLE?

It is used to change text style like text height, text font.

Step 1: Ribbon: Annotation tab ØText Text Østyle

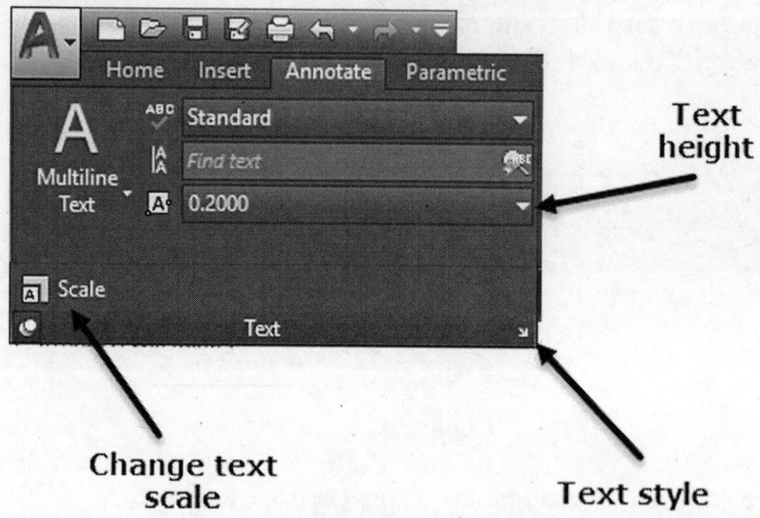

Figure 193 text style tool icon

Text style

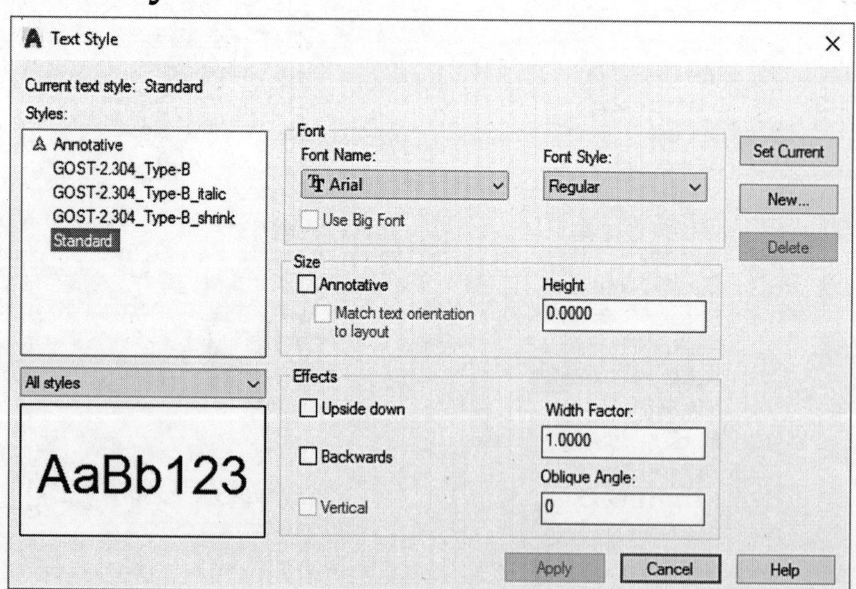

Figure 194 text style option

What do you mean by DIMENSIONING?

It is a command with the help of which we can draw the current viewport, change current text style, undo the recently created objects, etc.

Command: DIM & DIM1 Enter

Dimensioning mode command equivalents	
Dimensioning mode Command	**Equivalent Command**
ALIGNED	DIMALIGNED
ANGULAR	DIMANGULAR
BASELINE	DIMBASELINE
CENTER	DIMCENTER
CONTINUE	DIMCONTINUE
DIAMETER	DIMDIAMETER
HOMETEXT	DIMEDIT Home
HORIZONTAL	DIMLINEAR Horizontal
LEADER	LEADER
JOG	DIMJOGGED
NEWTEXT	DIMEDIT New
OBLIQUE	DIMEDIT Oblique
ORDINATE	DIMORDINATE
OVERRIDE	DIMOVERRIDE
RADIUS	DIMRADIUS
RESTORE	-DIMSTYLE Restore
ROTATED	DIMLINEAR Rotated
SAVE	-DIMSTYLE Save
STATUS	-DIMSTYLE Status
TEDIT	DIMTEDIT
TROTATE	DIMEDIT Rotate
UPDATE	-DIMSTYLE Apply
VARIABLES	-DIMSTYLE Variables
VERTICAL	DIMLINEAR Vertical

What do you mean by LINEAR?

We use linear command, to create a linear dimension with a vertical, horizontal, or rotated dimension line.

Step 1: Ribbon: Annotate tab ➢ Dimensions panel ➢ Linear

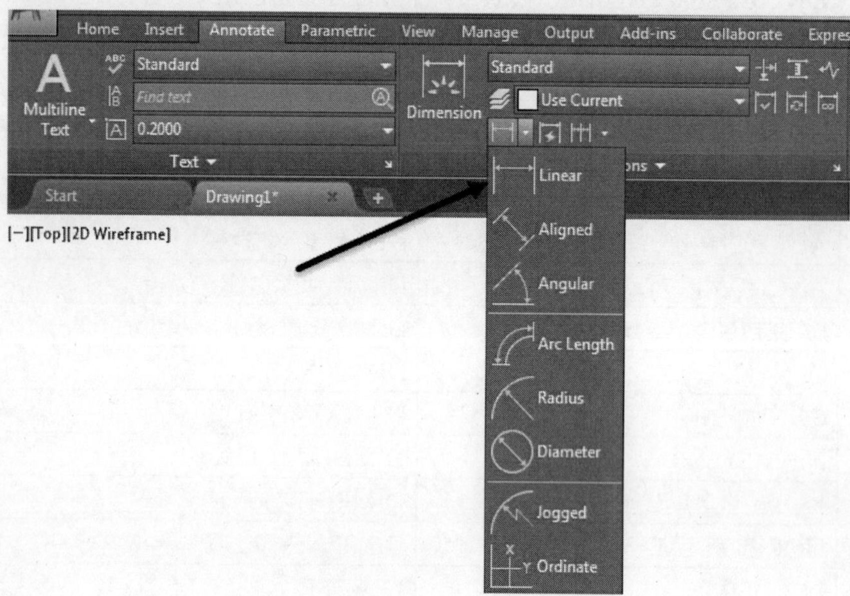

Figure 195 linear dimension tool icon

OR

Command: DIMLIN Enter

Step 2: Pick first point and Pick second point then give direction and click.

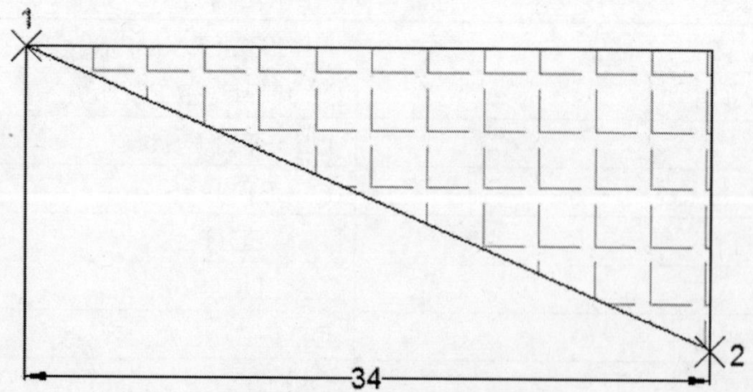

Figure 196 use of linear dim

What do you mean by ALIGNED?

It is a command to create a linear dimension in aligned position.

Step 1: Ribbon: Annotate tab ➢ Dimensions panel ➢ Aligned

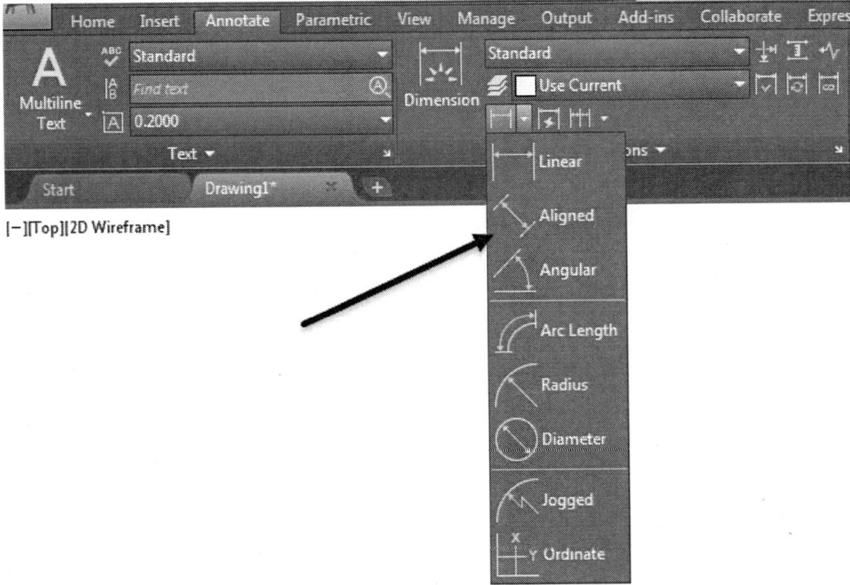

Figure 197 aligned dimension tool icon

OR

Command: DIMALI Enter

Step 2: Pick first point and Pick second point then give direction and click.

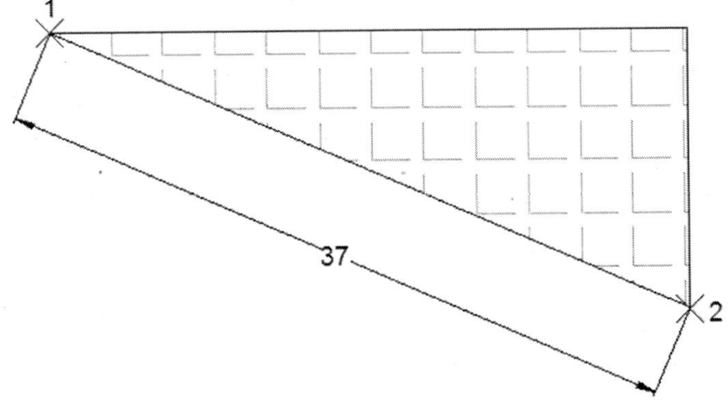

Figure 198 use of aligned dim

What do you mean by ANGULAR?

It is a command to measure Angle of object.

Step 1: Ribbon: Annotate tab ➢ Dimensions panel ➢ Angular

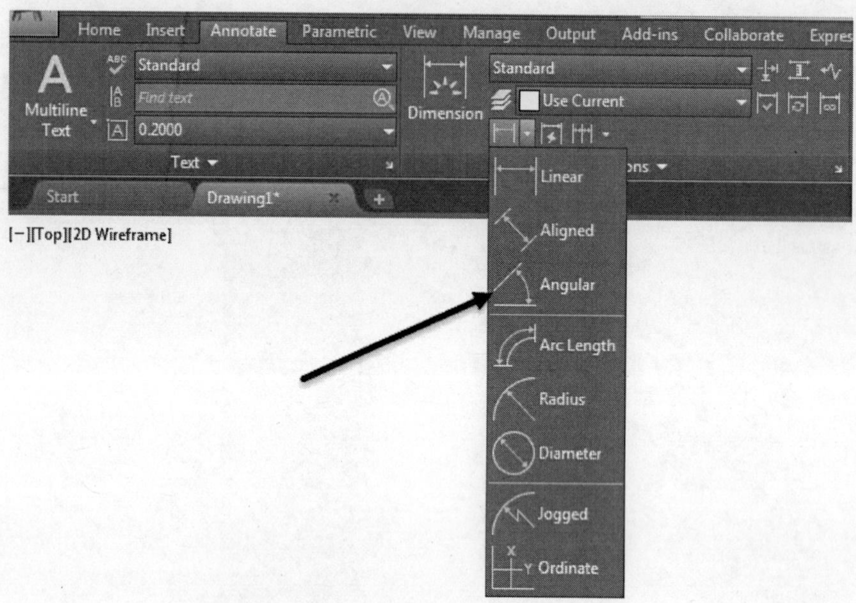

Figure 199 *angular dimension tool icon*

OR

Command: DIMANG Enter

Step 2: Select first object and select second object then click.

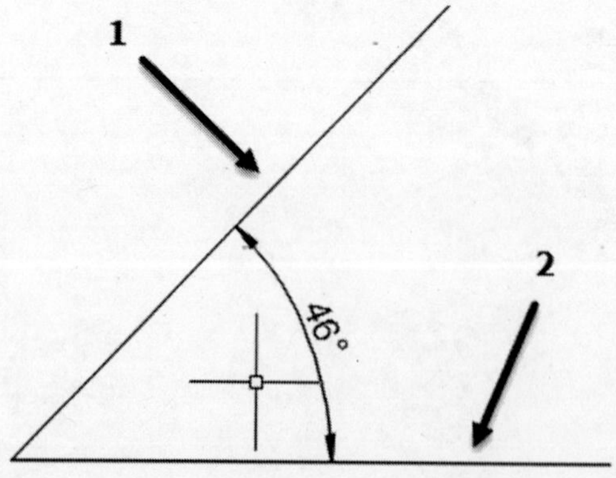

Figure 200 *use of angular dim*

What do you mean by ARC LENGTH?

It is a command to measure the length of a simple arc or polyline arc.

Step 1: Ribbon: Annotate tab ➢ Dimensions panel ➢ Arc length

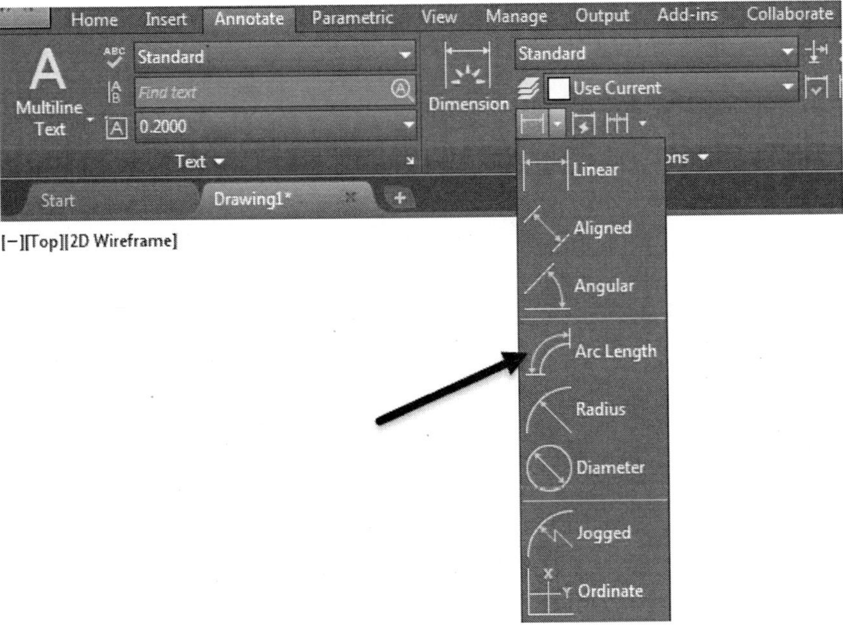

Figure 201 arc length tool icon

OR

Command: DIMARC Enter

Step 2: Select Arc then give direction and click.

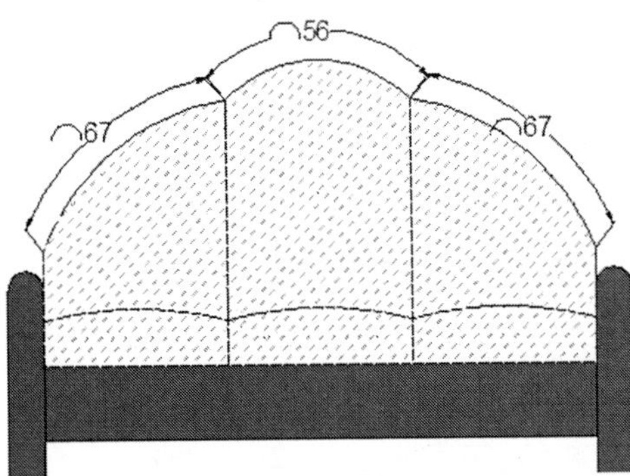

Figure 202 use of arc length

What do you mean by RADIUS?

As we all know, radius is the distance between the centre point and the point on the circle or the half of the diameter. It is a command to measure the radius of a selected circle or arc and display the dimension text having a radius symbol in front of it.

Ribbon: Annotate tab ➢ Dimensions panel Ø Radius

Figure 203 radius tool icon

OR

Command: DIMRAD Enter

Step 2: Select Circle or Arc and give direction then click.

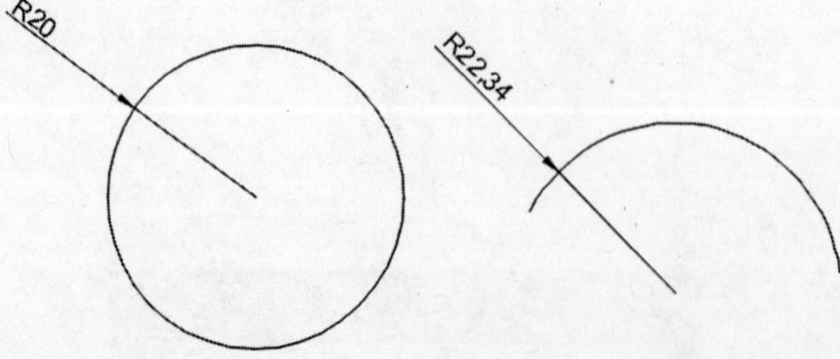

Figure 204 use of radius dim

What do you mean by DIAMETER?

It is a command to measure the diameter of the selected circle or arc, display the dimension text with diameter symbol in front of it and can relocate the resulting diameter dimension.

Step 1: Ribbon: Annotate tab ➢ Dimensions panel ➢ Diameter

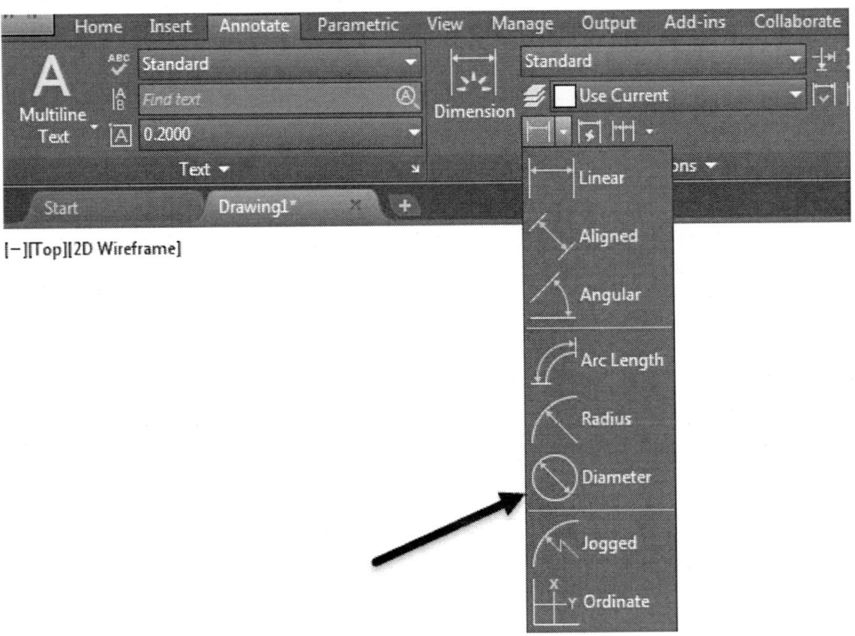

Figure 205 diameter tool icon

OR

Command: DIMDIA Enter

Step 2: Select Circle or Arc and give direction then click.

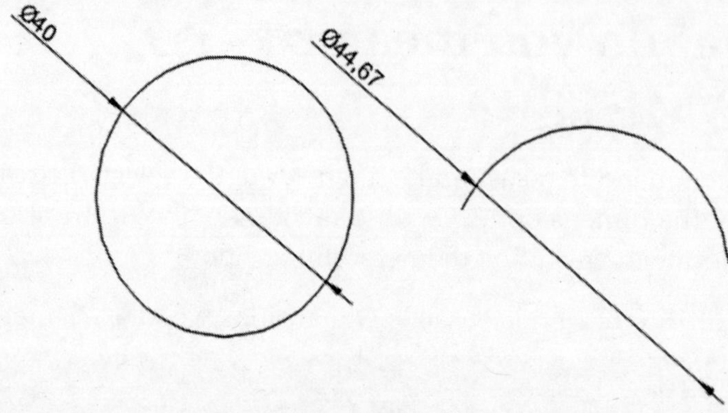

Figure 206 use of diameter

What do you mean by JOGGED RADIUS DIMENSION?

It is a command that measures the radius of the selected object and displays a radius symbol with dimension text.

Step 1: Ribbon: Annotate tab ➢ Dimensions panel ➢ Jogged

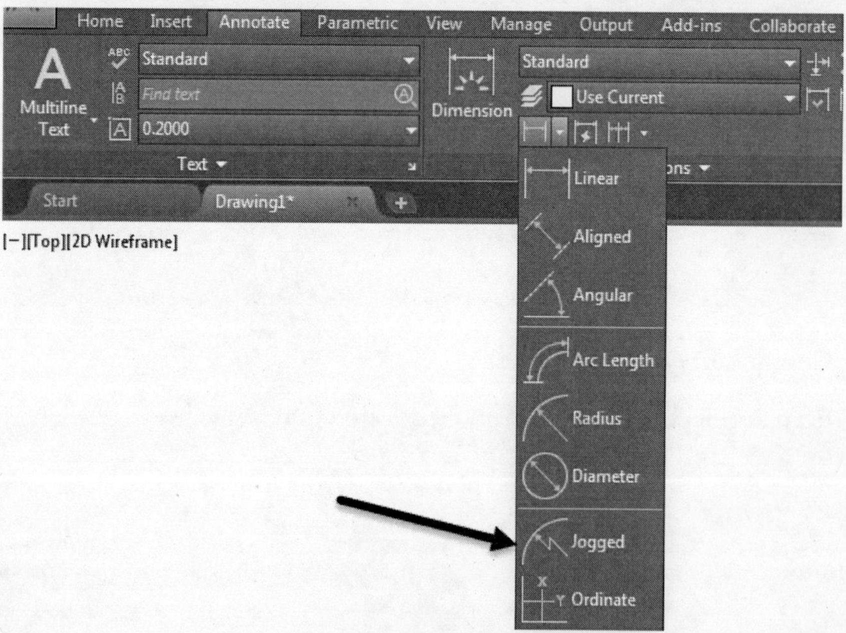

Figure 207 jogged tool icon

OR

Command: DIMJOGGED Enter

Step 2: Pick first arc then pick second point override center.

Step 3: Pick third point for text location then pick fourth point for direction.

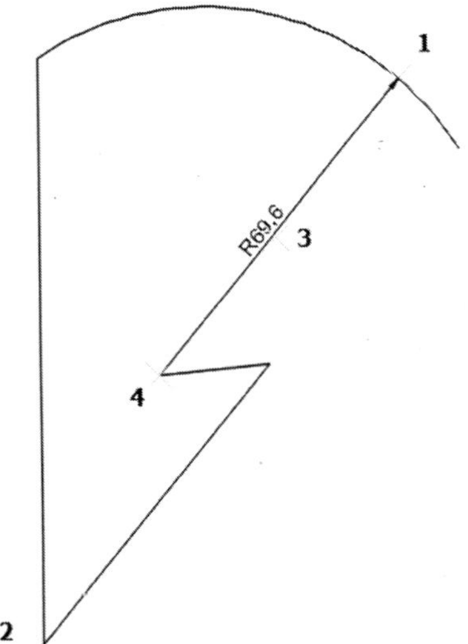

Figure 208 *use of jogged*

What do you mean by ORDINATE?

It is a command to measure horizontal or vertical distance from the point of origin (0, 0).

Step 1: Ribbon: Annotate tab ➤ Dimensions panel ØOrdinate

Figure 209 ordinate tool icon

OR

Command: DIMORD Enter

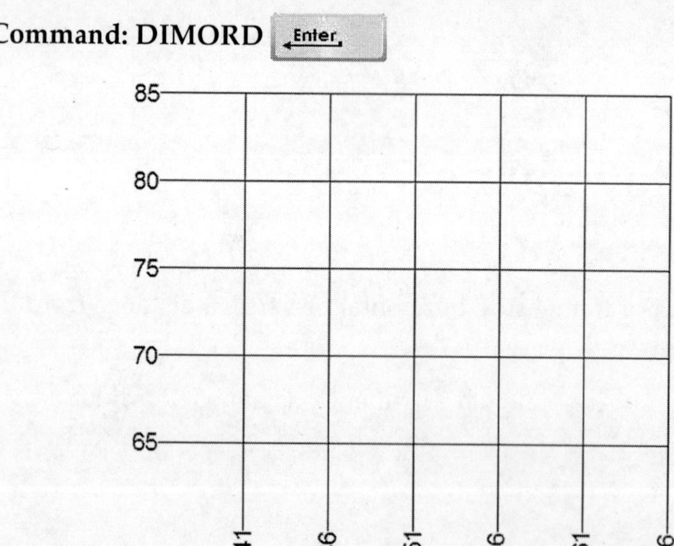

Figure 210 use of ordinate

What do you mean by QUICK DIMENSION?

It is a command which quickly creates multi-dimensions of the selected objects, particularly useful for dimensioning a series of circles and arcs, for creating a series of baseline.

Continuous

Creates a series of continued dimensions.

Ordinate

Creates a series of ordinate dimensions.

Staggered

Creates a series of staggered dimensions.

Radius

Creates a series of radius dimensions.

Edit

Edit a series of dimensions. When we are ready to add or remove points from existing dimensions.

Baseline

Creates a series of baseline dimensions.

Datum Point

Sets a new datum point for baseline and ordinate dimensions.

Diameter

Creates a series of diameter dimensions.

Settings

Sets the default object snap for specifying extension line origins. We get the following prompt:

Step 1: Ribbon: Annotate tab ➢ Dimensions panelØQuick Dimension

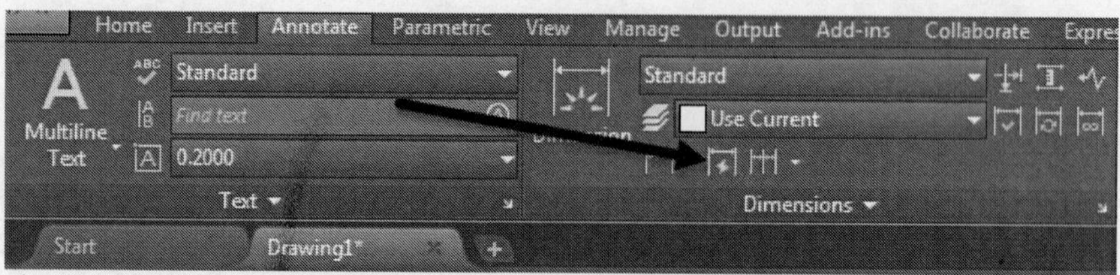

Figure 211 *quick dim tool icon*

OR

Command: QDIM Enter

Step 2: Select geometry to dimension: **Select all object then** Enter

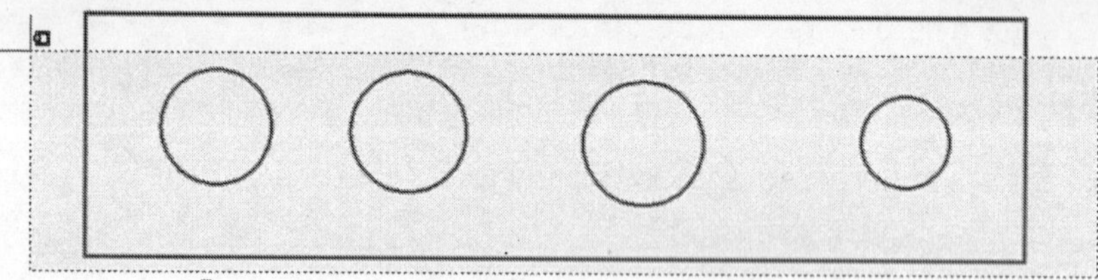

Figure 212 *select all object*

Step 3: Specify dimension line position, or [Continuous/ Staggered/ Baseline/ Ordinate/ Radius/ Diameter/ datumPoint/ Edit/ seTtings]: **Give direction and click**

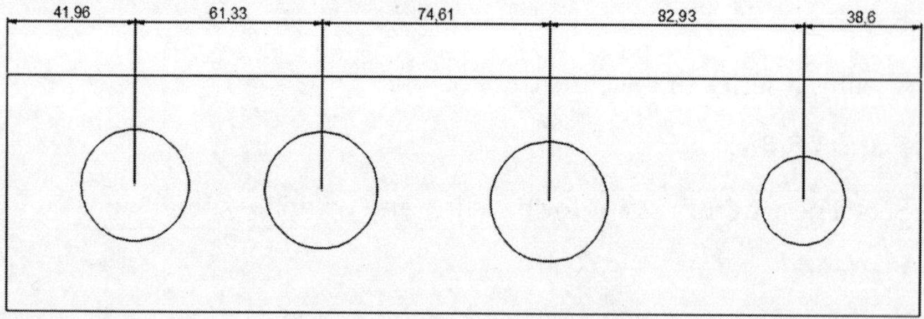

Figure 213 *use of quick dim*

What do you mean by CONTINUE?

It is a command to create an extension line automatically from the last selected linear, angular or ordinate dimension.

Step 1: Ribbon: Annotate tab ➢ Dimensions panel ➢ Continue

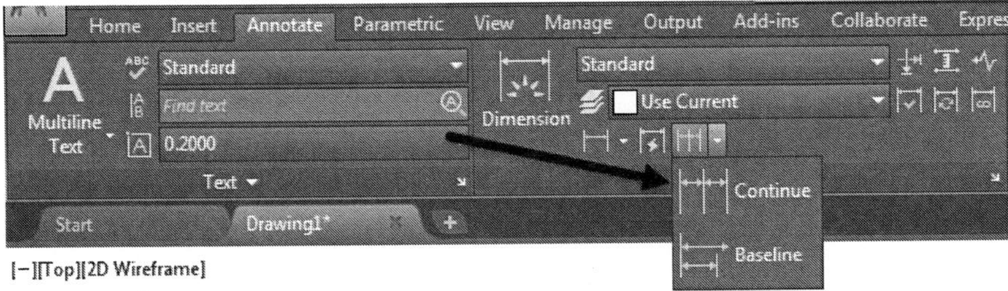

Figure 214 continue dim tool icon

OR

Command: DIMCONT Enter

Step 2: Pick third point, pick fourth point and pick fifth point.

(First of all use different dimension command like aligned then use continue dimension)

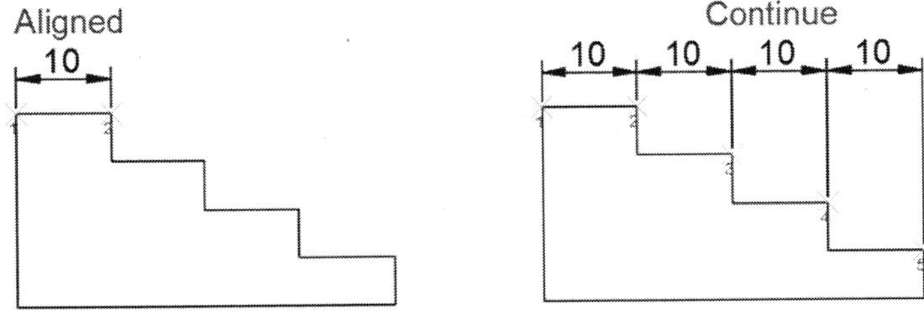

Figure 215 use of continue dim

What do you mean by BASELINE?

It is a command to create angular, linear and ordinate dimension from the baseline of the selected dimension.

Step 1: Ribbon: Annotate tab ➢ Dimensions panel ➢ Baseline

Figure 216 baseline dim tool icon

OR

Command: DIMBASE Enter

Step 2: Select base dimension line and then click next point.

Figure 217 use of baseline dim

What do you mean by CENTRE MARK?

It is a command to create a centre point in a circle or arc.

Step 1: Ribbon: Annotate tab ➢ Centerlines ➢ Center Mark

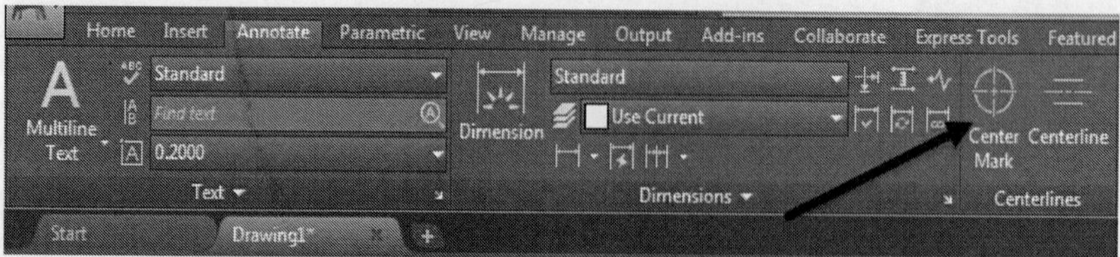

Figure 218 center mark tool icon

Step 2: Select arc or circle: **Select circle**

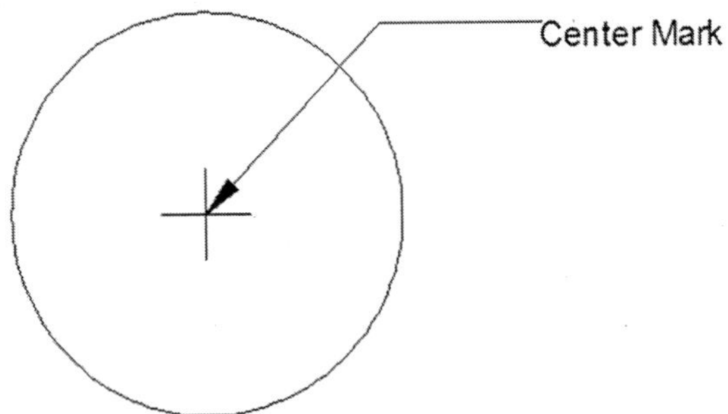

Figure 219 use of center mark

What do you mean by CENTRE LINE?

It is a command to create a centerline in a line.

Step 1: Ribbon: Annotate tab ➢ Centerlines ➢ Center Line

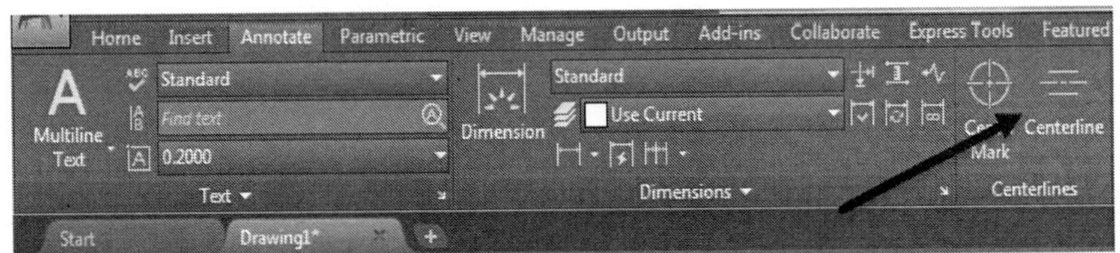

Figure 220 center line tool icon

Step 2: Select first line then select second line.

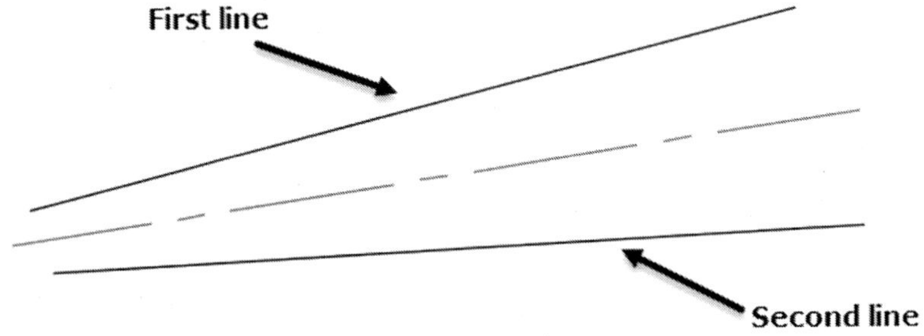

Figure 221 use of center line

What do you mean by INSPECTION DIMENSION?

It is a command to inspect the dimension given I the drawing so as to maintain the standard of the dimensions.

Step 1: Ribbon: Annotate tab ➢ Dimensions panel ➢ Inspect

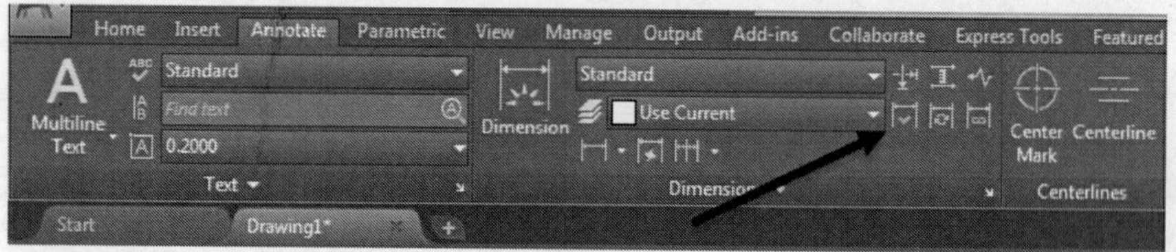

Figure 222 inspection tool icon

OR

Command: DIMINSPECT Enter

Step 2: Select dimension then and set inspection rate.

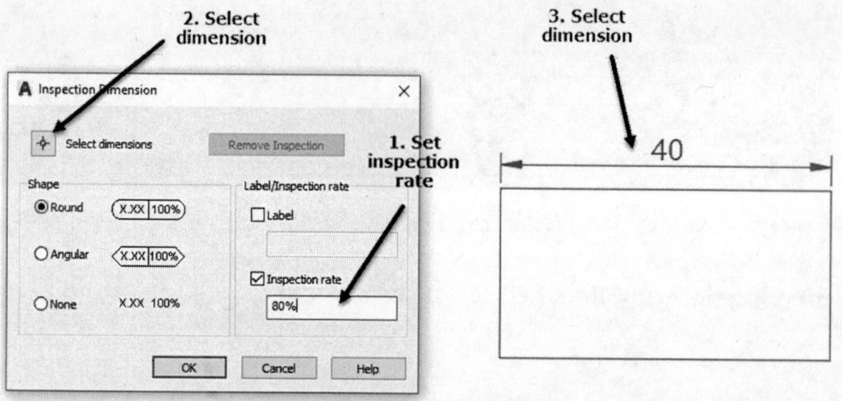

Figure 223 inspection dimension setting tab

Then click OK

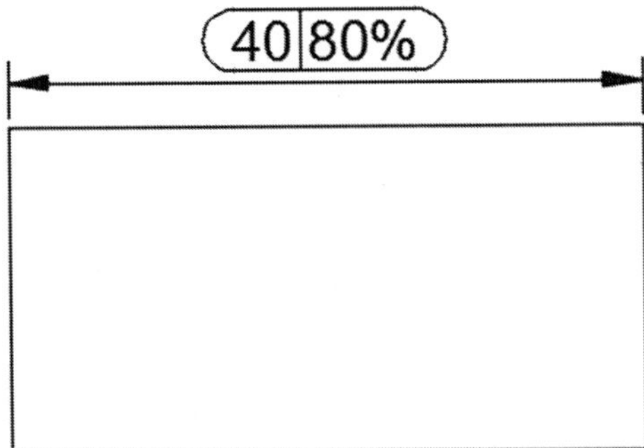

Figure 224 use of inspection dim

What do you mean by DIMENSION BREAK?

It is a command to break or restore the dimension or extension lines when they cross each other.

Step 1: Ribbon: Annotate tab ➢ Dimensions panel ➢ Break

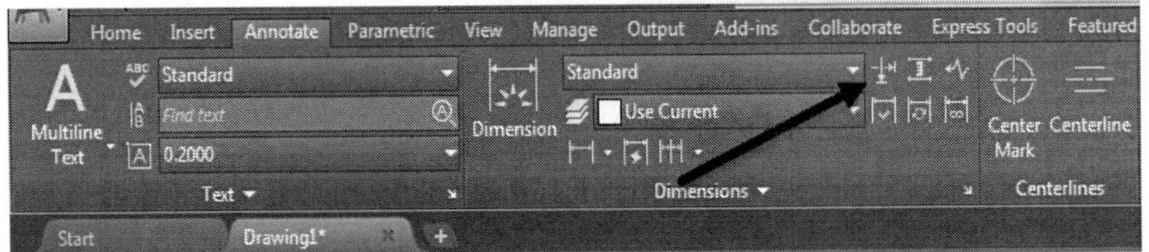

Figure 225 break dimension tool icon

OR

Command: DIMBREAK Enter

Step 2: Select dimension then Enter

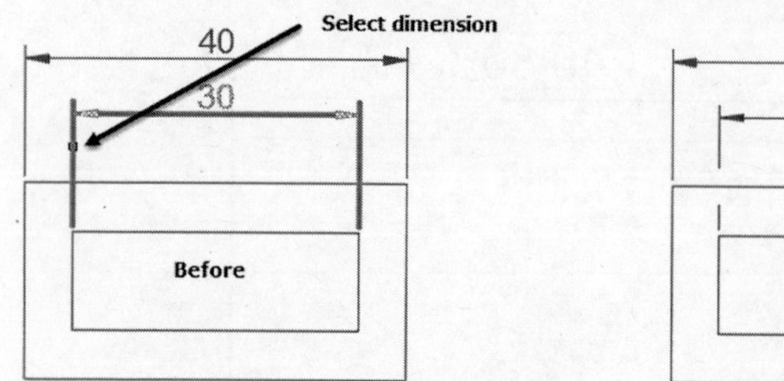

Figure 226 use of break dim

What do you mean by DIMENSION SPACE?

It is a command to adjust the spacing or distance between linear or angular dimensions.

Step 1: Ribbon: Annotate tab ➢ Dimensions panel ➢ Adjust Space

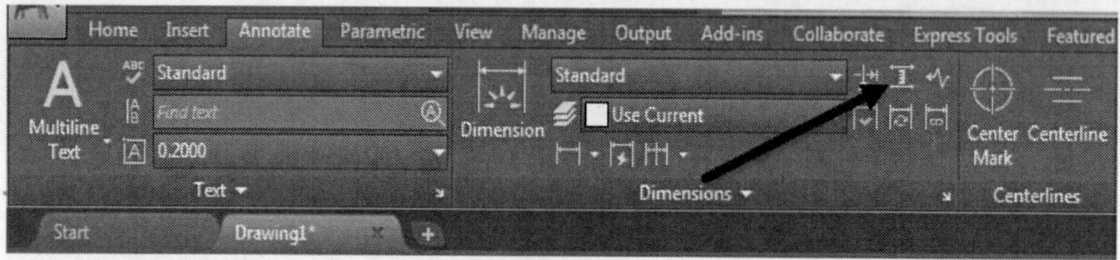

Figure 227 dimension space tool icon

OR

Command: DIMSPACE Enter

Step 2: Select first reference dimension and select second dimension then Enter

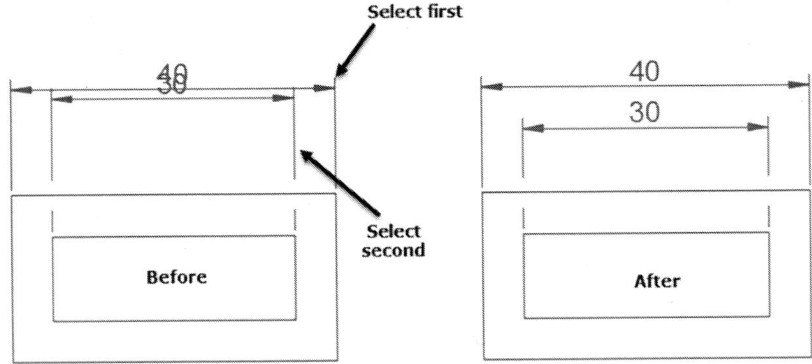

Figure 228 use of dimension space

When do we use DIM STYLE?

When we need to change the dimension setting and have control over the dimension used in the drawing, we use 'DIM Style". It stands for Dimension Style, by using 'dimstyle' we can create dimension styles and specify the format of dimensions quickly.

Like: Text height, Arrow size and precision etc.

Step 1: Ribbon: Annotate tab ➤ Dimensions panel ➤ Dimension Style

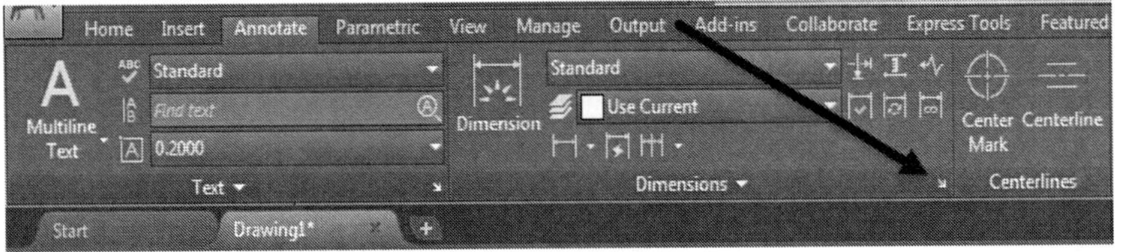

Figure 229 dimension style tool icon

OR

Command: D Enter

Step 2: Click modify button then select any tab like text, arrow etc.

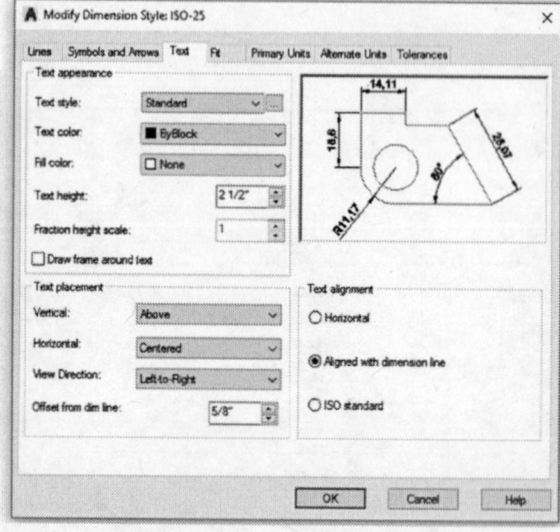

Figure 230 dimension style tab

What do you mean by QLEADER?

We use 'QLeader' to create leader annotation. By its help we can set location of set multiline text annotation and specify leader format

You can use QLEADER to

- Set the location where leaders attach to multiline text annotation
- Specify leader annotation and annotation format
- Constrain the angle of the first and second leader segments.
- Limit the number of leader points

Step 1: Command: LE Enter

Step 2: Specify first leader point, or [Settings]: **First point**

Step 3: Specify next point: **Second point**

Step 4: Specify text width: **0** Enter

Step 5: Enter first line of annotation text: **Wall 4.5″** Enter Enter

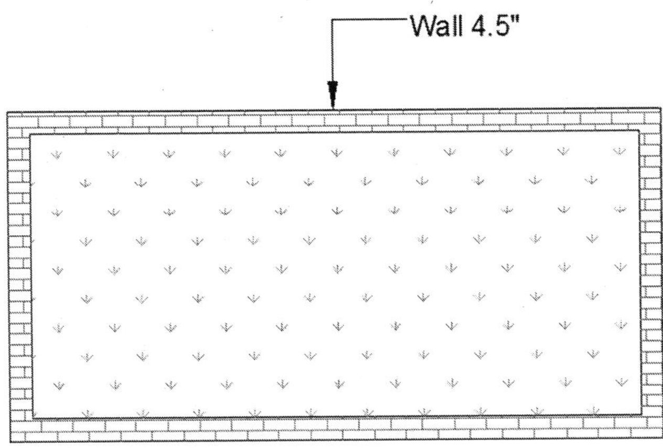

Figure 231 use of qleader

What do you mean by LEADER?

It is a command to create a line that can be connected to a feature by annotation. It also draws a leader line segment to the point specified.

Step 1: Command: LEAD Enter

Step 2: Specify leader start point: **Pick first point**

Step 3: Specify next point: **Pick second point**

Step 4: Specify next point or [Annotation/Format/Undo]: **Pick third point**

Step 5: Specify next point or [Annotation/Format/Undo]: **Pick fourth point**

Step 6: Specify next point or [Annotation/Format/Undo]: **A**

Step 7: Enter first line of annotation text or <option>: **Park**

Step 8: Enter next line of annotation text: Enter

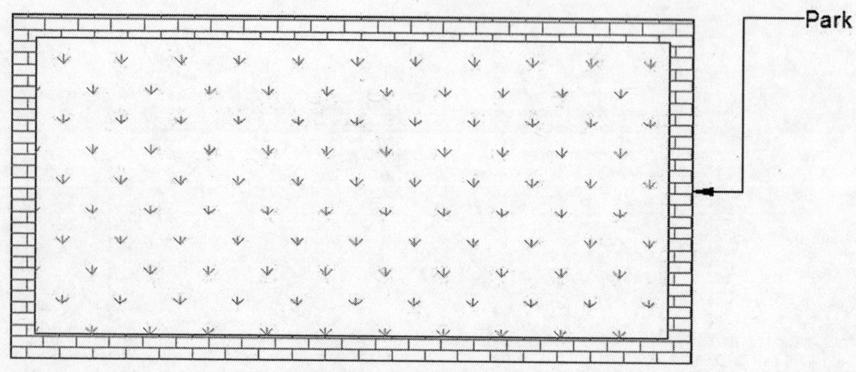

Figure 232 use of leader

What do you mean by TABLE?

It is a command to create several rows and columns in an empty table. We use table when we need to show the data input in tabular form.

Step 1: Ribbon: Home tab ➢ Annotation panel ØTables

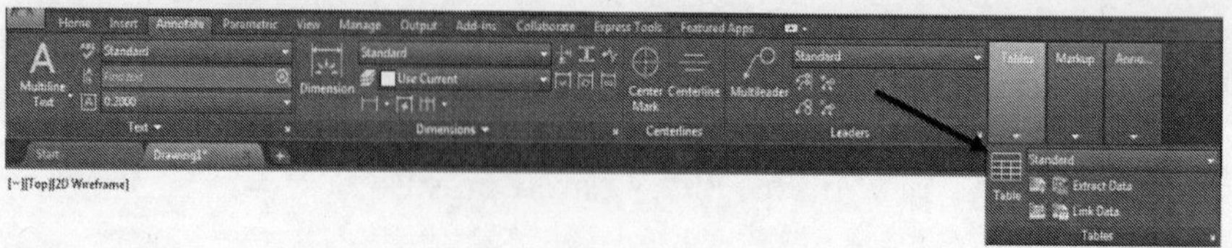

Figure 233 table tool icon

OR

Command: TB Enter

Step 1: Give the command 'TB' and press Enter.. An insert Table tab appears.

Step 2: If we have a table in excel then click the option of "from a data link" and browse the file and upload it. Else to create a new table select "Start from an empty table"

Step 3: Specify the requirements of the table in columns and rows settings.

Step 4: Click "preview" if you want a preview of your table, else click OK.

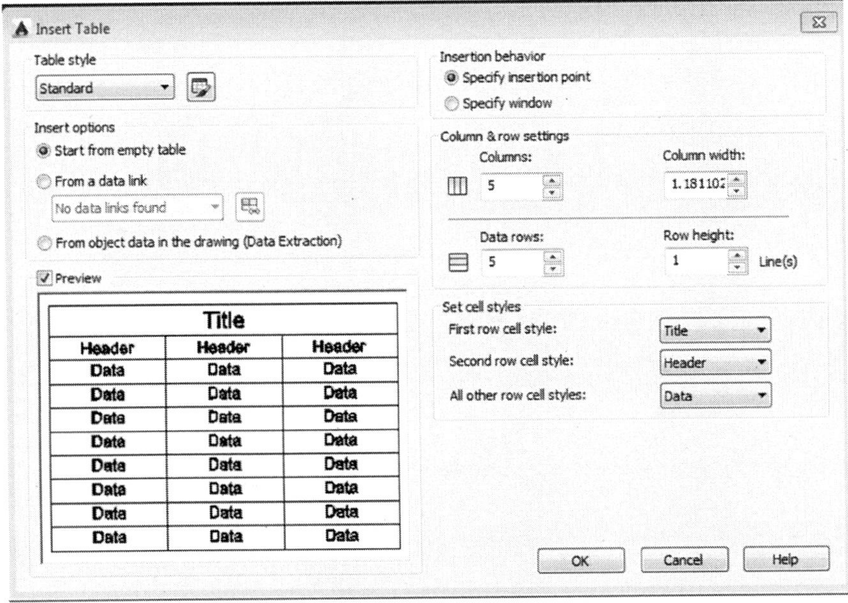

Figure 234 table tab

OR

Step 2: If you want link excel file so click from a data link.

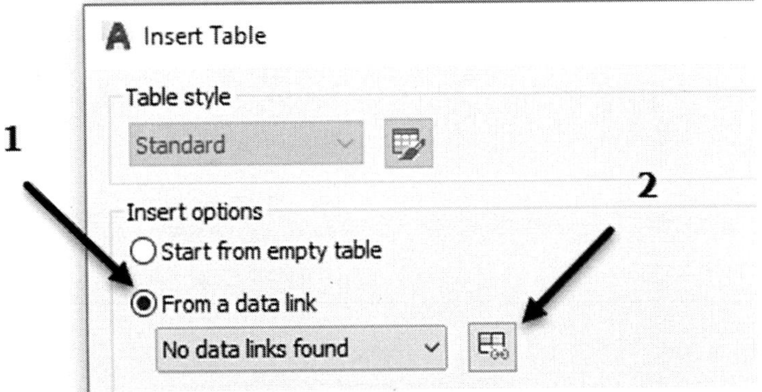

Figure 235 insert data link tab

Step 3: Create a new excel data link. Then give name and press OK.

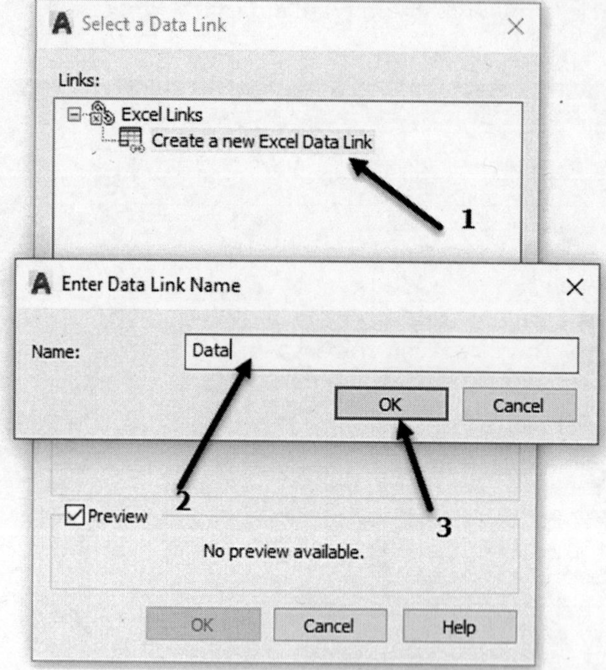

Figure 236 enter data link name

Step 4: Click browse then OK.

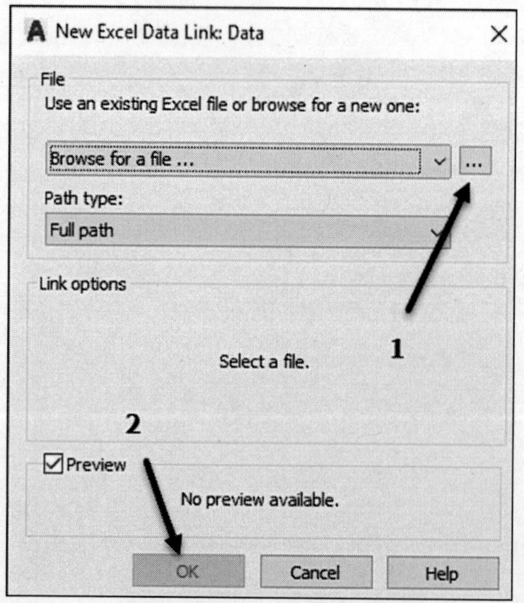

Figure 237 browse excel file

Step 5: Select Excel file then ok.

	A	B
1	Name	Designation
2	Linkan sagar	CAD Consultant
3	Simranjit	CAD Consultant
4	Anuj Kumar	PHP&UI
5	Nitish Bhardwaj	Embedded system
6	Vishal Gupta	coordinator
7	Devesh singh	coordinator
8	Mohammad Jawed Ali	system administrator
9	Ritu gupta	Head counsellor
10	Megha	counsellor
11	Ginni	counsellor
12	Aarushi	receptionist
13	Deep singh	Java trainer
14	Rajeev Shishodia	Java trainer
15	Pankaj Singh	.NET & Python
16	Kuldeep Shishodia	Networking
17	Vivek jha	C/C++
18	Punit katiyar	PHP
19	Shashank	Digital marketing

Figure 238 insert excel data

What do you mean by Smart Dimension?

Smart Dimension tool is recently introduce in AutoCAD 2017.

This tool is use to show the dimension of an object. This tool has an existing feature by which you can check any dimension of an object. While in normal dimension tool, the dimensions of an object is different like aligned, linear, radius etc. but Smart dimension lonely work on behalf of all dimension.

Step 1: **Ribbon:** Annotate ➢ Dimensions ➢ Dimension.

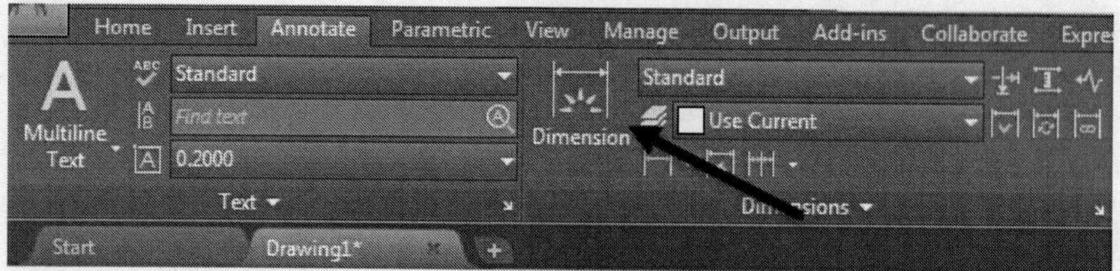

Figure 239 *smart dimension tool icon*

Step 2: Select object.

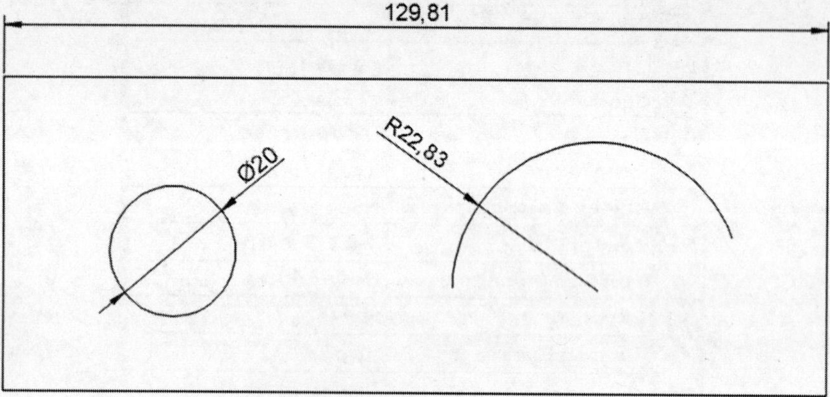

Figure 240 *all dimension use*

CHAPTER 6
Inquiry

What do you mean by LIST?

When we need to know the all properties of an object, we use command LIST. It lists all information of the selected objects such as what type of object it is (whether it is a circle, arc, block etc.), what is its color, its axis, its thickness, location of its end points, elevation from z-axis.

Following information we can get through command LIST:

- Line weight, Color, line type.
- How thick the object is..?.
- Z Coordinate elevation.
- Extrusion direction (UCS coordinates), with different Z (0, 0, 1) axis.
- Information related to a particular object type such as for dimensional constraint objects, name, and value; LIST displays the constraint type, reference type (yes or no), expression.

Step 1: Select object then LI Enter

```
        at point  X=2030.7185  Y=  50.4044  Z=   0.0000
        at point  X=1682.4570  Y=  50.4044  Z=   0.0000
Command: LI
LIST
Select objects: 1 found
Select objects:
                  LWPOLYLINE  Layer: "Road"
                            Space: Model space
                   Color: 19,155,72    Linetype: "BYLAYER"
                   LineWeight: 0.50 mm
                   Handle = d73
            Closed
    Constant width    0.0000
              area   62978.5030
         perimeter   1058.1966
          at point  X=1682.4570  Y= 231.2413  Z=   0.0000
          at point  X=2030.7185  Y= 231.2413  Z=   0.0000
          at point  X=2030.7185  Y=  50.4044  Z=   0.0000
          at point  X=1682.4570  Y=  50.4044  Z=   0.0000
```

Figure 241 *rectangle list and detail*

What do you mean by ANGLE?

We use command ANGLE to know the angle between points, circle, or arc.

Step 1: Ribbon: Home tabØUtilities panel ➢ Angle

Step 2: Select arc, circle, line or <Specify vertex>: **Select arc**

Angle=130°

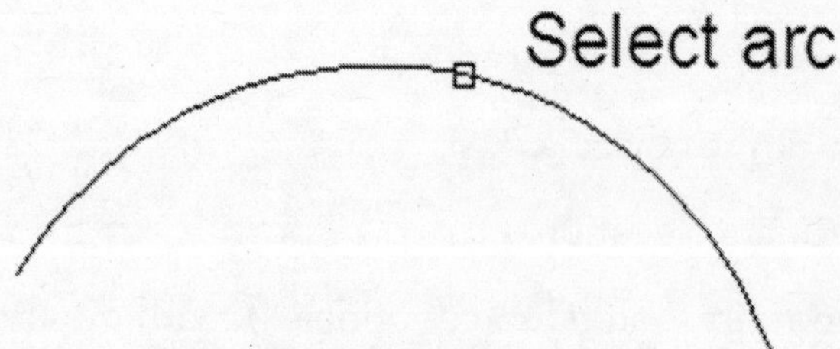

Figure 242 *select arc*

What do you mean by DIST?

DIST is an inquiry command which lists the distance between any two selected points in our command bar.

Step 1: DI Enter then click first point.

Step 2: Click second click.

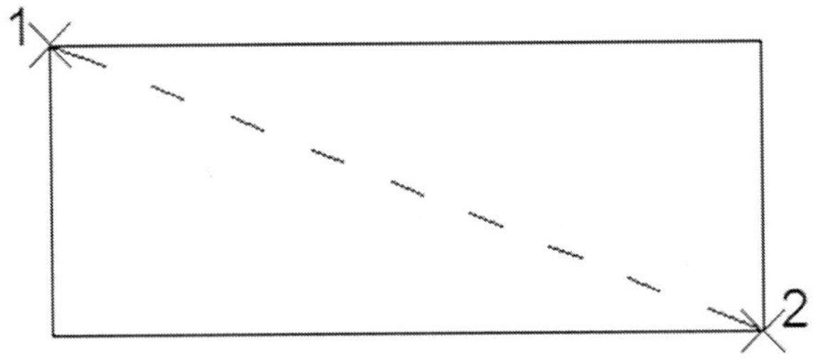

Figure 243 pick point

And press F2 key

```
AutoCAD Text Window - Drawing1.dwg
Edit
Command: *Cancel*

Command: *Cancel*

Command:
Command:
Command: *Cancel*

Command: *Cancel*

Command: *Cancel*

Command:
Automatic save to C:\Users\sagar\appdata\local\temp\Drawing1_1_1_2937.sv$ ...

Command:
Command: DI DIST
Specify first point:
Specify second point or [Multiple points]:
Distance = 26.9258,  Angle in XY Plane = 338,  Angle from XY Plane = 0
Delta X = 25.0000,  Delta Y = -10.0000,   Delta Z = 0.0000

Command:
```

Figure 244 List detail tab

What do you mean by VOLUME?

We use volume command, to compute volume of a defined object.

Step 1: Ribbon: Home tabØUtilities panelØVolume

Step 2: Click first point.

Step 3: Click second point.

Step 4: Click third point.

Step 5: Click forth point.

Step 6: T Enter for total.

Step 7: 5 Enter for height.

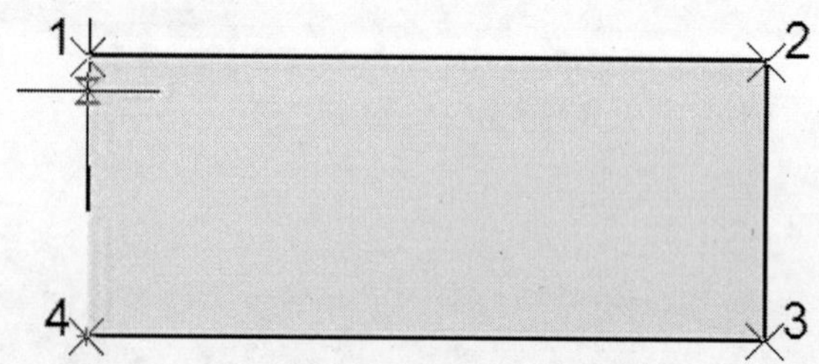

Figure 245 use of volume tool

Volume=1250.00

What do you mean by AREA?

We use the command area to calculate the area of an object or shape. Using this command, we can calculate the area of the object such as circle or by selecting the various points of a given object etc.

Step 1: AA Enter.

Step 2: Click first point.

Step 3: Click second point.

Step 4: Click third point.

Step 5: Click forth point.

Step 6: T Enter for total.

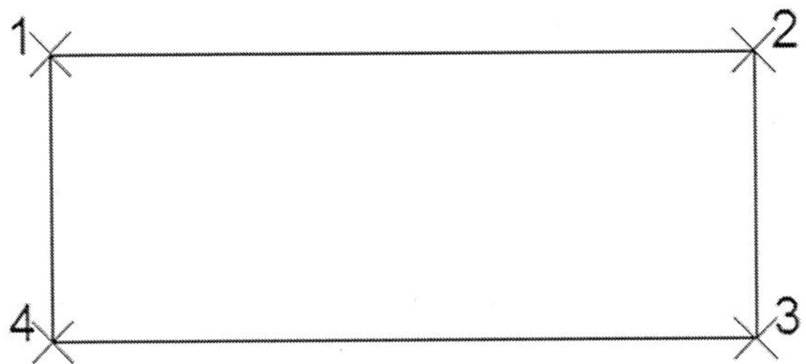

Figure 246 *use of area tool*

And press F2 key

AutoCAD Text Window - Drawing1.dwg

Edit

```
Specify next point or [Arc/Length/Undo/Total] <Total>: t

Area = 250.0000, Perimeter = 70.0000
Command: Specify opposite corner or [Fence/WPolygon/CPolygon]:
Command: AREA

Specify first corner point or [Object/Add area/Subtract area] <Object>: *Canc

Command: Specify opposite corner or [Fence/WPolygon/CPolygon]:
Command: *Cancel*

Command: aa AREA
Specify first corner point or [Object/Add area/Subtract area] <Object>:
Specify next point or [Arc/Length/Undo]:
Specify next point or [Arc/Length/Undo]:
Specify next point or [Arc/Length/Undo/Total] <Total>:
Specify next point or [Arc/Length/Undo/Total] <Total>: t

Area = 250.0000, Perimeter = 70.0000

Command:
```

Figure 247 *area list tab*

CHAPTER 7
Parametric

What is meant by PARAMETRIC DRAWINGS?

By using Parametric constraints, we can force an object to behave the way we want it to. If we need an object to behave the same way as other we need to set a constraint on it to do the same. For example, if we need a pair of line to always remain parallel to one another we can select constraint parallel, then even if we change the position of any one object the other will also change accordingly being always parallel to the first.

In the Parametric tool panels, Constraints are divided into three sections:

GEOMETRIC CONSTRAINTS

DIMENSIONAL CONSTRAINTS

MANAGE

Ribbon: Parametric

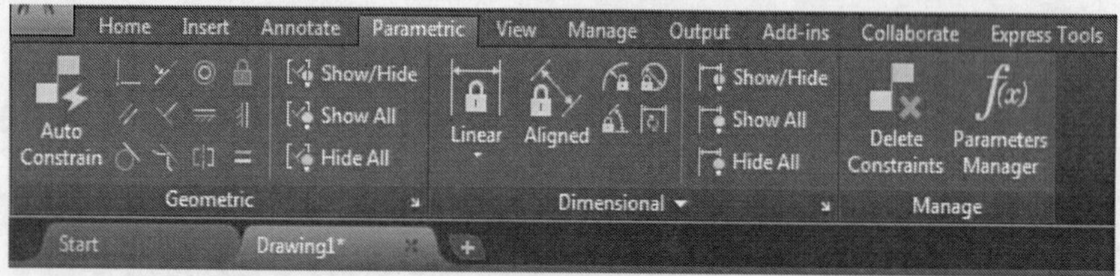

Figure 248 parametric tab

Menu: Parametric

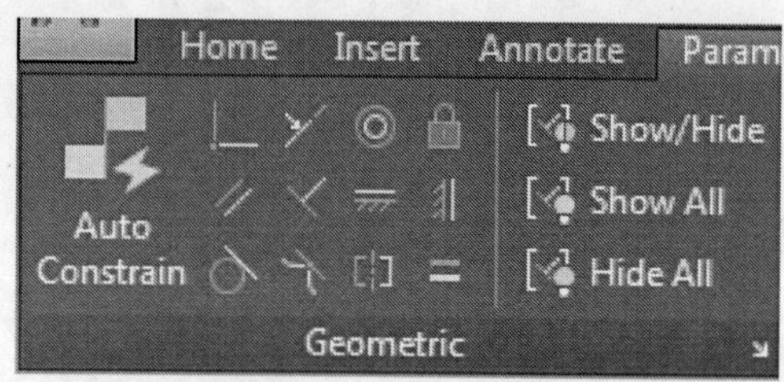

Figure 249 geometric panel

Geometric Constraints: Constrains a object based on geometric properties: Vertical, horizontal, etc.

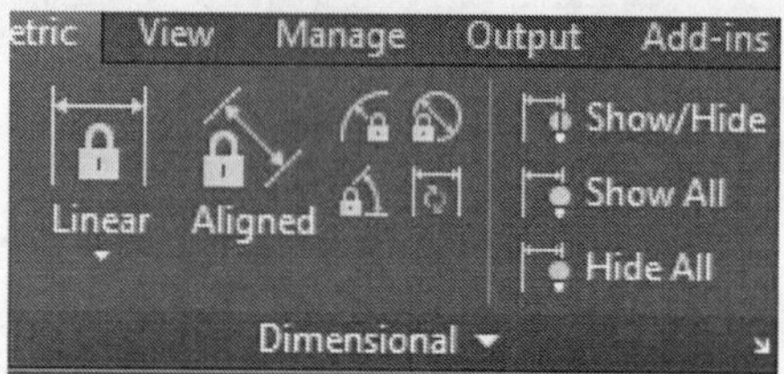

Figure 250 dimensional panel

Dimensional Constraints: Dimensional Constraints an object based on a set length or radius.

GEOMETRIC CONSTRAINTS

Ribbon: Parametric ➢ Geometric

Menu: Parametric ➢ Constraints

Geometric constraints associate geometric objects together. For example, If we have a symmetric drawing and later we make a change in the drawing, now the work will no longer remain symmetric, to maintain symmetricity of the drawing we apply the constraints symmetry and select the objects that we require to keep symmetrical.

Let's say we have a rectangle. As for rectangle, sides have to be perpendicular to each other. But in case during the design, we may need to change the position of a vertex. If we extend one of the rectangle vertex, then it would not remain a rectangle anymore. As AutoCAD is not aware that we want to keep it as a rectangle.

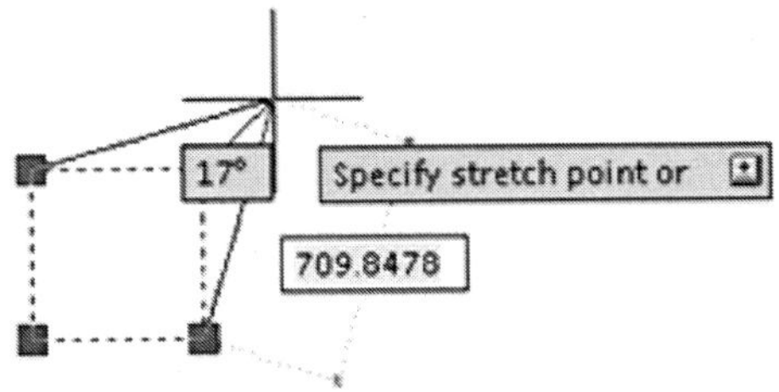

Figure 251 before geometric

To prevent this, in AutoCAD, we apply perpendicular constraints, ensuring that we want them always perpendicular to each other. So now we add a perpendicular constraint to the two sides. Now, try to stretch the vertex again.

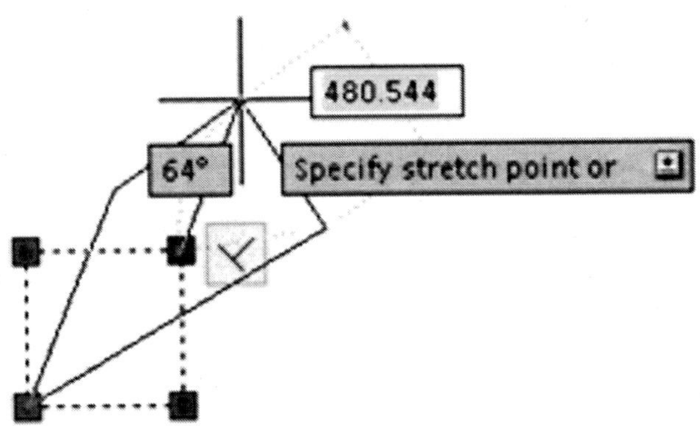

Figure 252 after geometric

As we can see, the two sides are perpendicular to each other. But the other edges don't. So, we need to add all constraint to keep it a rectangle.

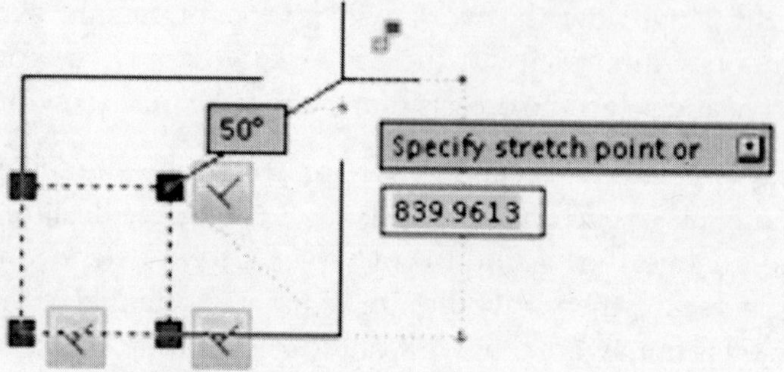

Figure 253 complete use geometric

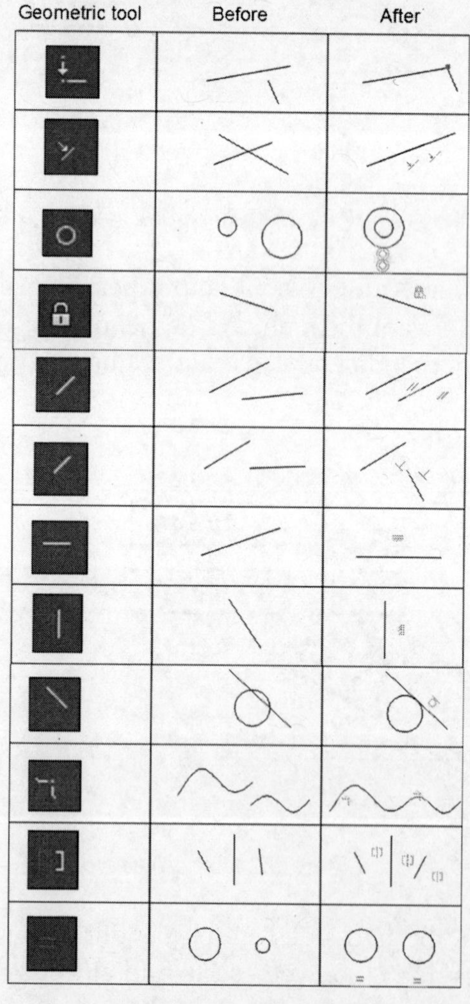

Figure 254 use of geometric

DIMENSIONAL CONSTRAINTS

Dimensional constraints are different to geometrical; these are used in making changes to what we have already worked with. If we have a drawing and we need to make amendments in the dimensions of the objects we use dimensional constraints

Instead of making a line vertical (for example), we can make a line 10 units long and make it stay that way until we change it. We can add more than one dimensional constraint on certain objects.

Draw a random angled line on the screen. Pick on the Aligned constraint icon. Aligned Pick two points on the line.

Notice that even if we have our Osnaps off, we can only pick the endpoints and midpoint on the line. After selecting the 2 points, we can now enter a length that we want the distance between those points to be.

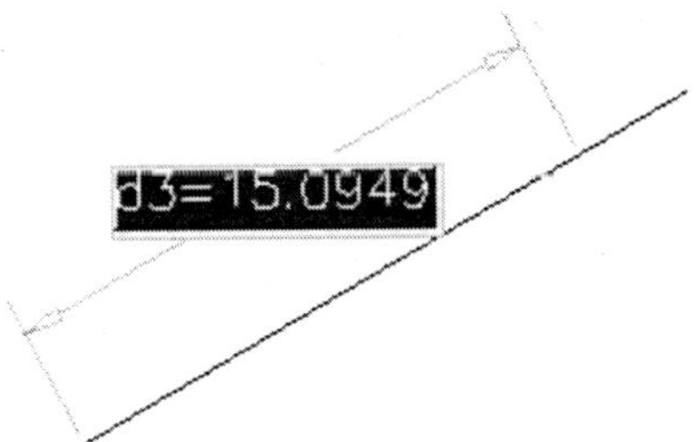

***Figure 255** dimensional sample*

With the constraint still highlighted, enter a number. D3 in this example refers to the 3rd dimensional constraint in the drawing. If we add a constraint from end to middle, add another from end to end (or vice versa). Notice that the constraint will be double the first one. If we change one, the other will change accordingly.

How to MANAGE CONSTRAINTS

In the third column of parametric toolbar we have 'manage' section. In this section we can perform two operations, we can use "parameters manager" to generate excel sheets of all the constraints used and secondly "delete constraints" to remove unnecessary constraints. By using Parameter manager, the excel sheet of parameter is generated, using this sheet we can also make changes in the sheet that are simultaneously applied on the objects in the drawing.

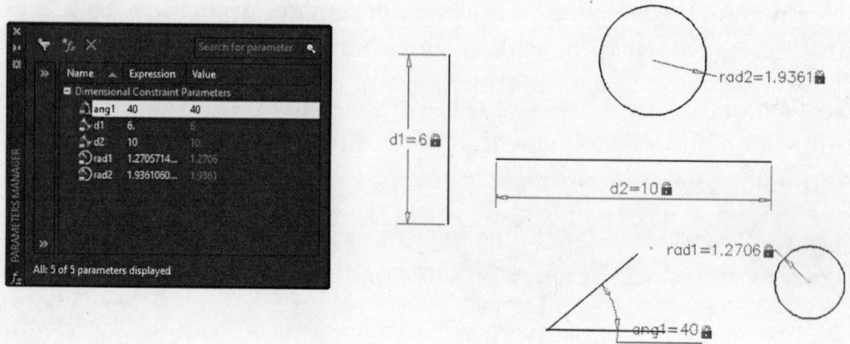

Figure 256 *Manage option*

CHAPTER 8
Setting & Option

What do you mean by INFER CONSTRAINT?

It a helping type of tool for applying geometrical constraints while creating and editing geometrical objects. We can also use it as parametric constraint and also creates line infer on and off.

INFER CONSTRAINT command automatically applies constraints between the object or points associated with object snaps and the object we are creating or editing.

Similarly AUTOCONSTRAIN command, constraints are applied only if the objects meet the constraint conditions.

With Infer Constraints turned on, to infer geometric constraint we specify the object snap while creating geometry. However, the following object snaps are not supported: Apparent Intersection, and Quadrant, Extension, Intersection

The following constraints cannot be implied:

- Smooth

- Symmetric
- Equal
- Concentric
- Fix
- Collinear

Toolbar: Status bar ➤ Infer

Create a line infer off and create a line infer on.

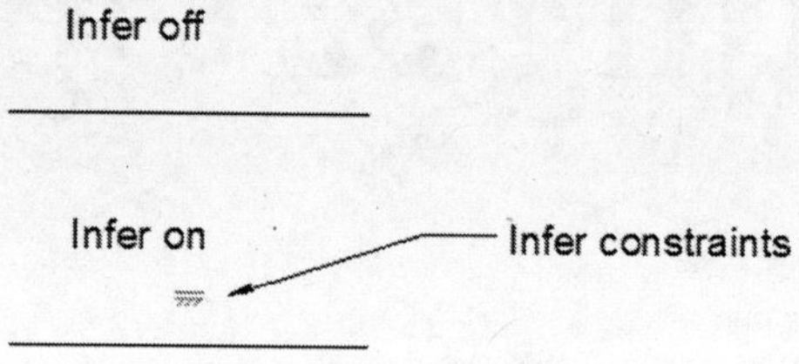

Figure 257 use of infer

Right click for Infer setting

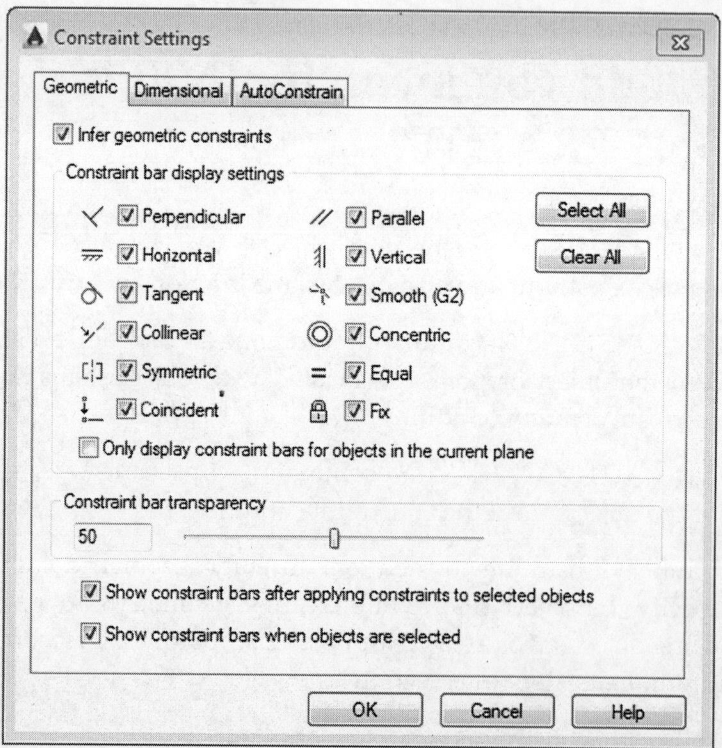

Figure 258 infer option

What do you mean by GRID & SNAP?

The grid is a pattern of straight lines that crosses over each other, forming square. In AutoCAD it is infinite in the given workspace. Grid helps us in aligning objects and visualizing the distances between them. Horizontal lines are said to be minor grid lines and vertical lines are said to be major grid lines.

Snap mode limits the movement of the crosshairs since it is defined. With Snap mode on, the cursor will follow an invisible rectangular grid. Snap is helpful in specifying precise points with the arrow keys.

Both are independent to each other but sometimes we use them simultaneously.

Toolbar: Status bar ➢ Grid or Snap

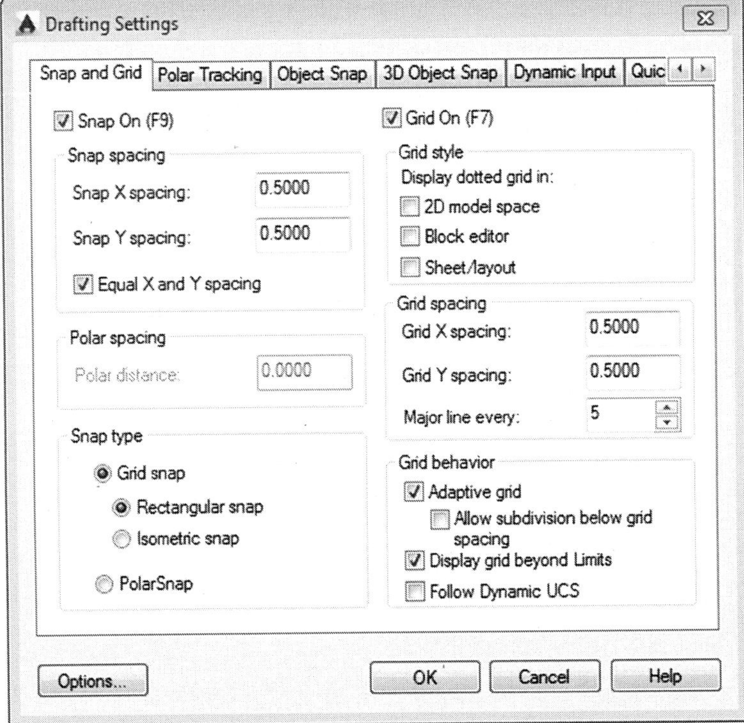

Figure 259 grid and snap setting

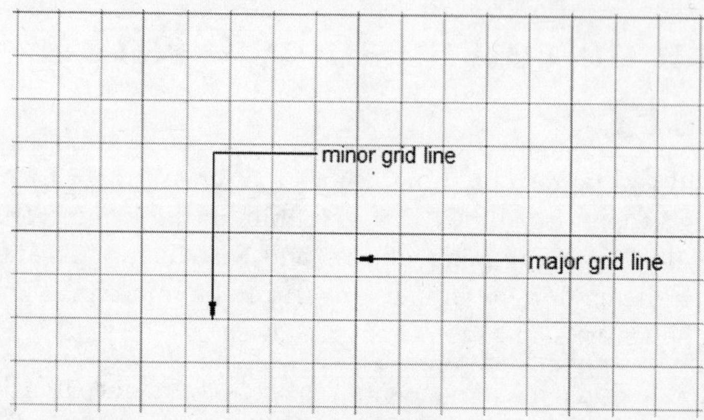

Figure 260 grid

What do you mean by OSNAP?

"OSNAP" means object snap. The Object Snaps are drawing tool that help us in drawing accurately. Osnap specifies us to *snap* onto a particular point location while picking a point. For example, using Osnap we can sharply pick the end point of a line or the center of a circle. Osnap in AutoCAD is so essential that we cannot draw faultlessly without them.

Toolbar: Status bar ØOsnap

ENDPOINT: The Endpoint command snaps to the end points of arcs, line and to polyline vertices.

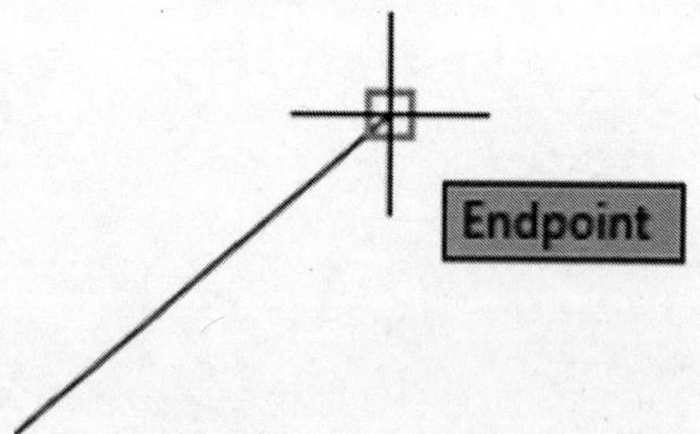

Figure 261 endpoint

MIDPOINT: The Midpoint command snaps to the mid-point of lines and arcs and to the mid-point of polyline segments.

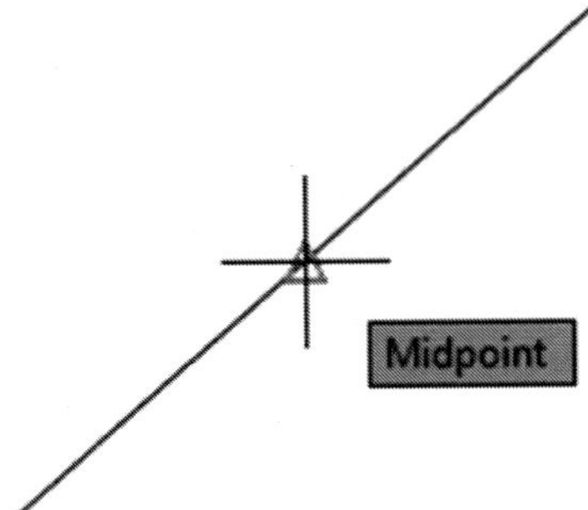

Figure 262 midpoint

INTERSECTION: The Intersection command snaps to the physical intersection of any two drawing sheet.

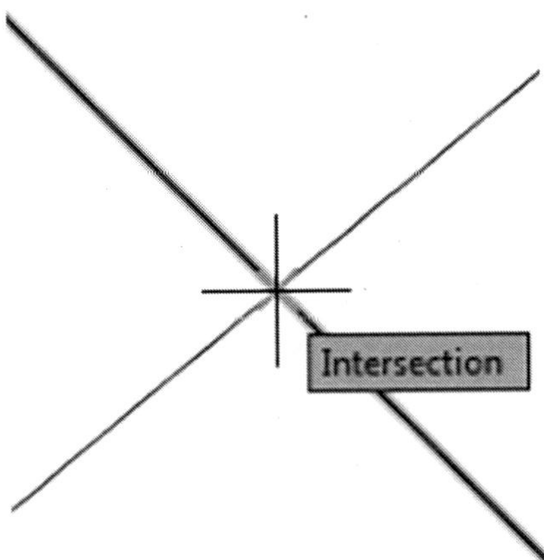

Figure 263 intersection

APPARENT INTERSECT: Apparent Intersection command snaps to the point where objects seem to intersect in the current view.

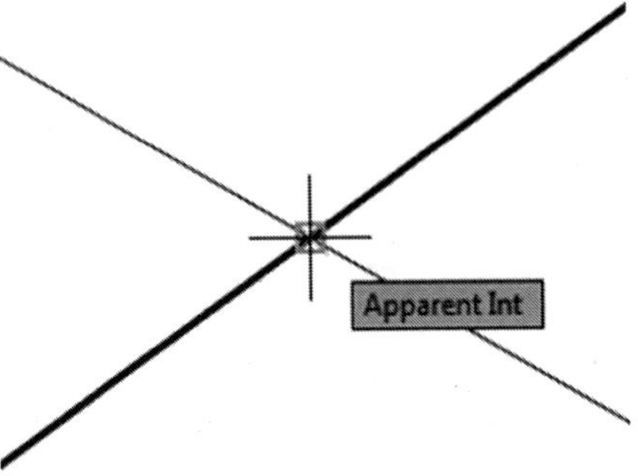

Figure 264 APPARENT INTERSECT

EXTENSION: The Extension command helps to snap to some point along the imaginary extension of the arc, the line, or polyline segment.

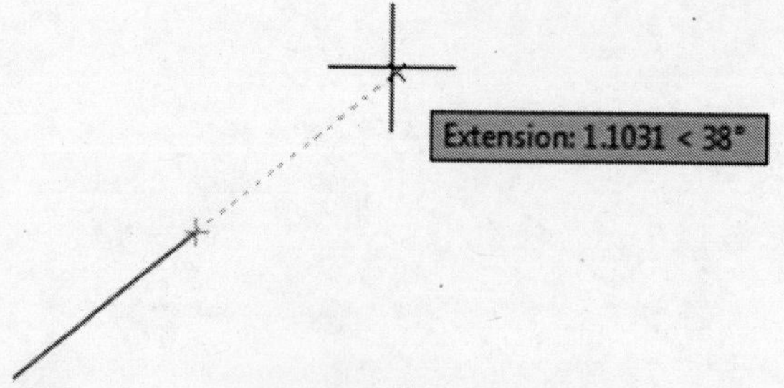

Figure 265 EXTENSION

CENTRE: The Centre command snaps to the center of a circle, arc, an object or polyline arc segment.

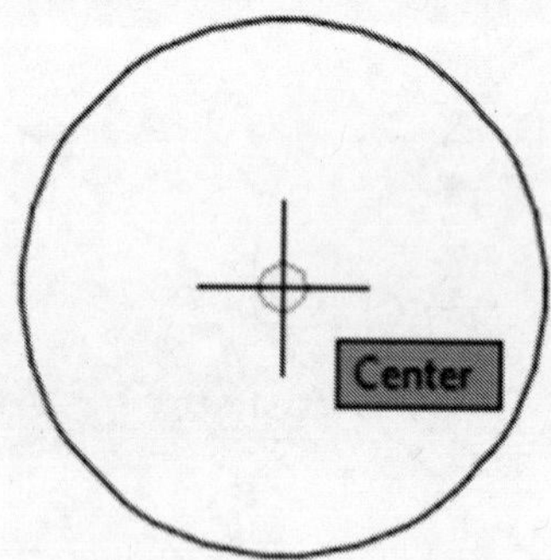

Figure 266 CENTRE

QUADRANT: The Quadrant command locates the four circle quadrant points located at east, north, west and south or 0, 90, 180 and 270 degrees respectively.

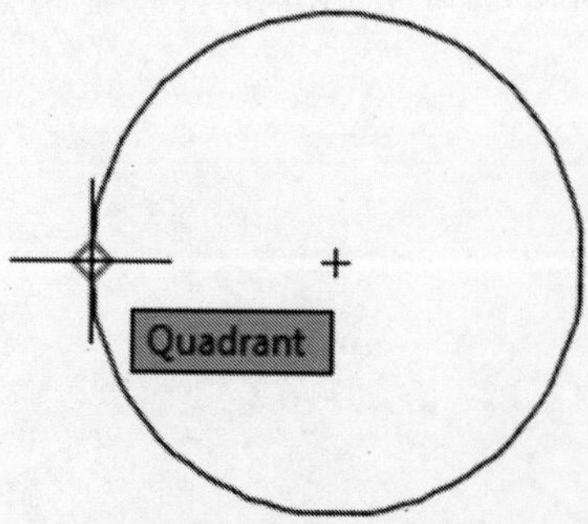

Figure 267 QUADRANT

TANGENT: The Tangent command snaps to a tangent point on a circle.

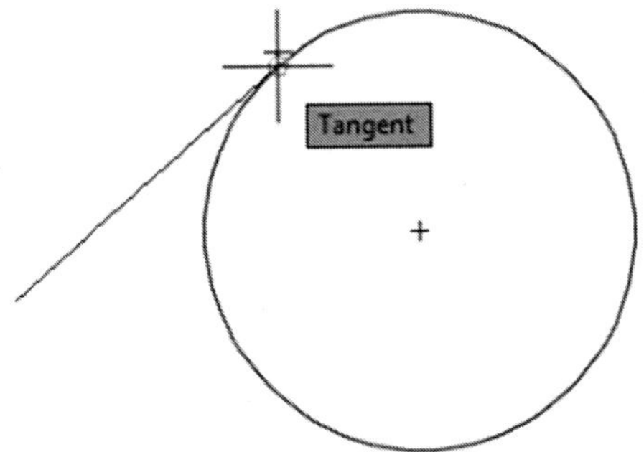

Figure 268 TANGENT

PERPENDICULAR: The Perpendicular command snaps to a point where it forms a perpendicular line with the selected object.

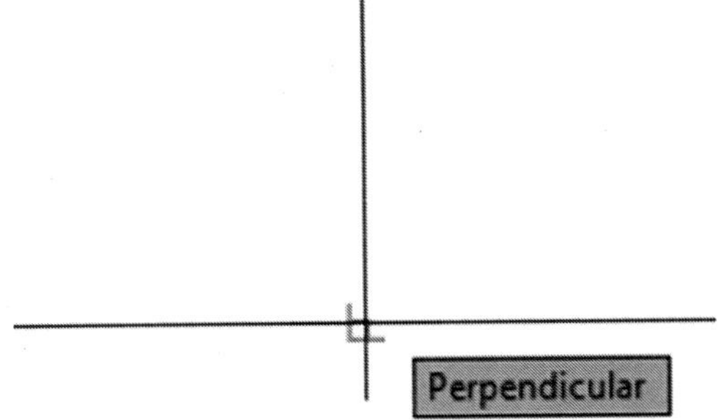

Figure 269 PERPENDICULAR

PARALLEL: The parallel command is used to draw a line parallel to a line segment.

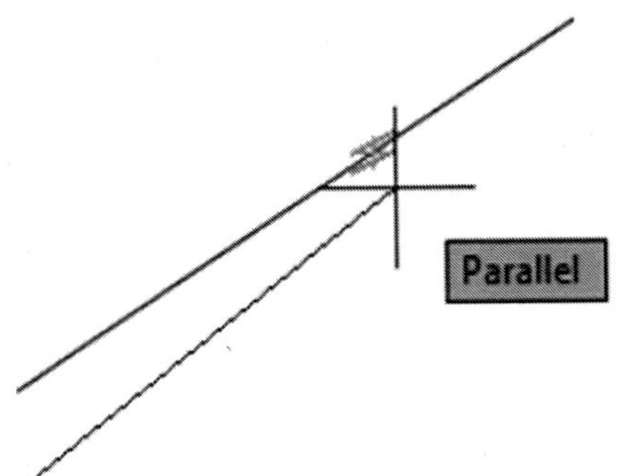

Figure 270 PARALLEL

INSERT: The Insert command snaps to the insertion point of the text, block or image.

Figure 271 insert

NODE: The Node command snaps to the centre of a Point object.

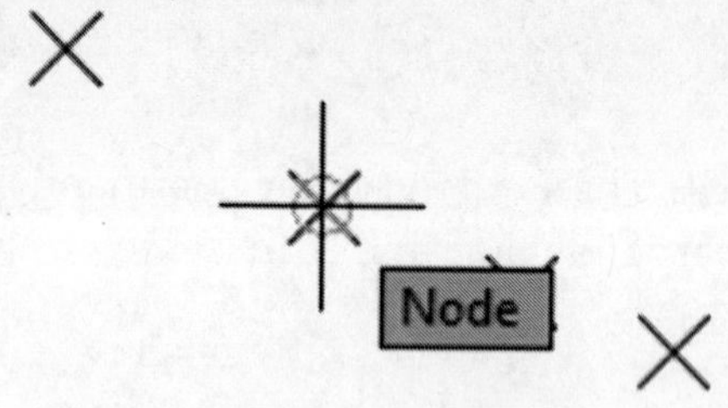

Figure 272 node

NEAREST: The nearest command snaps the nearest point on the drawing sheet.

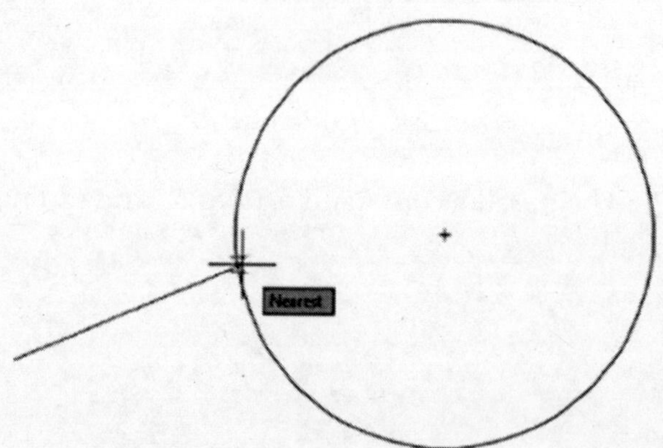

Figure 273 NEAREST

Geometric Center: Snaps to the Geometric center point of polyline, 2D polyline and 2D spline.

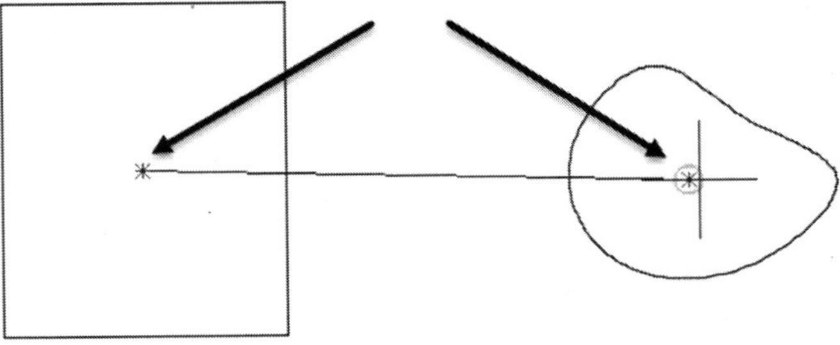

***Figure* 274** *Geometric Center*

What do you mean by POLAR?

It is a helping type of tool used to define an angle and to draw using angles. It setting contains two types of angles:

- INCREMENT ANGLE
- ADDITIONAL ANGLE

Increment angle is the angle that is shown in the drawing as a multiple of it, but additional angle we take more than one and they can be easily seen in the drawing.

Toolbar: Status bar ØPolar

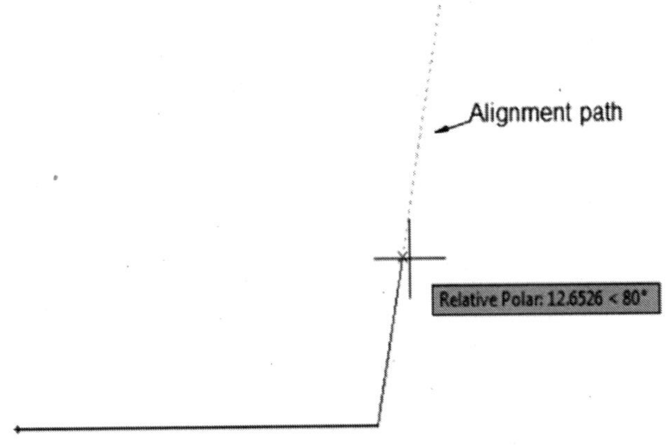

***Figure* 275** *polar*

What do you mean by ORTHO?

It is a setting by which cursor movement is constrained to vertical and horizontal direction only. We use it often when we specify the distance and angle between two points.

Toolbar: Status bar ØOrtho

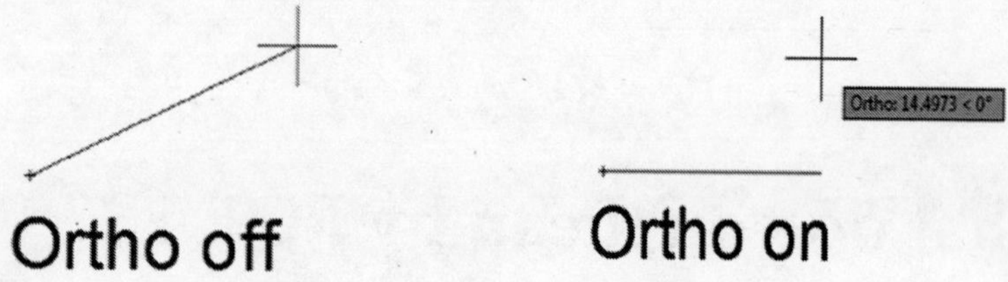

Figure 276 ortho

What do you mean by OTRACK?

It is a command that hover over the reference point until the Otrack box appears. Otrack point can be changed whenever needed.

Toolbar: Status bar ØOtrack

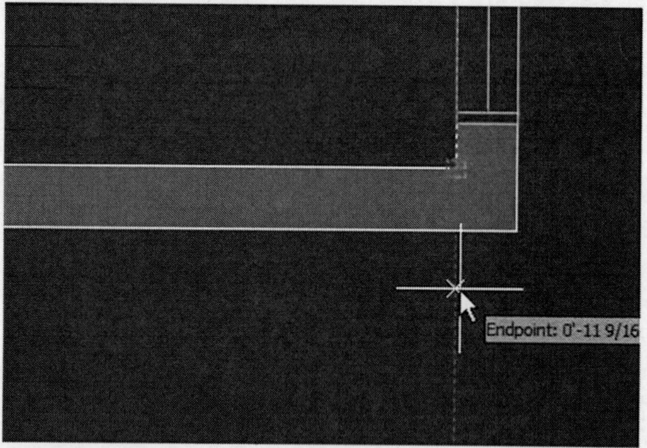

Figure 277 otrack

What do you mean by LWT?

It is a command used to increase and decrease the pixels of the line segment.

Toolbar: Status bar ➢ **Lwt**

Figure 278 use of LWT

What do you mean by DYN?

It is a setting in the status bar which acts as a command interface near the cursor so as to keep the focus in the drafting area.

Toolbar: Status bar ➢ **Dyn**

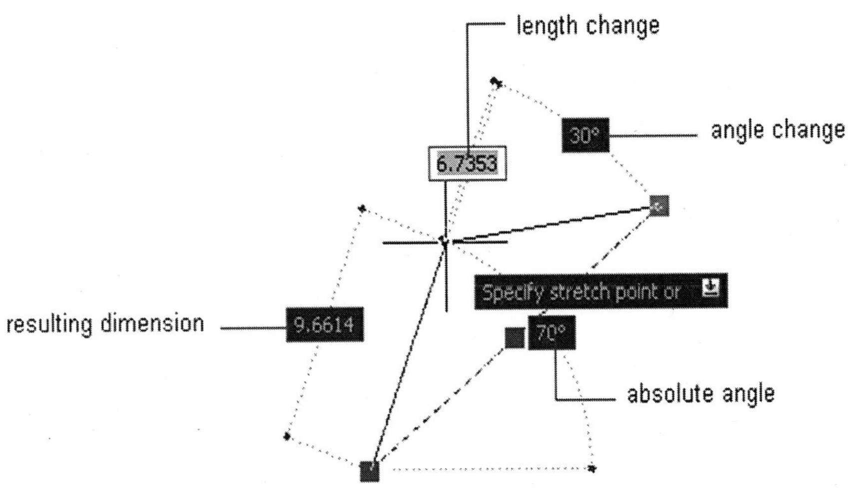

Figure 279 use of dyn

What do you mean by QP (Quick properties)?

It is used to observe the properties of the required object such as color, layer, linetype, centre x, centre y, circumference, area, diameter, radius.

Toolbar: Status bar ØQP Enter

Select object then modify properties like radius, color etc.

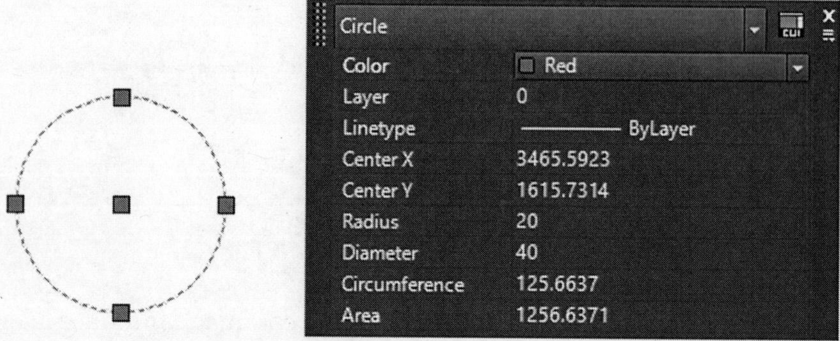

Figure 280 *use of quick properties*

What do you mean by COLOUR?

It is a display type of tool which is used in interface elements so that the elements used can be distinguished from one another.

Command: OP Enter

1 Click display tab

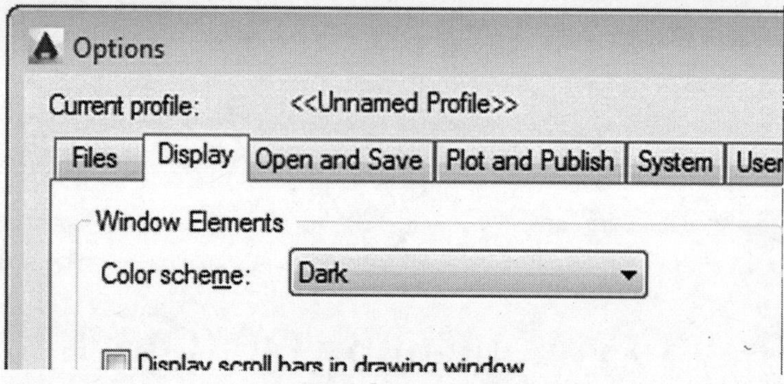

Figure 281 *display tab*

2 Click Colors

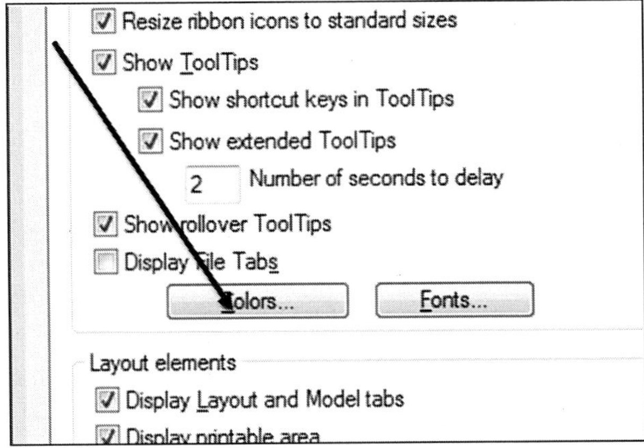

Figure 282 color tab

3 Chose interface element & color

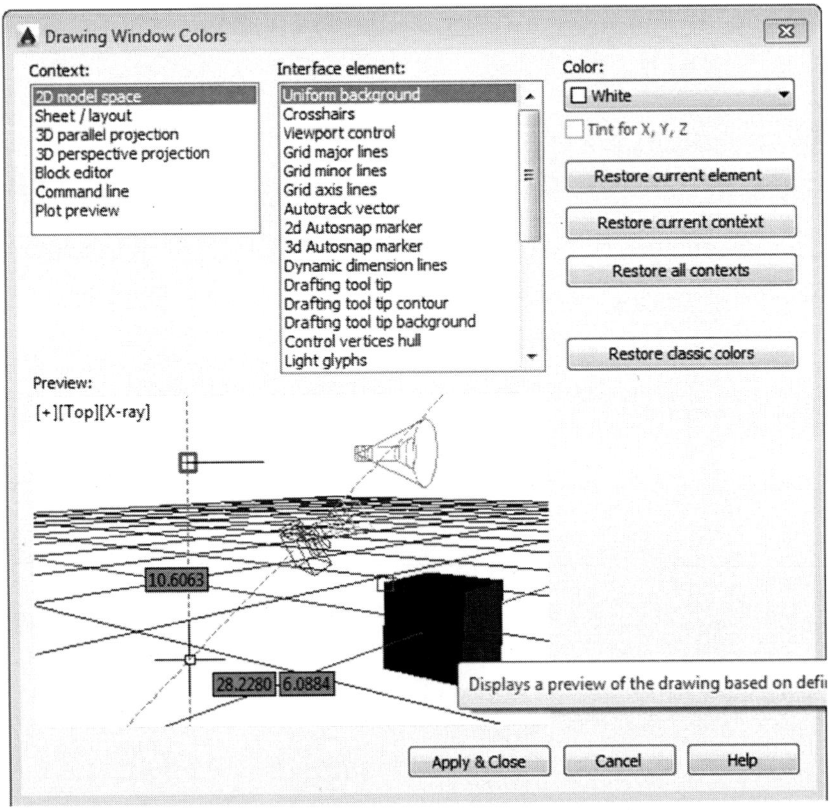

Figure 283 color choice

4 Click apply & close

5 Click apply & ok

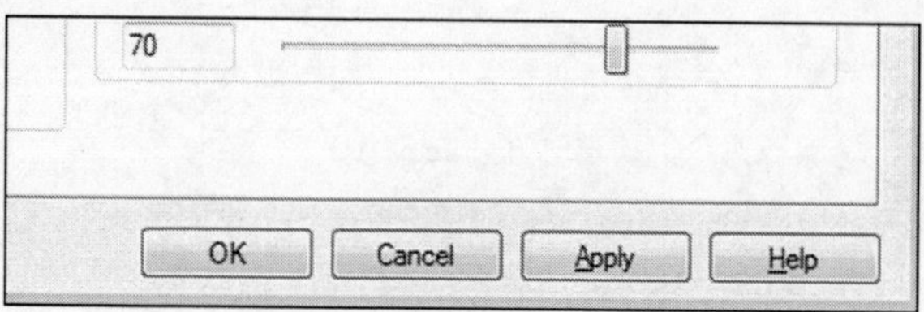

Figure 284 Click ok

What do you mean by UI COLOUR CHANGES

It is the latest setting in the AUTOCAD 2022 used to change the color to light and dark version so as to be identified easily in dark. It decreases the contrast between the elements used (tools) and workspace. It also helps in Lessing the strain on the user.

Command: OP Enter

1 **Click display & Chose color scheme.**

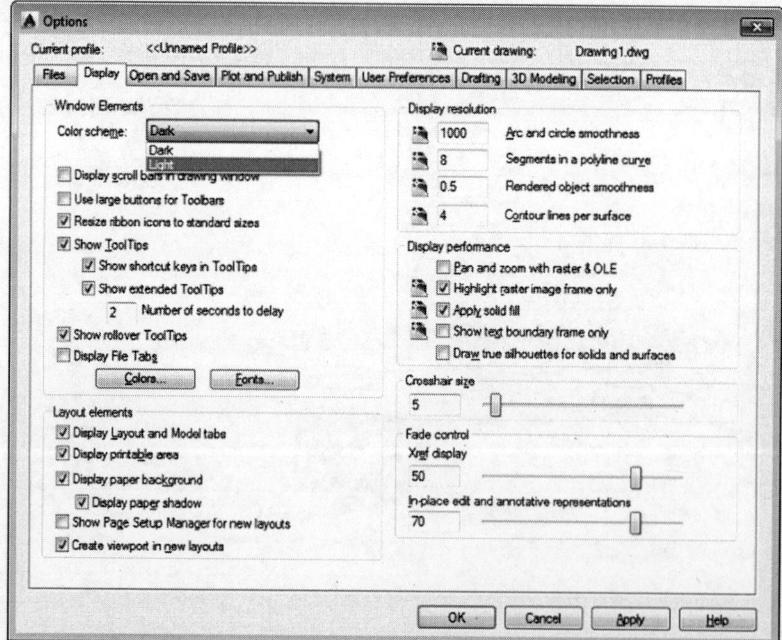

Figure 285 color scheme

Dark

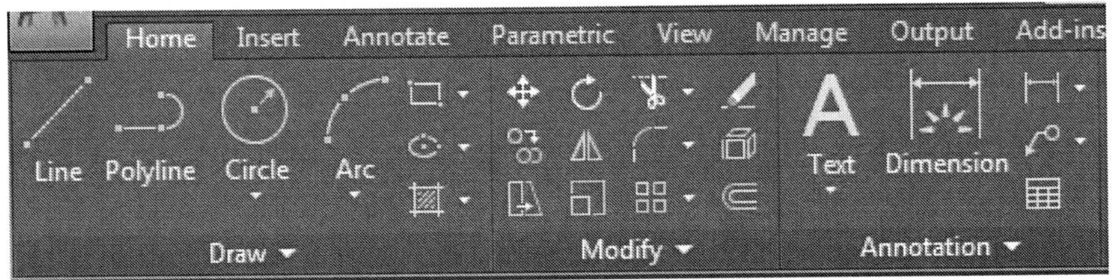

Figure 286 dark effect

Light

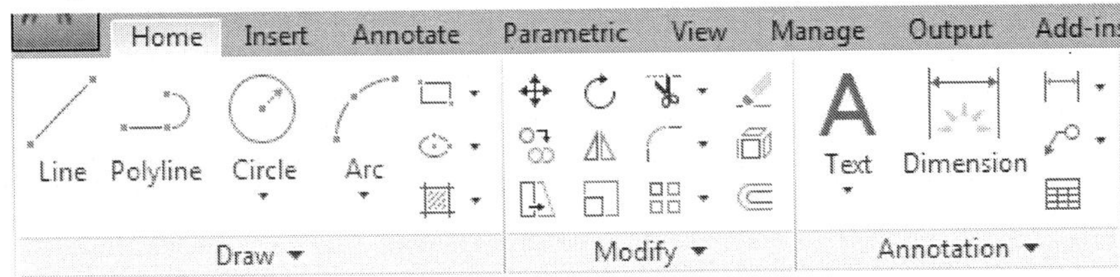

Figure 287 light affect

What do you mean by PAN?

It is a command to move view planar to the home screen.

Menu: View ØZoomØPan

Command: P Enter

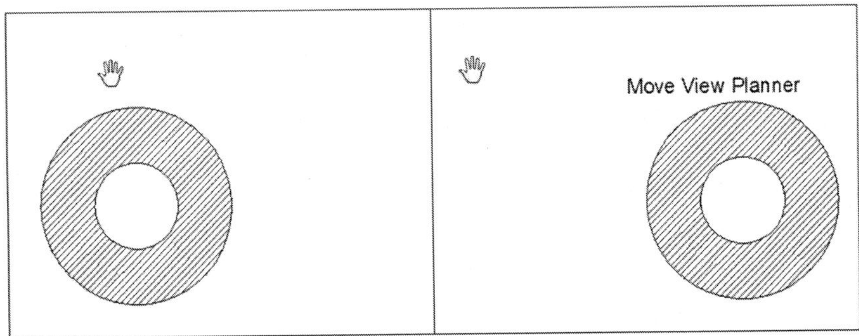

Figure 288 pan use

What do you mean by STEERING WHEELS?

It is a navigation wheel to have a watch on the drawing made in 2-d or 3-d. some of the tools in the navigation wheel are:

***Figure 289** STEERING WHEELS icon*

- **ZOOM:** *To show a smaller area of an image at higher magnification or a larger area at a lower magnification.*
- **REWIND:** It restores the most recent view. By clicking and dragging left or right, we can move backward or forward respectively.
- **PAN:** By panning we can reposition the current view.
- **ORBIT:** Rotates the current view around a fixed pivot point.

- **WALK:** Pretend walking through a model.
- **CENTRE:** To adjust the center of the current view by specifying a point on a model or change the target point used for some of the navigation tools.
- **UP/DOWN:** Slides the current view of a model along the Z axis of the model.

LOOK: Turns around the current view.

Command: WHEEL 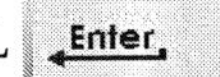

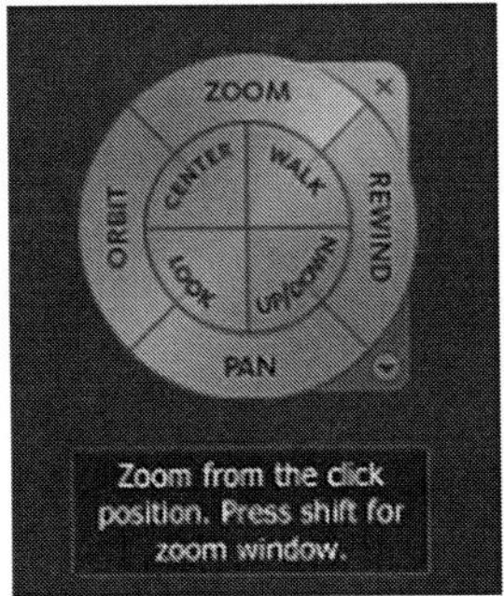

Figure 290 STEERING WHEELS

What do you mean by GRIPS EDITING?

It is an editing option for the grip in the line. In editing the grip, we can change the size and color of the grip.

Command: GR Enter

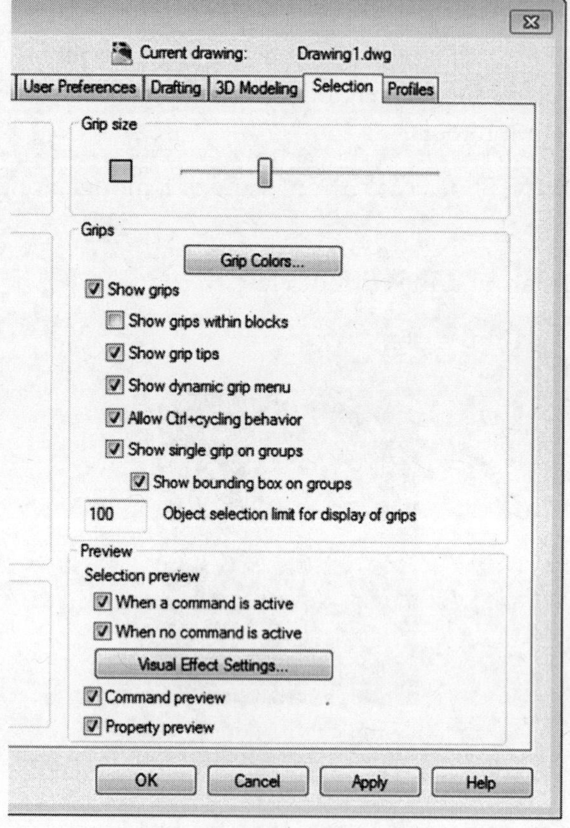

***Figure 291** grip setting*

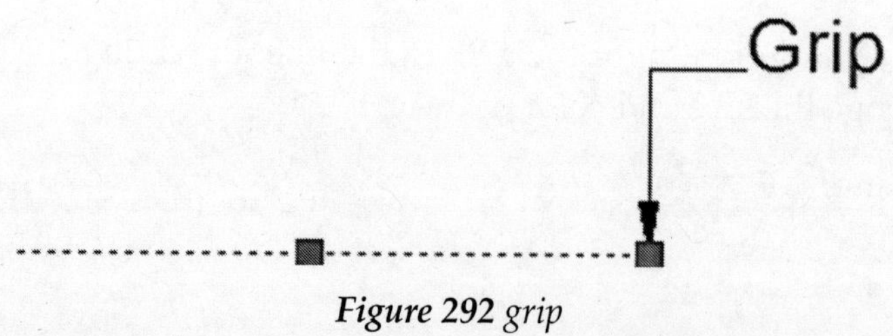

***Figure 292** grip*

What do you mean by REGEN?

It is a command to regenerate the entire drawing in the current viewport.

Menu: View ØRegen

Command: RE Enter

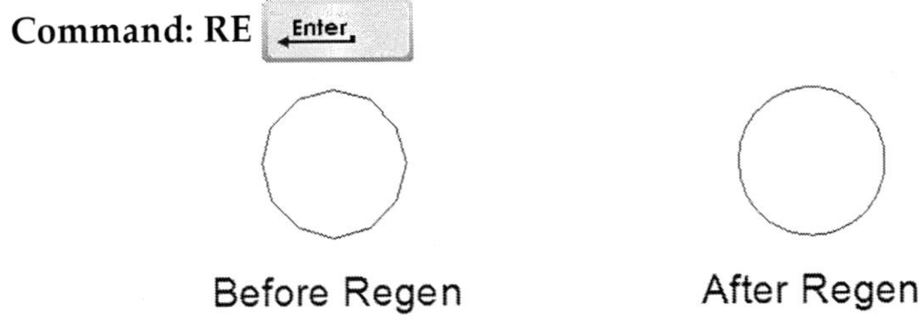

***Figure 293** use of regen*

What do you mean by MULTLINE STYLE?

It is a command to set the elements and the properties of the new multiline style or it can change them for the existing multiline style.

Menu: Format ➢ Multiline Style

Command: MLSTYLE Enter

without line

with line

***Figure 294** multiline style*

What do you mean by POINTSTYLE?

It is a command that shows and can change the current point style and size of the point style.

Menu: Format ØPoint Style

Command: PTYPE Enter

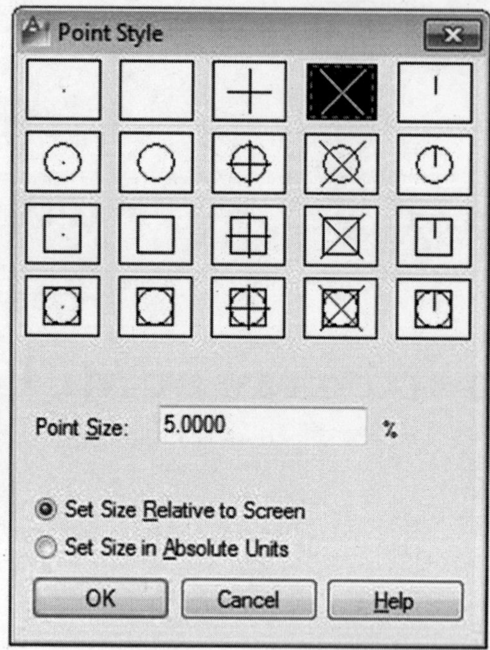

Figure 295 point style option

What do you mean by TABLESTYLE?

The overall look of the table is denoted by table style. We can use the default table style, STANDARD, or create own table styles.

When we create a new table style, we can specify a starting table. Once the table is selected, you can specify the structure and contents to copy from that table to the table style.

Ribbon: Annotate tab ØTables panel ØTables style

Menu: Format ØTables style

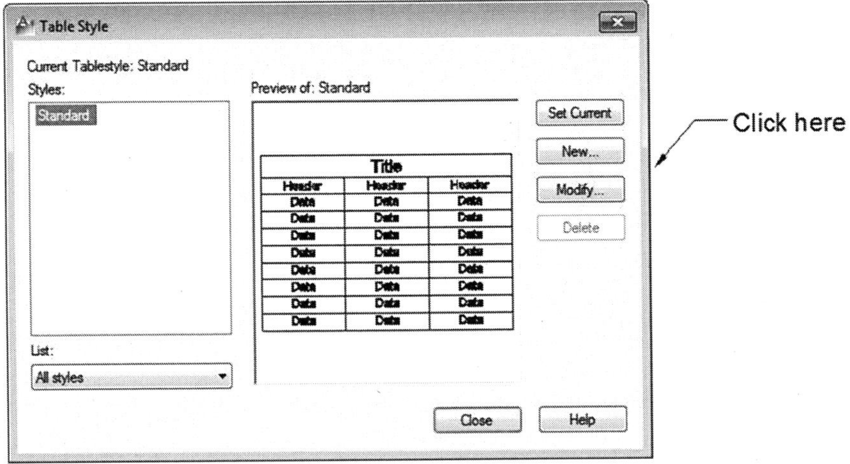

Figure 296 *table style tab*

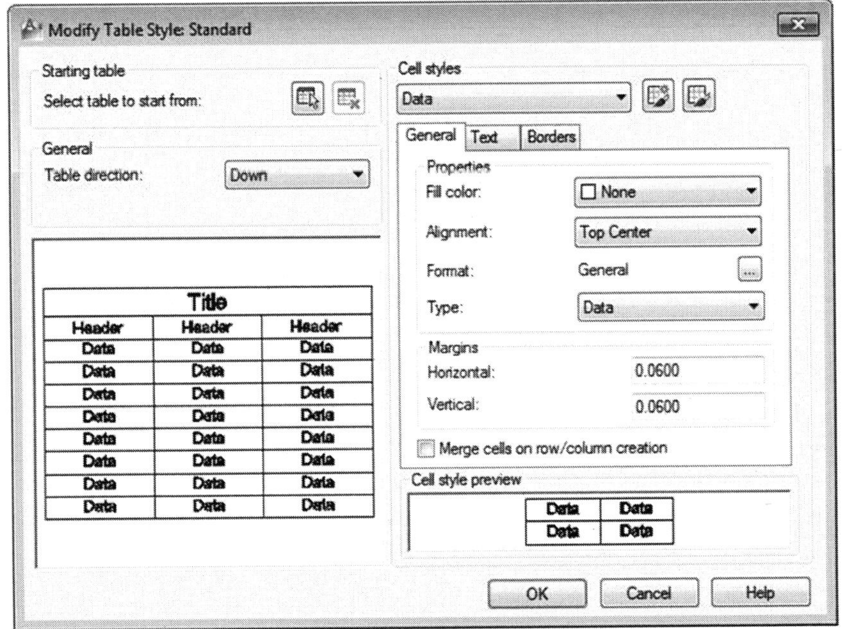

Figure 297 *table modify tab*

What do you mean by BACKGROUND MASK?

It is a command which is used for mtext for applying background mask. In background mask dialogue box, we can specify border offset and can fill color. It can also be applied in dimension objects.

Right click and click Background Mask.

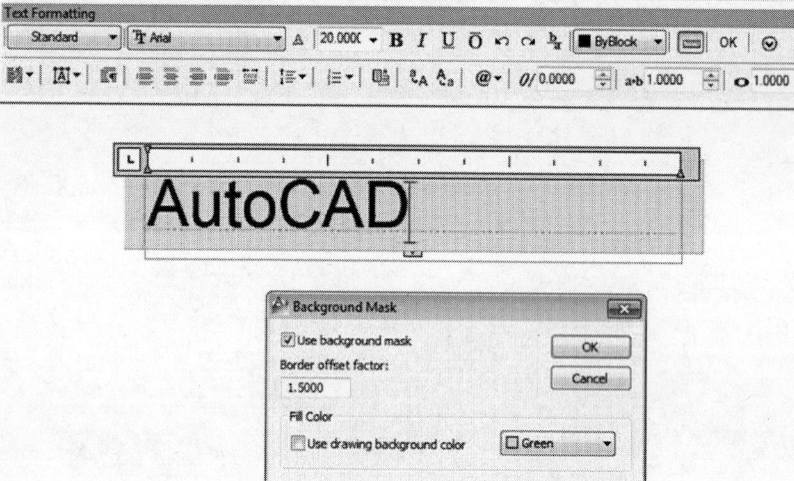

Figure 298 text background color

When do we use UNITS?

When we begin our new work we start by setting up the units of measurement in which we need to work. When we give the command for unit, we see the Drawing Units dialogue box. The dialogue box is divided into four main sections, namely 'Length,' 'Angle,' 'Insertion Scale.' In "Length" we select our linear units whereas in "Angles," we select our angular units. We can make amendments for linear units and angular units independently and in both sections we can also control the type and precision required. In the Angle section we can also specify the direction of angle as per our requirement and ease.

LINEAR UNITS

The default unit for length is "Decimal." The AutoCAD 2022 provides five different linear unit types in its box. Brief necessary description of the different units is provided in the table below.

Unit Type	1.5 Drawing Units	1500 Drawing Units	Description
Decimal	1.5000	1500.0000	Metric or SI units
Scientific	1.5000E+00	1.5000E+03	Decimal value raised to a power
Engineering	0′-1.5000″	125′-0.0000″	Feet and decimal inches
Architectural	0′-1 1/2″	125′-0″	Feet and fractional inches
Fractional	1 ½	1500	Whole numbers and fractions

ANGULAR UNITS

As linear, the default angular unit is also decimal and in general circumstances it is not required to be changed. We will find five different angular units provided to us in the units dialogue box. Below is a table describing the necessary description of the types of angular units?

Unit Type	12.5 Angular Units	180 Angular Units	Description
Decimal Degrees	12.500	180.000	Metric units
Deg/Min/Sec	12d30′0″	180d0′0″	Degrees, Minutes and Seconds
Grads	13.889g	200.000g	400 grads = 360 degrees
Radians	0.218r	3.142r	2 Pi radians = 360 degrees
Surveyor	N 77d30′0″ E	W	Compass bearings

What do you mean by LAYERS?

It is a command having large space where all types of object are placed, and the basic designing is done on it…

On starting AutoCAD default layer is only shown which is set current. The person using it defines the various different layers .the object defined is only seen on the layer, the layer itself is not seen. Layer is invisible matter…..

Ribbon: Home tab ➢ Layers panel ➢ Layer Properties Manager

Menu: Format ➢ Layer

Command: LA Enter

1. **Choose:** Format, Layer.

   Or

2. **Type:** LAYER at the command prompt.

   Command: **LAYER (or LA)**

   Or

3. **Pick:** the layers icon from the Layer Control box on the object properties toolbar.

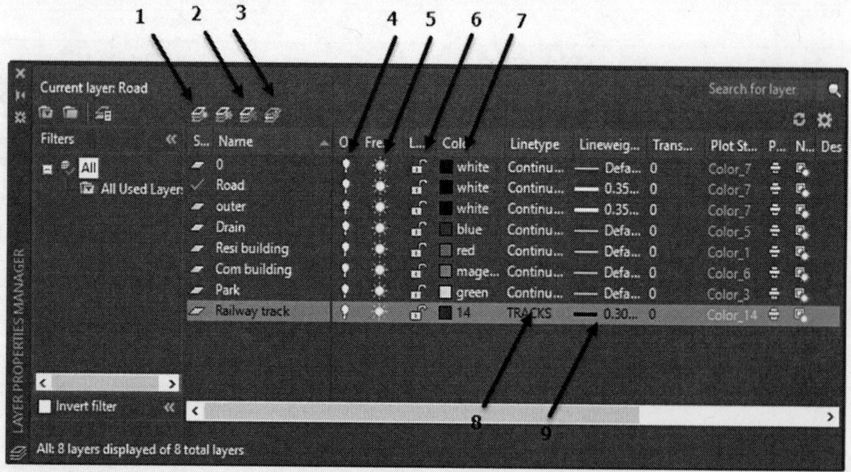

Figure 299 layer setting tab

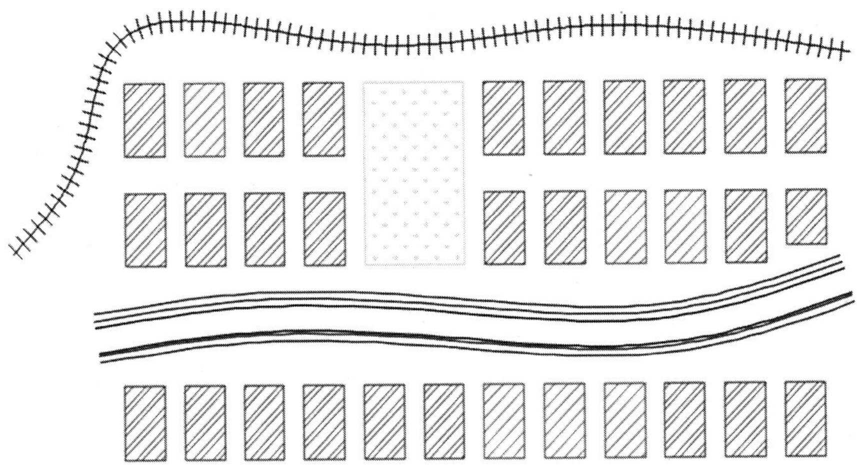

***Figure 300** layer use*

New Creates new layers.

? Lists layers, with states, colors and linetypes.

Make Creates a new layer and makes it current.

Set Sets current layer.

ON Turns on specified layers.

OFF Turns off specified layers.

Color Assigns color to specified layers.

Ltype Assigns linetype to specified layers.

Freeze Completely ignores layers during regeneration.

Thaw Unfreezes specified layers Ltype.

Lock Makes a layer read only preventing entities from being Edited but available visual reference and osnap functions.

Unlock Places a layer in read write mode and available for edits.

Plot Turns a Layer On for Plotting

No Plot Turns a Layer Off for Plotting

LWeight Controls the line weight for each layer

TIP:

Layers can be set using the command line prompts for layers. To use this,

Type –LAYER or -LA at the command prompt

1. **Type** Command: **-LAYER** or **LA**
2. **Type** One of the following layer options ?/Make/Set/New/ON/OFF/Color/Ltype/Freeze/Thaw:

Changing the Layer of an Object

1. **Click** Once on the object to change.
2. **Select** the desired layer from the Layer Control Box, AutoCAD will move the object to the new layer.

What do you mean by PURGE?

Purge is basically a command for removing unused named items from a drawing...

It can remove block definition, layers, dimension style, linetypes, empty text objects and text style.

Menu: Application menu ➢ Drawing Utilites ØPurge

Command: PU Enter

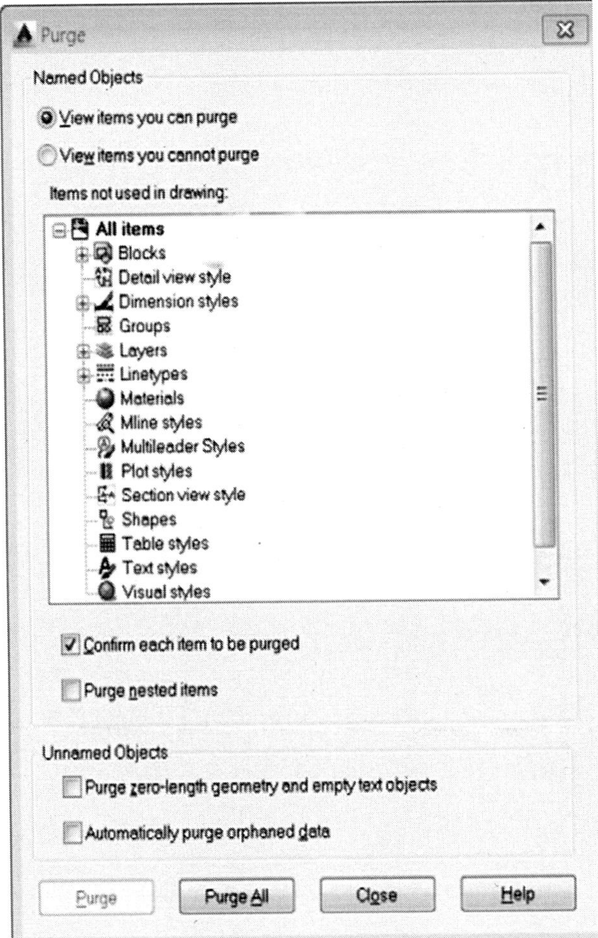

Figure 301 *purge tab*

CHAPTER 9

3D Modeling & View

BOX

Box is a 3D object. It can be create on X and Y plane and its height create on Z axis. Solid box create by this command.

Step 1: Ribbon- Home tab- Modeling- Box

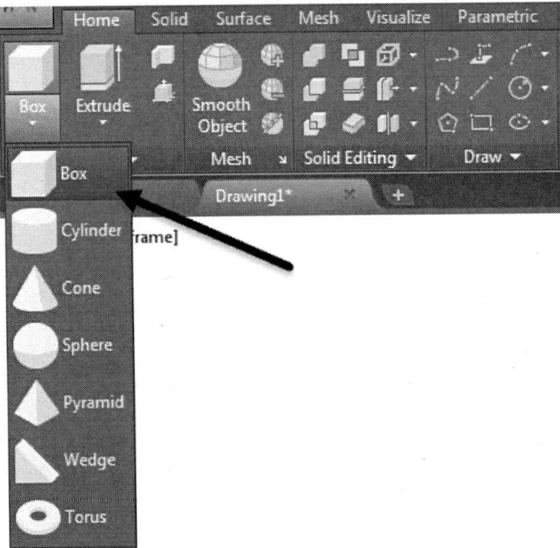

***Figure 302** box tool icon*

Step 2: Click first point for first corner.

Step 3: L Enter for box length.

Step 4: 60 Enter for length.

Step 5: 30 Enter for width.

***Figure 303** box length and width*

Step 6: 30 Enter for height.

***Figure 304** box*

CYLINDER

Cylinder command is like a circular pipe. To create cylinder we must have radius and height. After creating cylinder on x and y plane give height on z axis.

Step 1: Ribbon ➢ Home tab ➢ Modeling ➢ Cylinder.

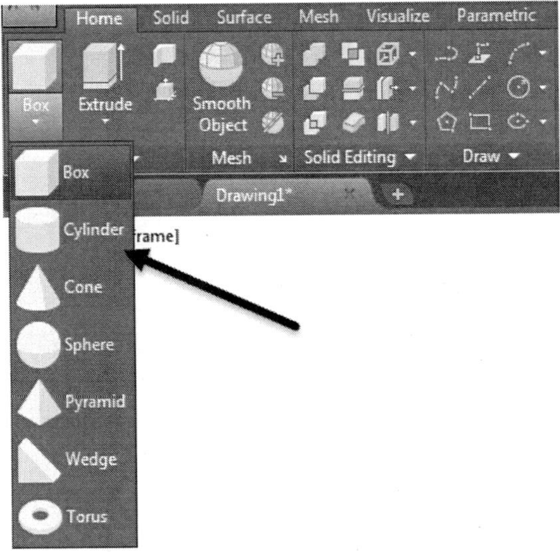

Figure 305 cylinder tool icon

Step 2: Click point for center point.

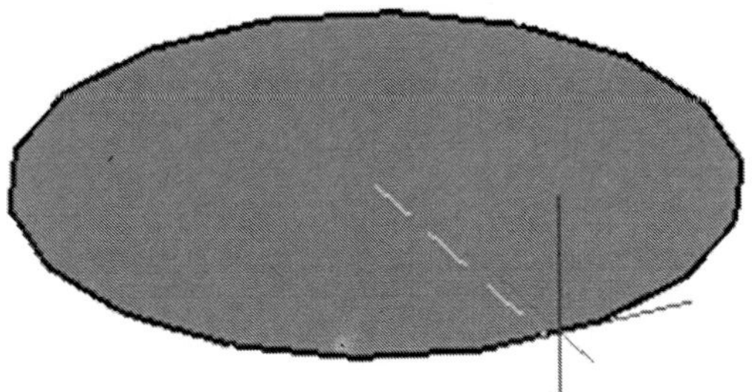

Figure 306 cylinder with radius

Step 3: 20 Enter for base radius.

Step 4: 30 Enter for height.

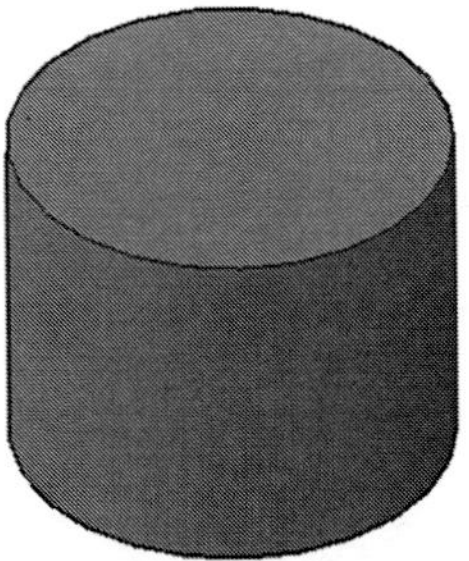

Figure 307 cylinder

HELIX

Helix command creates a spring. Firstly give base radius, top radius and height as well as turns to the use of helix.

Step 1: Ribbon ➢ Home tab ➢ Draw ➢ Helix.

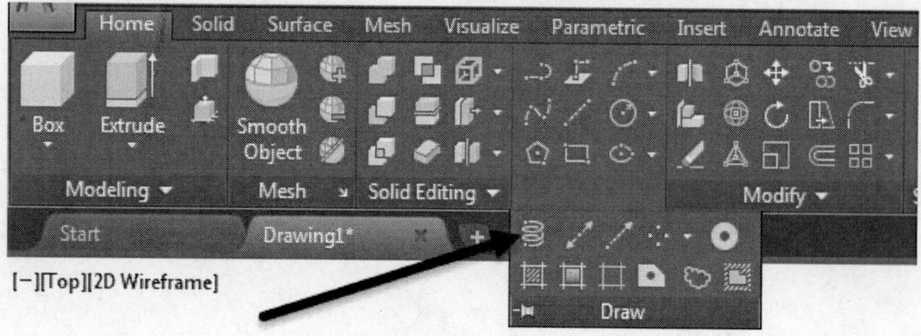

Figure 308 helix tool icon

Step 2: Click point for center base point.

Step 3: 20 Enter for base radius.

Step 4: 30 Enter for top radius.

Step 5: T Enter for helix turns.

Step 6: 10 Enter for turns.

Step 7: 50 Enter for height.

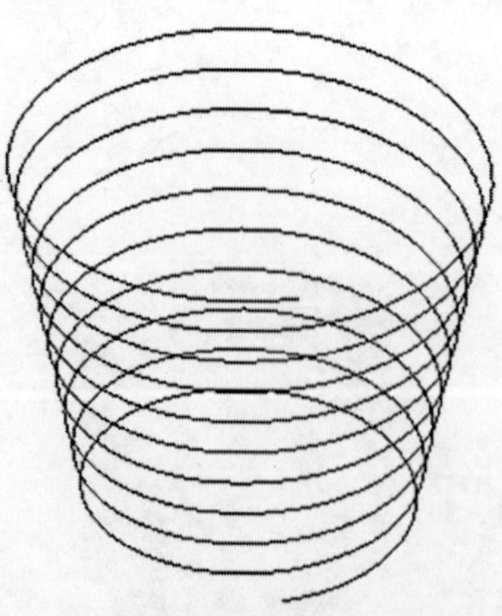

Figure 309 helix

CONE

Cone command is used to create circular cone. To create cone firstly give radius after that give height of cone.

Step 1: Ribbon ➢ Home tab ➢ Modeling ➢ Cone.

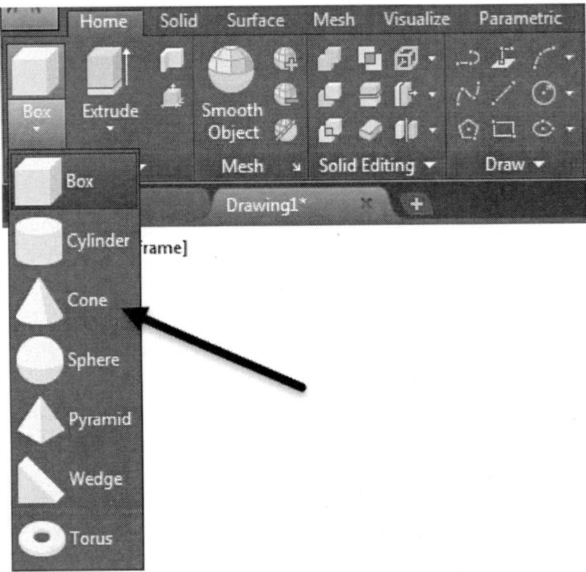

Figure 310 cone tool icon

Step 2: Click point for center point.

Step 3: 20 Enter for cone radius.

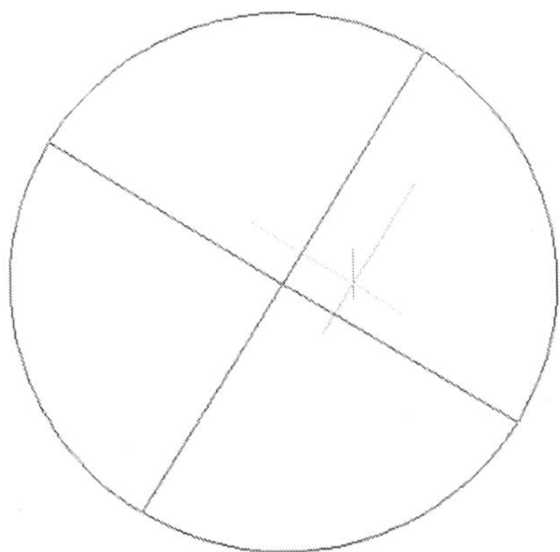

Figure 311 cone radius

Step 4: 40 Enter for cone height.

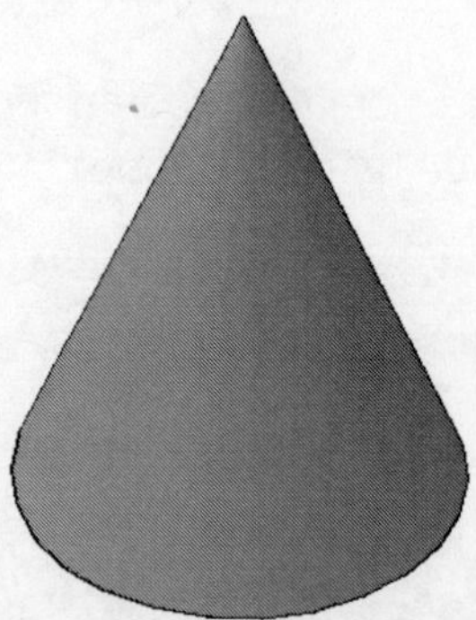

***Figure 312** cone*

TORUS

Torus command is used to create tube and give radius of circular tube and then give radius its thickness.

Step 1: Ribbon ➤ Home tab ➤ Modeling ØTorus.

***Figure 313** torus tool icon*

Step 2: Click point for center point.

Step 3: 20 Enter for torus radius.

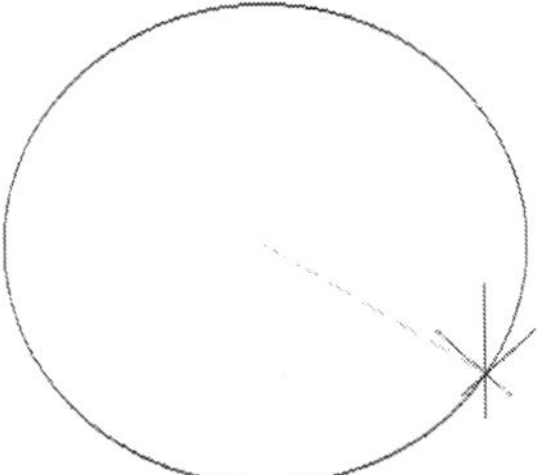

Figure 314 torus radius

Step 4: 5 Enter for tube radius.

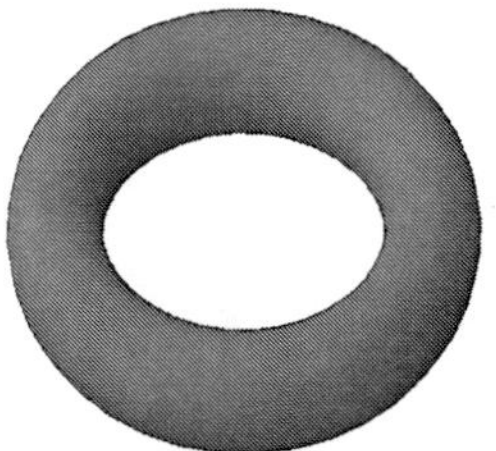

Figure 315 torus

PYRAMID

Pyramid command is just like cone, but cone is circular while pyramid have edge, it has at least 3 edge and can up to maximum 32.

Step 1: RibbonHome tab ➢ Modeling ØPyramid.

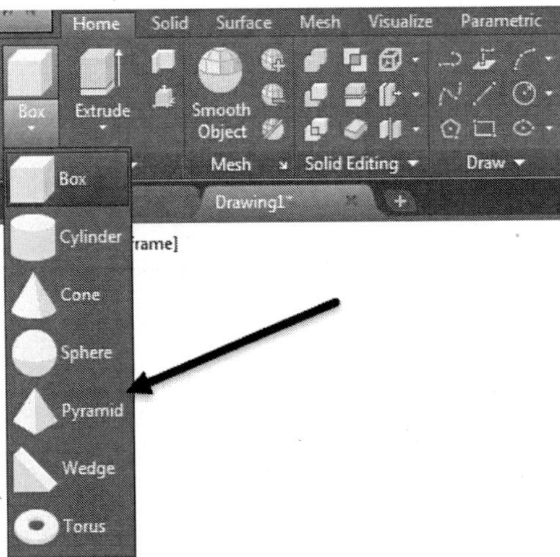

Figure 316 pyramid tool icon

Step 2: Click point for center point.

Step 3: 10 Enter for base radius.

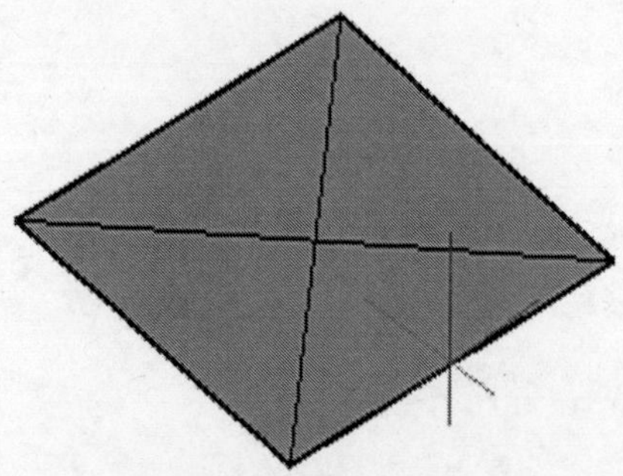

Figure 317 *pyramid base radius*

Step 4: 20 Enter for height.

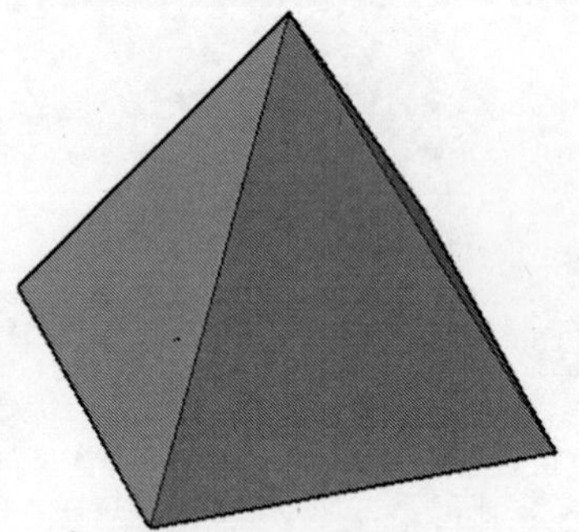

Figure 318 *pyramid*

WEDGE

Sphere command act like a ball, and create just like circle. But circle is 2d object while sphere is a circular shape solid 3d object, and created by giving center and radius.

Step 1 Ribbon ➢ Home tab ➢ Modeling ØWedge.

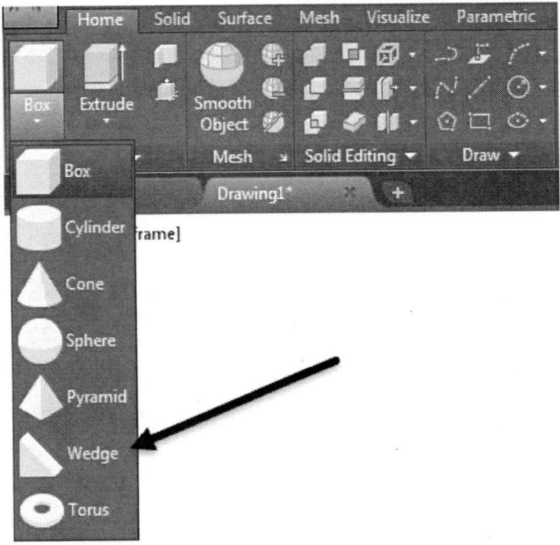

Figure 319 wedge tool icon

Step 2: Click first point for wedge corner.

Step 3: L Enter for length option.

Step 4: 40 Enter for length.

Step 5: 20 Enter for width.

Figure 320 wedge length and width

Step 6: 15 Enter for height.

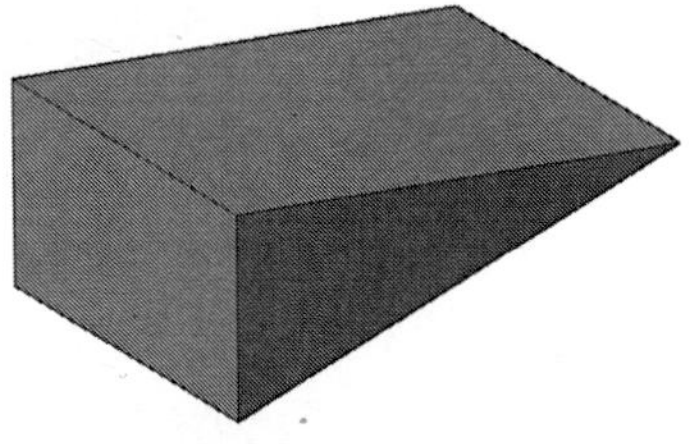

Figure 321 wedge

POLYSOLID

Polysolid command use just like Polyline, but polysolid is a 3d object so we also consider or give thickness and height.

It used to create wall or simple plane (surface).

Step 1: Ribbon ➢ Home tab ➢ Modeling ØPolysolid.

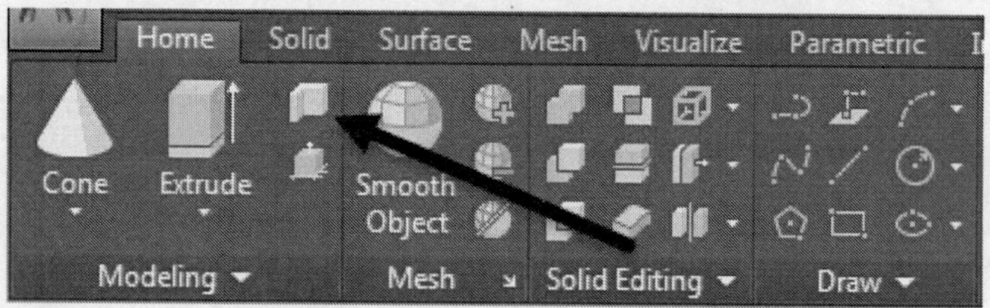

Figure 322 polysolid tool icon

Step 2: H Enter for height option.

Step 3: 10′ Enter for height.

Step 4: W Enter for width option.

Step 5: 9″ Enter for width.

Step 6: Click first point.

Step 7: Specify direction then 60′ Enter.

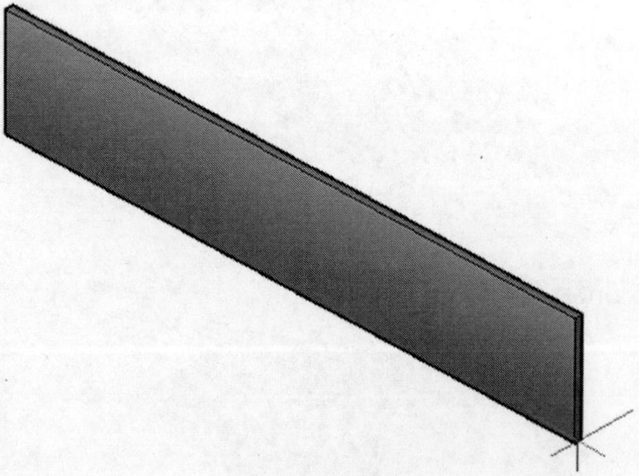

Figure 323 single polysolid

Step 8: Specify direction then 30′ Enter.

Step 9: Specify direction then 60′ Enter.

Step 10: C Enter for close.

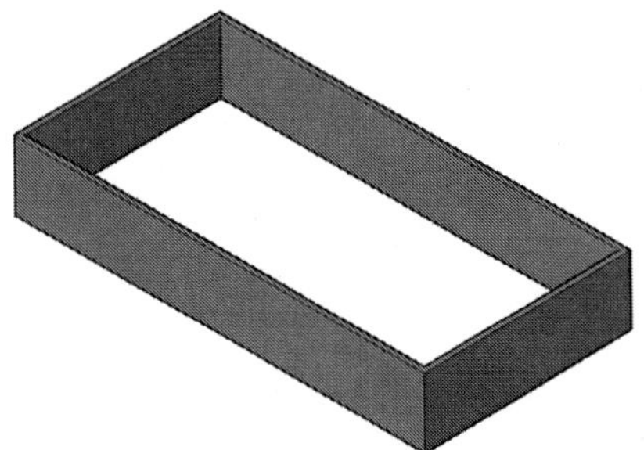

Figure 324 polysolid

SPHERE

Sphere command act like a ball, and create just like circle. But circle is 2d object while sphere is a circular shape solid 3d object, and created by giving center and radius.

Step 1: Ribbon ➢Home tab ➢Modeling ØSphere.

Figure 325 sphere tool icon

Step 2: Click point for center point.

Step 3: 20 Enter for radius.

Figure 326 *sphere*

EXTRUDE

Extrude command is used to increase the height of object like line, circle, rectangle, arc, spline etc.

That is by increasing height we convert those 2D object into 3D.

For example. If you take a circle and extend the height you can convert it in to cylinder (3D object) or convert a rectangle into box (I.e. 3D object)

Step 1: Ribbon ➢ Home tab ➢ Modeling ➢ Extrude.

Figure 327 *extrude tool icon*

Step 2: Select 2D object then Enter.

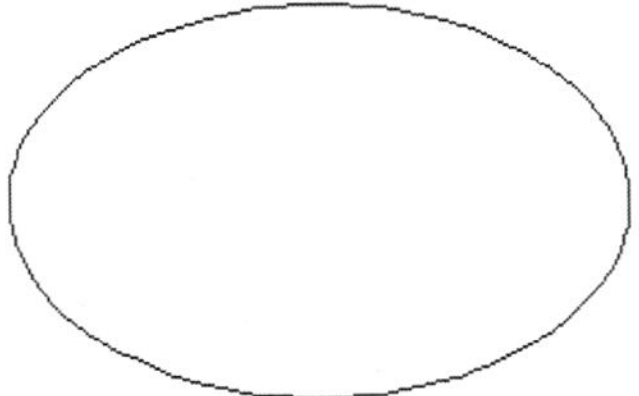

Figure 328 circle

Step 3: 30 Enter for extrude height.

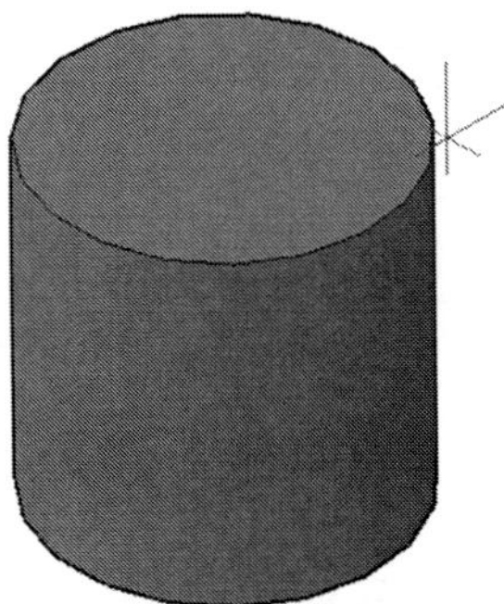

Figure 329 use of extrude

PRESSPULL

Presspull act like extrude command with a significancial difference, it allow to increase or decrease any face of the 3d object while extrude allow only increase in height of 2d.

Step 1: Ribbon ➢ Home tab ➢ Modeling ØPresspull.

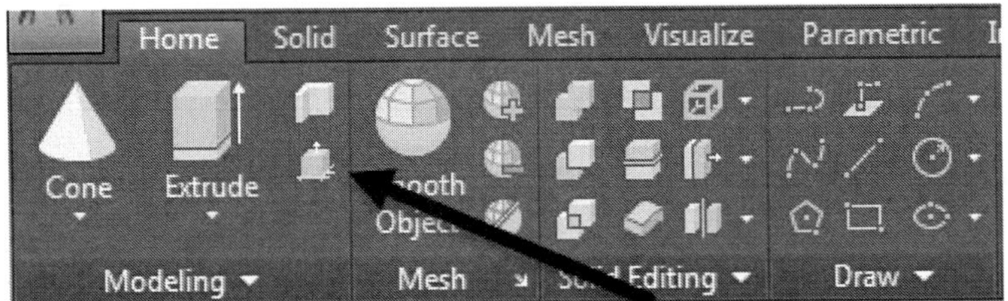

Figure 330 presspull tool icon

Step 2: Select face for presspull.

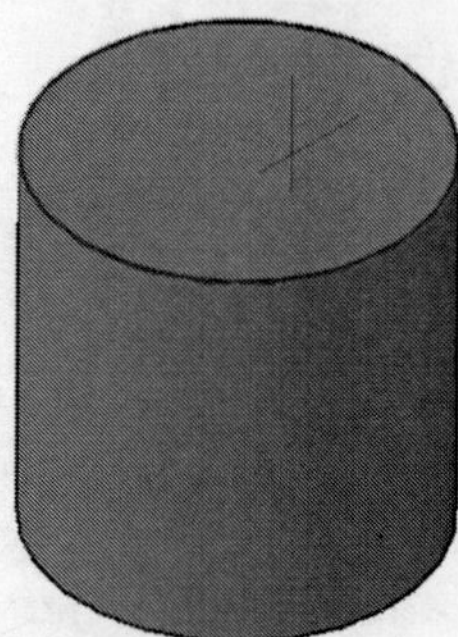

Figure 331 *cylinder*

Step 3: 10 Enter for extrusion height.

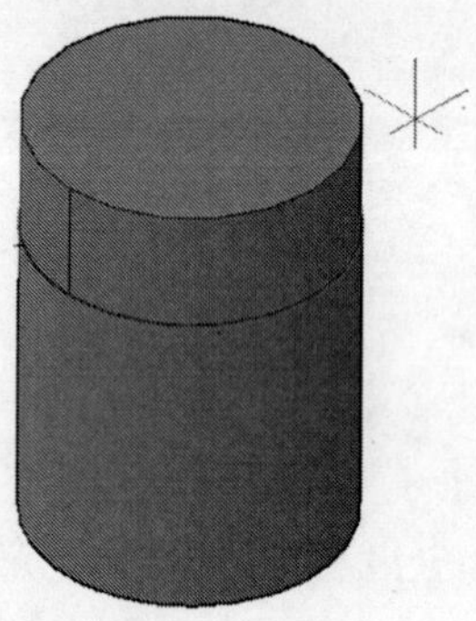

Figure 332 *increases height*

LOFT

Loft command is used to convert two or more than two 2d object into single 3d object. Loft command work on any 2d object which is built upon

Any 3rd object by selecting simultaneously both the object and then convert in single 3d object.

To use this command both object have different Z-axis (i.e. height must be different).

Step 1: Ribbon ➤ Home tab ➤ Modeling ➤ Loft.

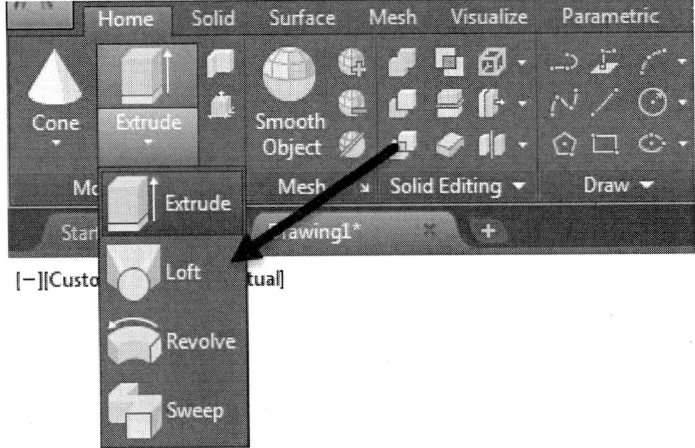

Figure 333 loft tool icon

Step 2: Select first object.

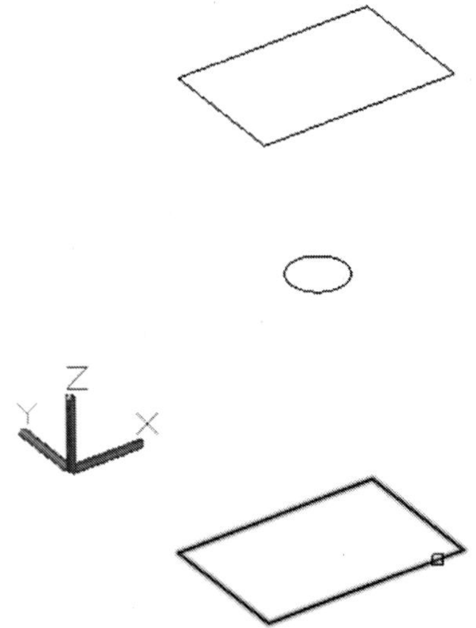

Figure 334 select first object

Step 3: Select second object.

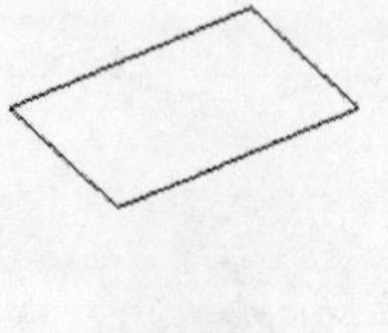

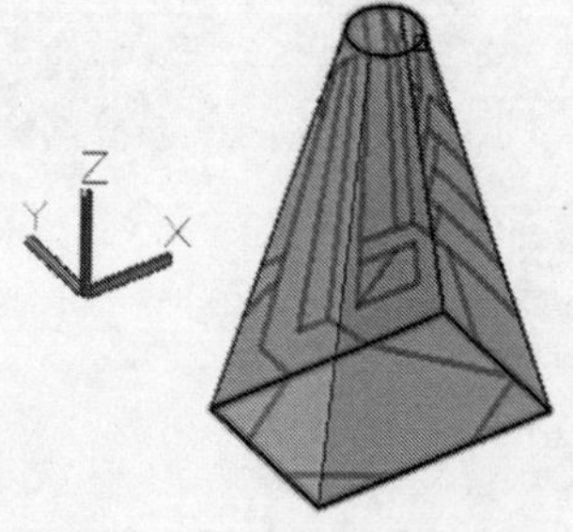

***Figure 335** Select second object.*

Step 4: Select third object.

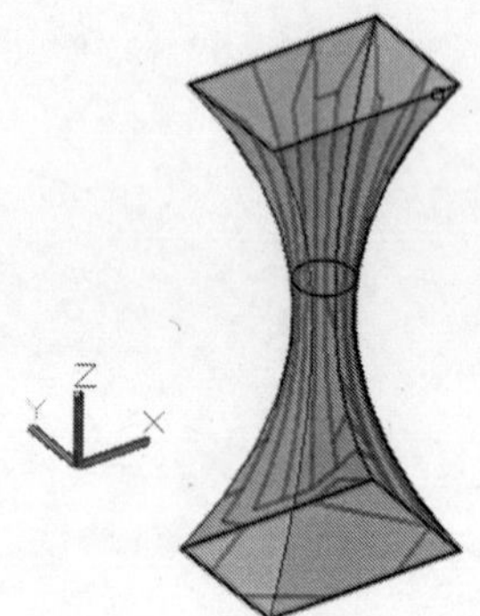

***Figure 336** Select third object.*

Step 5: Double enter.

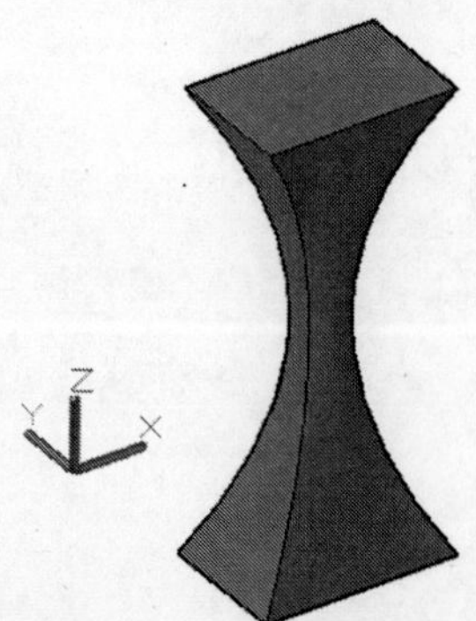

***Figure 337** loft object*

REVOLVE

Revolve command is use to convert a 2d object into 3d by revolving that object on one of any axis with respect to 2 distinguish point of that axes.

That is choose two different point on that targeted axis and revolve the object circle with respect to that point.

Step 1: Ribbon ➤ Home tab ➤ Modeling ØRevolve.

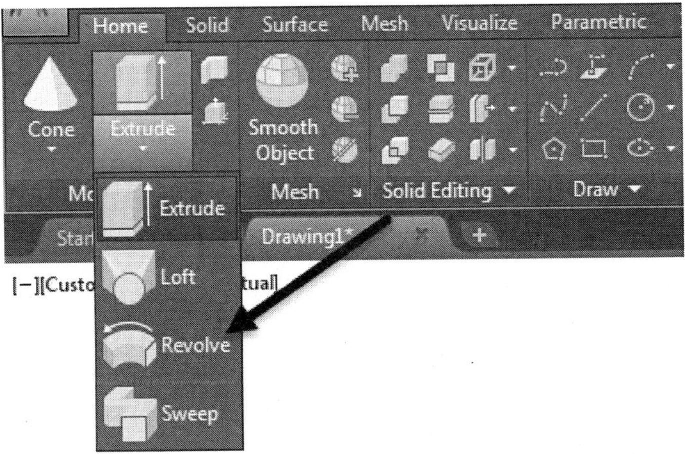

Figure 338 revolve tool icon

Step 2: Select 2D object then Enter.

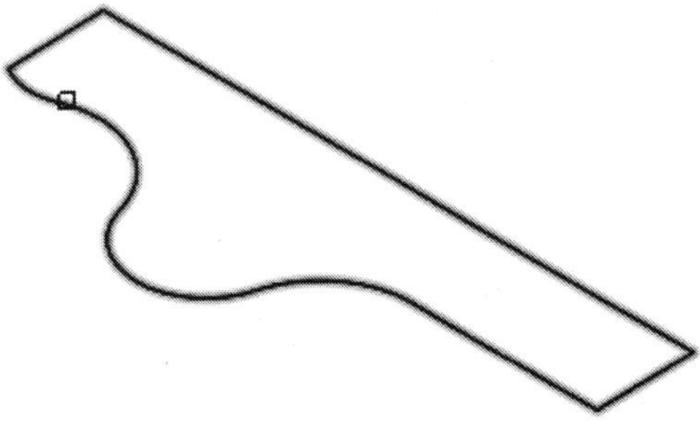

Figure 339 select object

Step 3: Click first point for Axis.

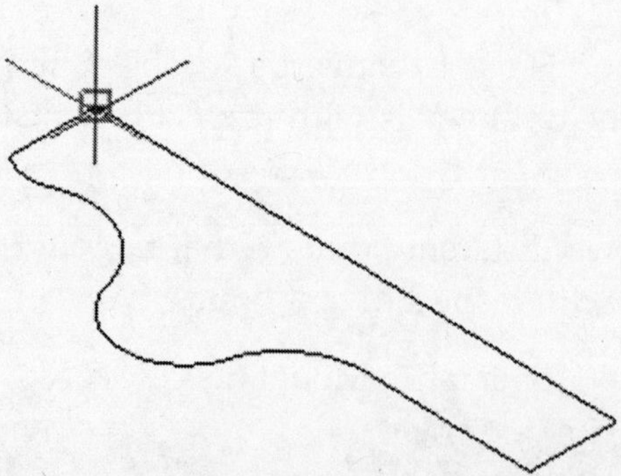

Figure 340 *specify axis first point*

Step 4: Click second point for Axis.

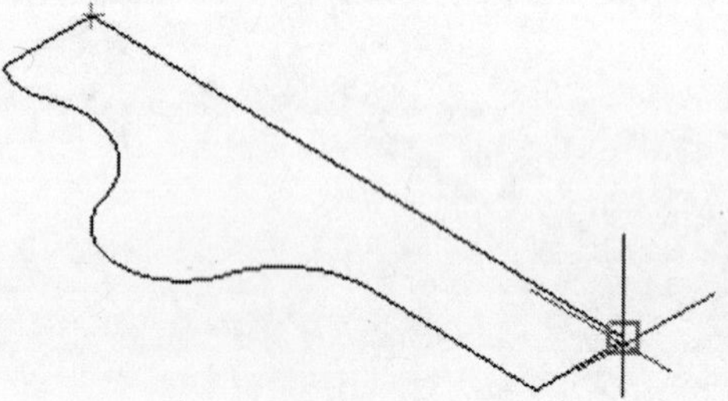

Figure 341 *specify axis second point*

Step 5: 360 Enter for Circular angle.

Figure 342 *revolve object*

SWEEP

Sweep command is used to convert into 3d object by sweeping anyone 2d object to another 2d object.

Step 1: Ribbon ➢ Home tab ➢ Modeling ØSweep.

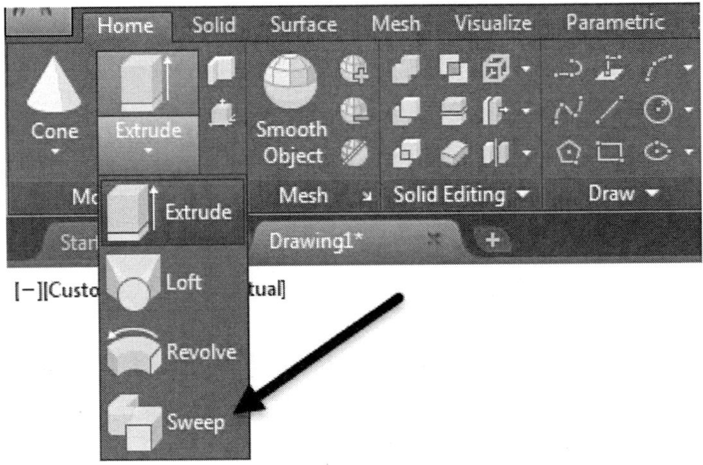

Figure 343 *sweep tool icon*

Step 2: Select object to sweep then Enter.

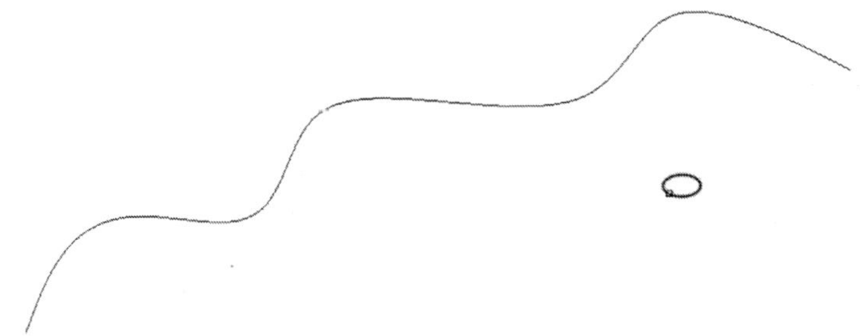

Figure 344 *select circle*

Step 3: Select sweep path.

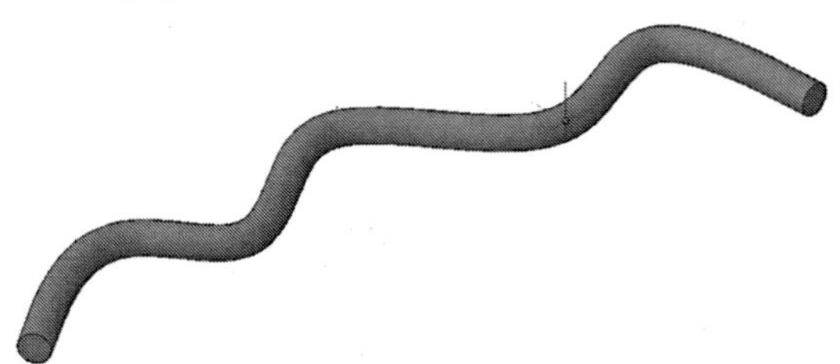

Figure 345 *sweep*

CHAPTER 10
3D Modify tools

3D MOVE

3d move command is use to move an object along any of the 3 axises. To do that select the object first then select 3d move object and you will found all 3 axes appear, now move the object along the desired axes by clicking on that axes and provide move distance manually.

Step 1: Ribbon ➢ Home tab ➢ ModifyØ3D move.

Figure 346 *3D move tool icon*

Step 2: Select object then Enter.

Step 3: Click Z Axis for Z direction move.

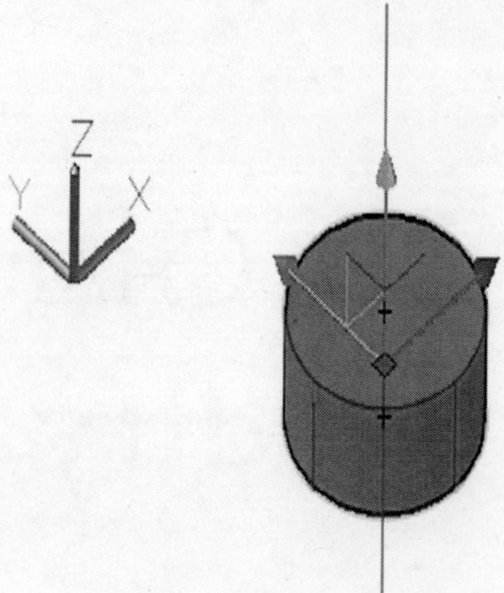

Figure 347 3D move object

Step 4: 20 Enter for distance.

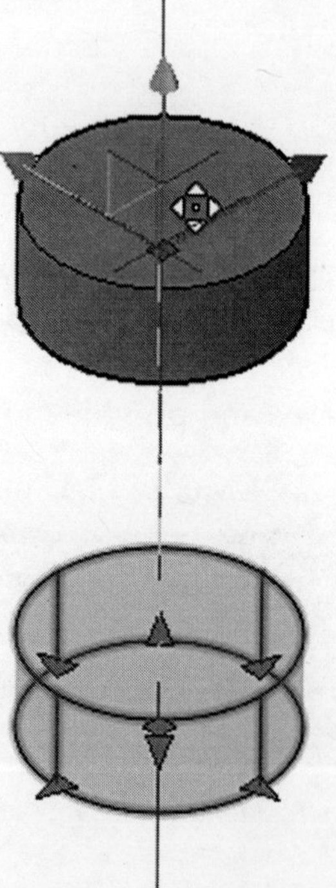

Figure 348 specify distance

3D ROTATE

3d rotate command is use to rotate an object along any of the 3 axises. To do that, select the object first then click on 3d rotate and you see object and found all 3 axes appear, now rotate the object along desired axes by click on that axes and enter the angle manually as

More you like to rotate from an angle.

Step 1: Ribbon ➢ Home tab ➢ Modify3D rotate.

Figure 349 3D rotate tool icon

Step 2: Select object then Enter.

Step 3: Click Axis for rotate.

Step 4: 90o Enter for rotate angle.

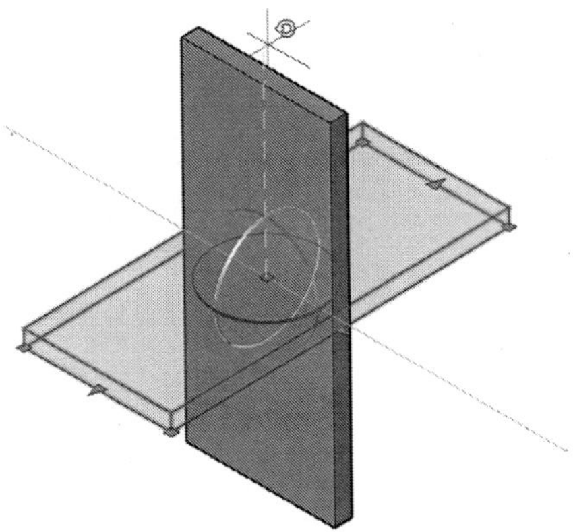

Figure 350 object rotate

3D SCALE

3d scale command is used to scale an object along any of three (x or y or z) axis, you can change scale according to length, width or height.

Step 1: Ribbon ➢ Home tab ➢ ModifyØ3D scale.

Figure 351 3D scale tool icon

Step 2: Select object then Enter.

Step 3: Click base point.

Step 4: Pick axis.

Step 5: R Enter for reference option.

Step 6: 1 Enter for reference length.

Step 7: 2 Enter for new length.

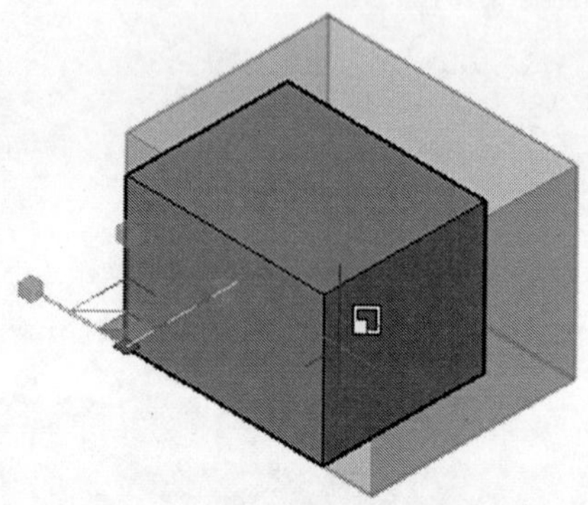

Figure 352 object scale

3D MIRROR

3D mirror command is used to create reflection or mirror object. But 3d mirror is different than Mirror, we can also mirror an object along z axis.

Step 1: Ribbon ➢ Home tab ➢ Modify Ø3D mirror.

Figure 353 3D mirror tool icon

Step 2: Select object then Enter.

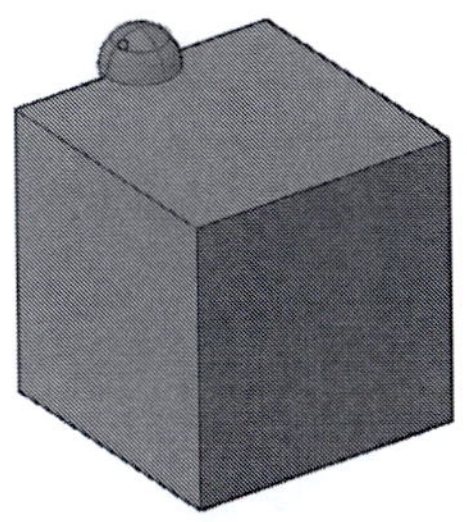

Figure 354 select sphere

Step 3: Click first base point.

Step 4: Click second point.

Step 5: Click third point.

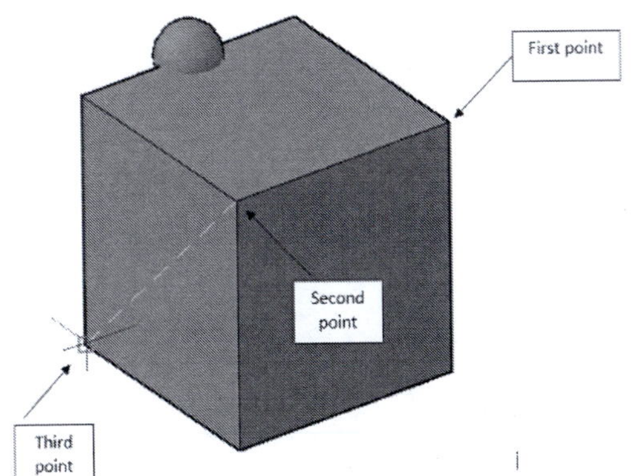

Figure 355 specify point

Step 6: N Enter for No, delete source object.

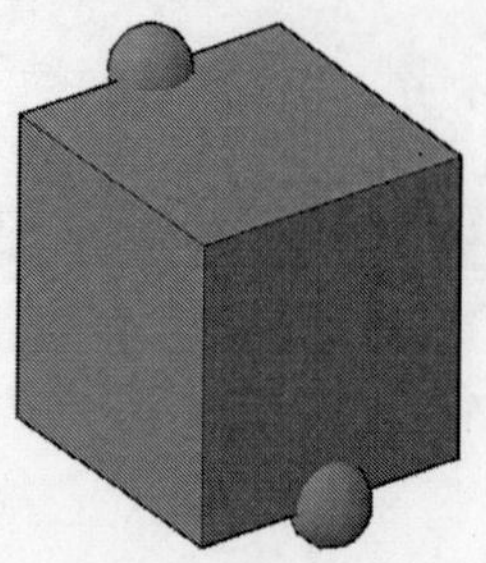

Figure 356 after 3d mirror

3D ARRAY

3D array command is used to create multiple copy of an object simultaneously along all of 3 axis.

Step 1: 3d array Enter.

Figure 357 3D array command

Step 2: Select object then Enter.

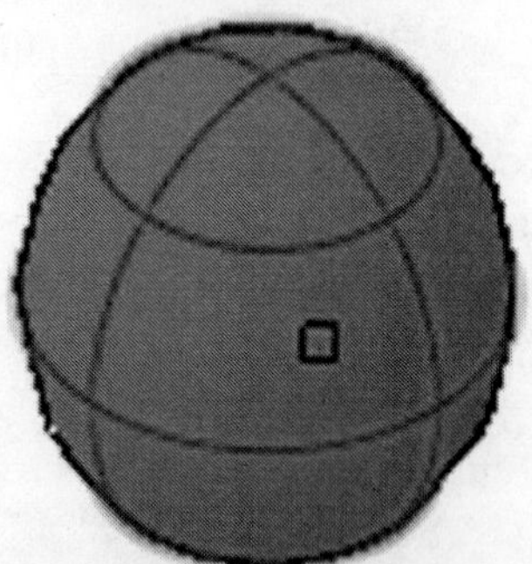

Figure 358 select sphere

Step 3: R Enter for rectangular option.

Step 4: 5 Enter for Rows number.

Step 5: 4 Enter for Columns number.

Step 6: 3 Enter for Levels number.

Step 7: 30 Enter for distance between rows.

Step 8: 30 Enter for distance between columns.

Step 9: 30 Enter for distance between levels.

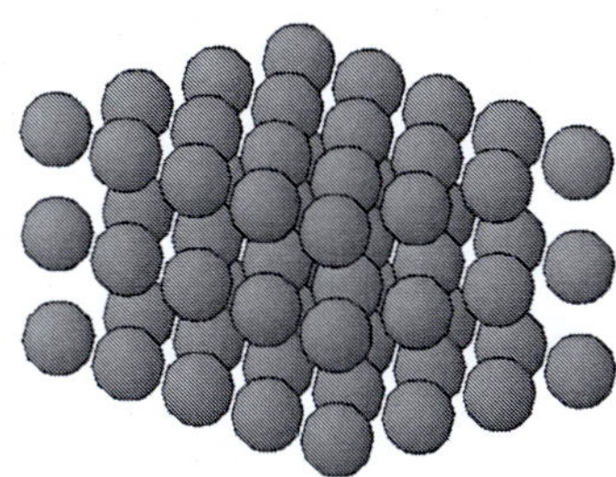

Figure 359 after array

SUBTRACT

Subtract command is used to cut the intersected part of the overlapping 3d object,

For example, if you have to make a circular hole in a box then you have to intersect an object of similar radius then subtract it.

Step 1: Ribbon ➢ Home tab ØSolid editing ØSubtract.

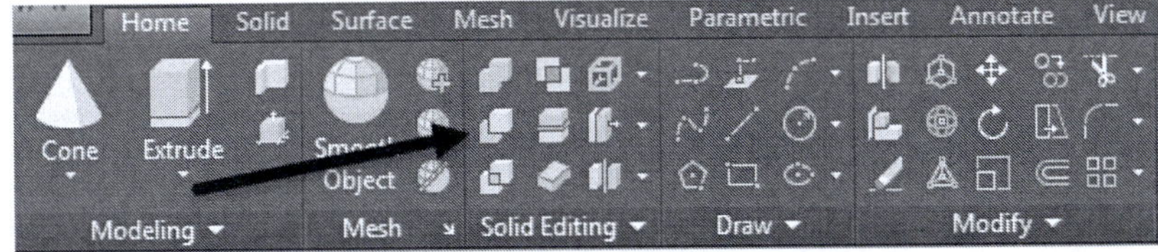

Figure 360 subtract tool icon

Step 2: Select first object then Enter.

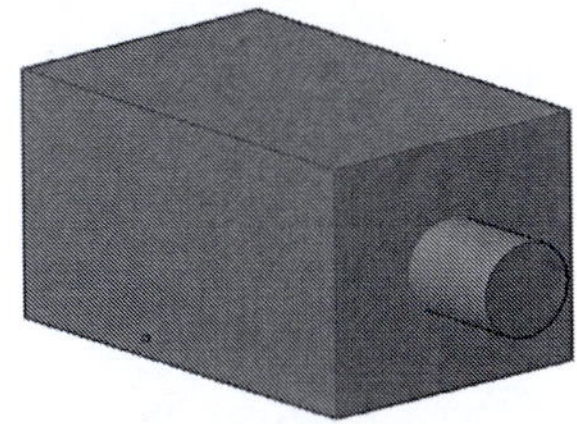

Figure 361 select box

Step 3: Select second object.

Figure 362 select cylinder

Step 4: Then Enter.

Figure 363 after subtract

UNION

Union command is use to joint or merge two or more than two 3d object. By applying this command all participated object are seems as a block.

Step 1: Ribbon ➤ Home tab ØSolid editing ØUnion.

Figure 364 union tool icon

Step 2: Select first object.

Step 3: Select second object.

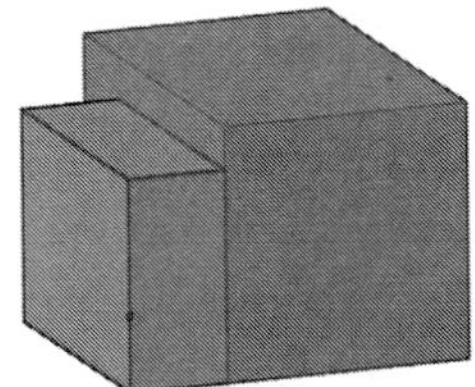

Figure 365 select object

Step 4: Then Enter.

Figure 366 after union

INTERSECT

Intersect command is use to cut the rest part (i.e. except intersected part) of two 3d object who is intersecting each other.

Step 1: Ribbon ➢ Home tab ØSolid editing ➢ Intersect.

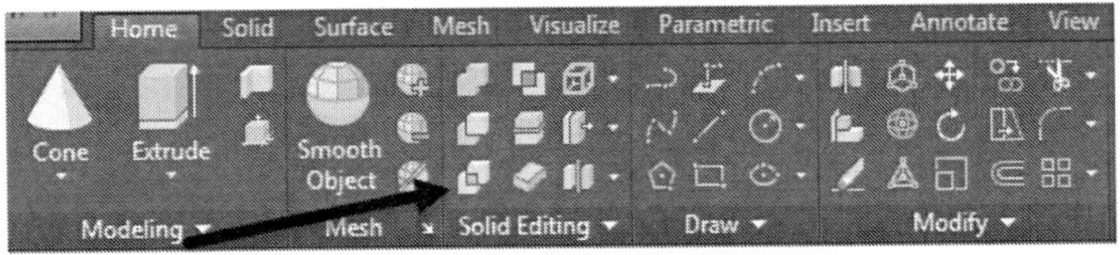

Figure 367 intersect tool icon

Step 2: Select first object.

Step 3: Select second object.

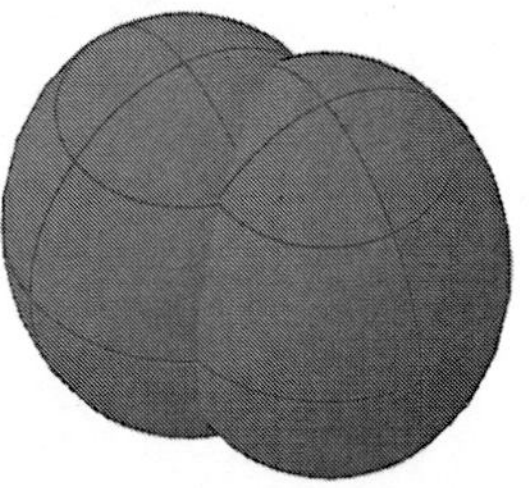

Figure 368 select sphere

Step 4: Then Enter.

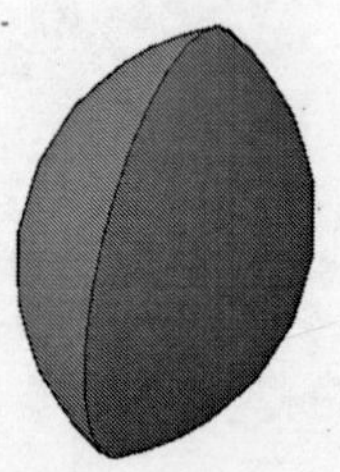

Figure 369 *after intersect*

SLICE

Slice command is use to cut an 3d Object, and remove the isolated part.

Step 1: Ribbon ➢ Home tab ØSolid editing ØSlice.

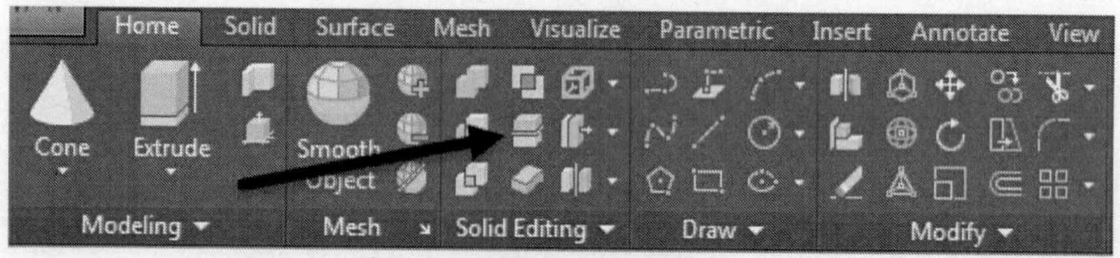

Figure 370 *slice tool icon*

Step 2: Select object then Press Enter.

Step 3: Pick first point.

Step 4: Pick second point.

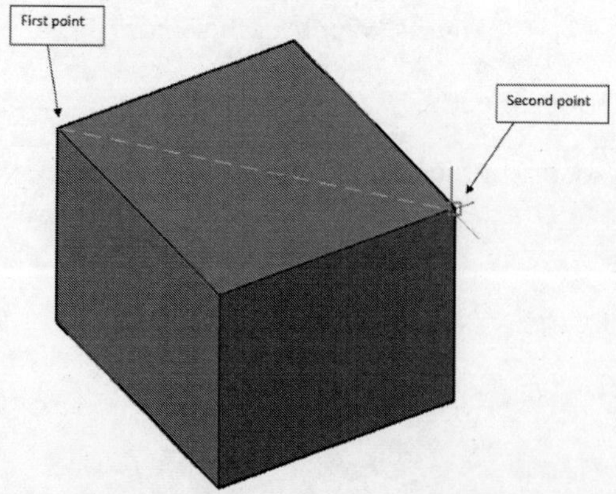

Figure 371 *specify slice points*

Step 5: Specify a point on desired side.

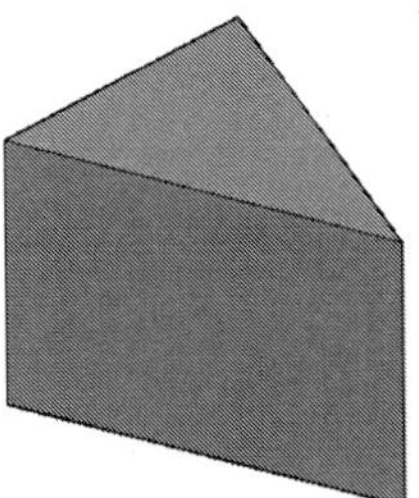

Figure 372 after slice

FILLET EDGE

Step 1: Ribbon- Solid- Solid editing- Fillet Edge.

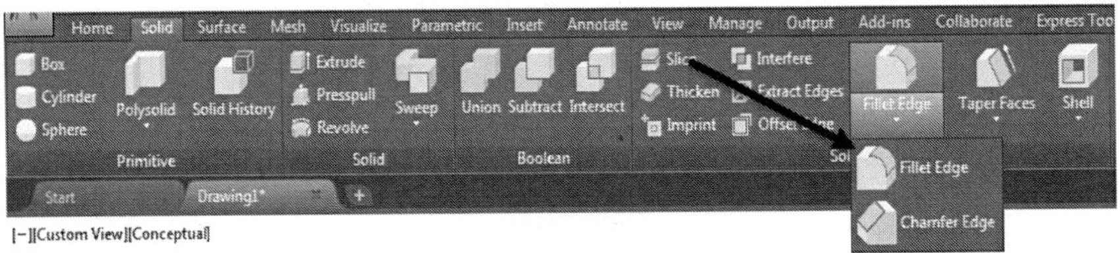

Figure 373 Fillet edge tool icon

Step 2: Select edge then Press Enter.

Step 3: R Enter for radius option.

Step 4: Enter for fillet radius then Press Enter.

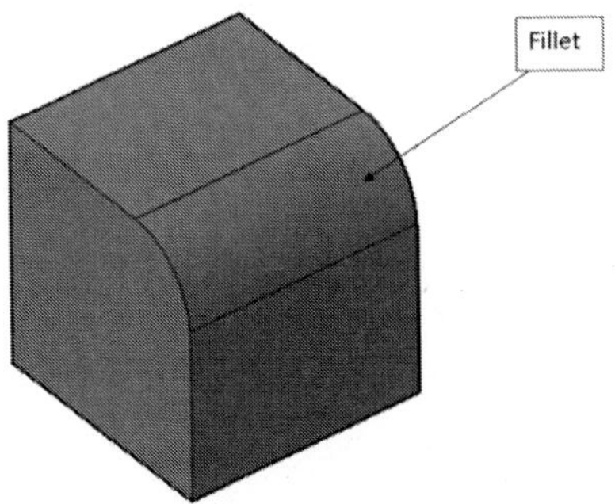

Figure 374 fillet use

CHAMFER EDGE

Step 1: Ribbon: Solid ØSolid editing ➤ Chamfer Edge.

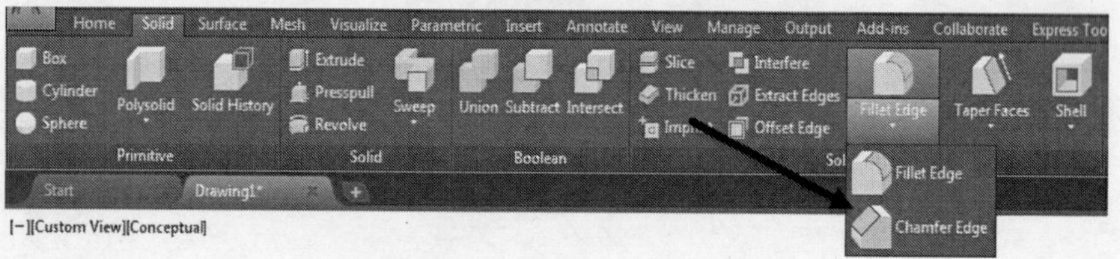

***Figure 375** chamfer edge tool icon*

Step 2: Select edge then Press Enter.

***Figure 376** select edge*

Step 3: D Enter for distance option.

Step 4: 2 Enter for base distance.

Step 5: 2 Enter for other distance then double Enter.

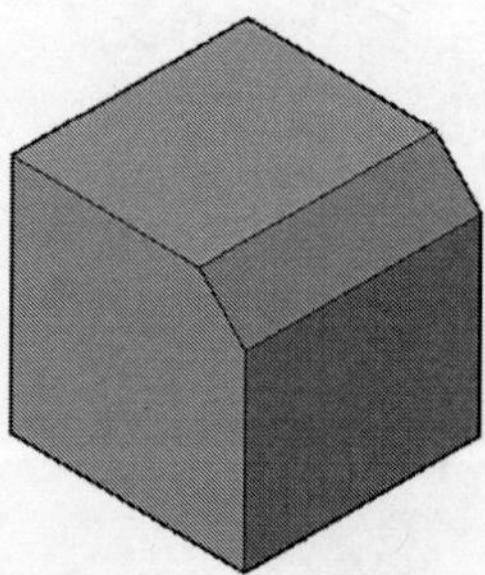

***Figure 377** after chamfer*

CHAPTER 11
3D Surface & Mesh

NETWORK

A network surface can be created between a network of curves or between the edges of other 3D surfaces or solids.

Step 1: Ribbon ØSurface ➢ Create ØNetwork.

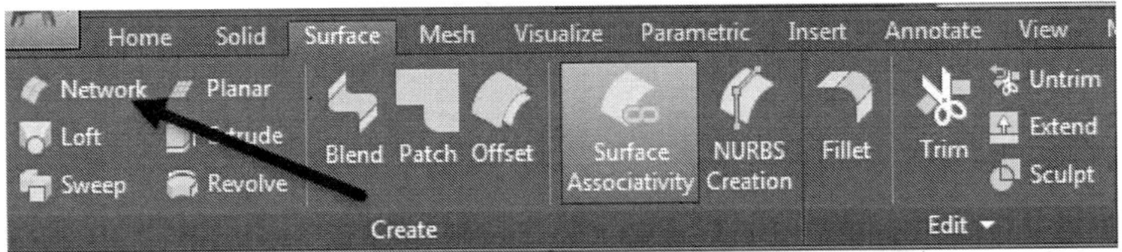

Figure 378 network tool icon

Step 2: Select all first direction edges then Press Enter.

***Figure 379** select all arc*

Step 3: Select all second direction edges then Press Enter.

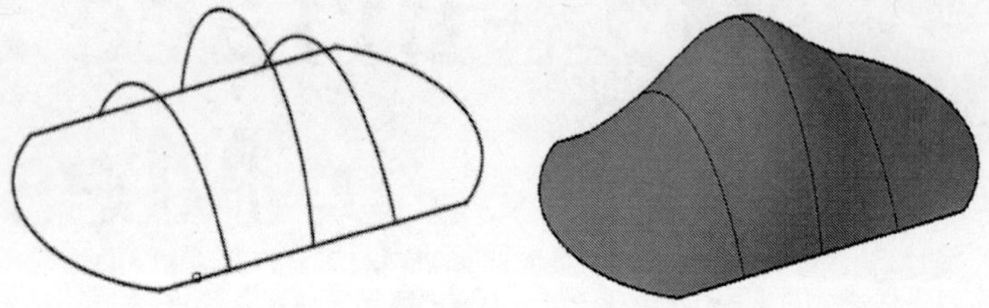

***Figure 380** select line*

PLANAR

Create planar surfaces in the space between edge sub objects splines and other 2D and 3D curve.

With PLANESURF, planar surfaces can be created from multiple closed objects and the edges of surface or solid objects. During creation, you can specify the tangency and bulge magnitude.

Step 1: Ribbon ØSurface ➤ Create ØPlanar.

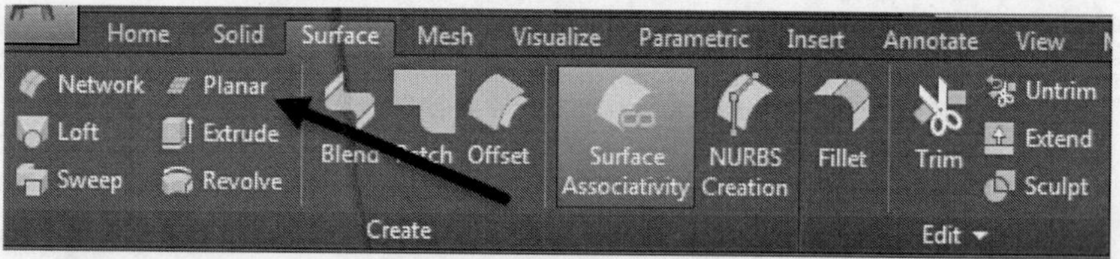

***Figure 381** planar tool icon*

Step 2: O Enter for object option.

Step 3: Select object then Press Enter.

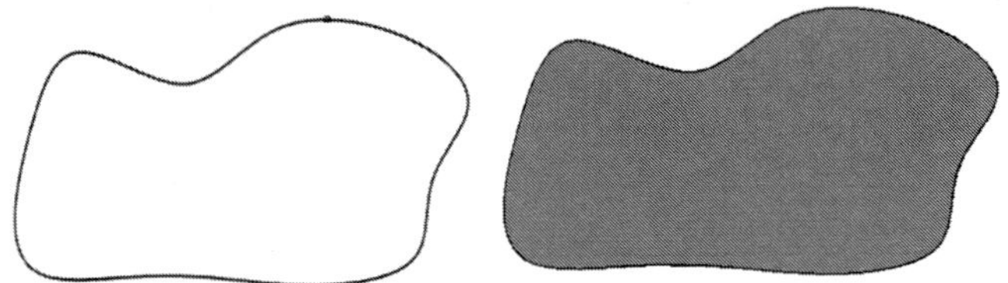

Figure 382 use of planar

SURFACE BLEND

Creates a continuous blend surface between two existing surfaces.

Step 1: Ribbon ØSurface ➢ Create ➢ Blend.

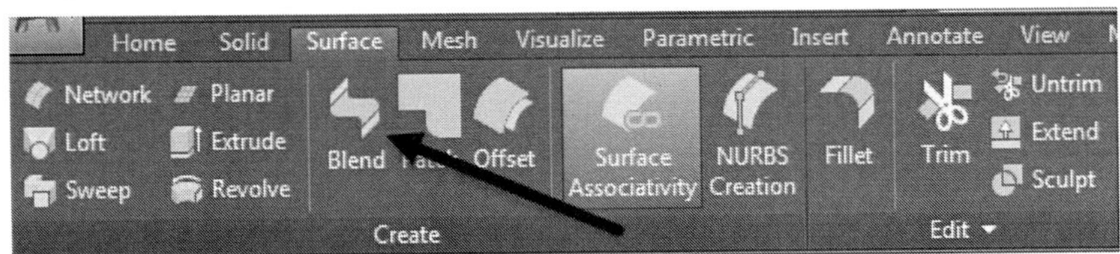

Figure 383 blend tool icon

Step 2: Select first edge then Press Enter.

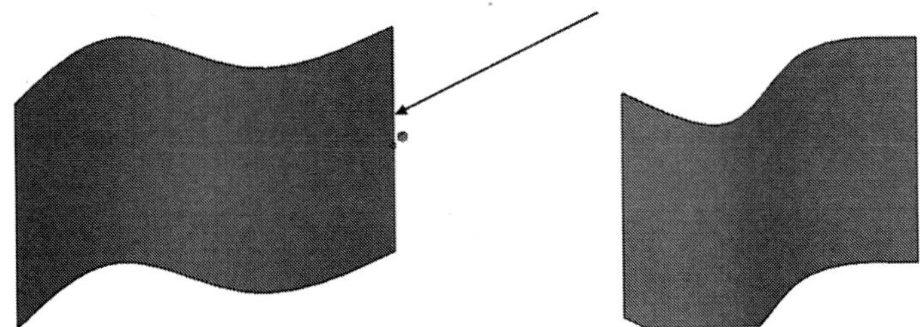

Figure 384 select edge of first surface

Step 3: Select second edge then Press Enter.

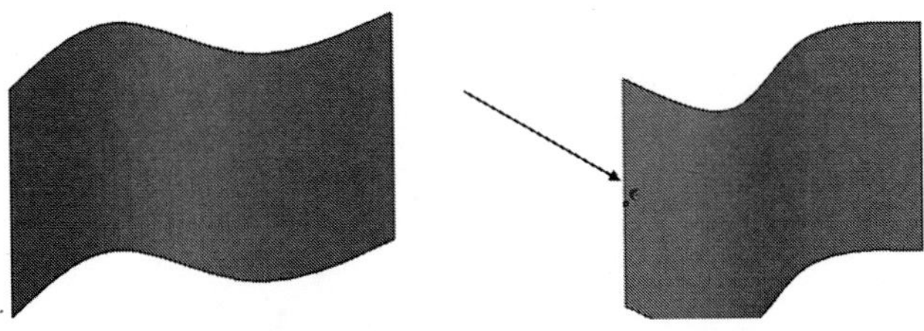

Figure 385 select edge of second surface

Step 4: Enter.

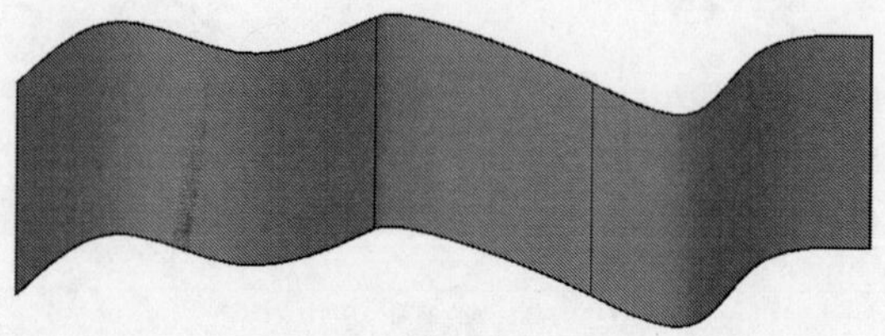

Figure 386 after blend

PATCH

Creates a new surface by fitting a cap over a surface edge that forms a closed loop.

Step 1: Ribbon ØSurface ➢ Create ØPatch.

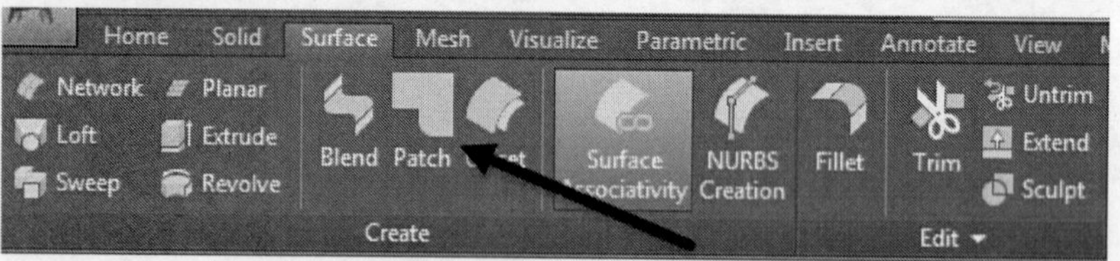

Figure 387 patch tool icon

Step 2: Select surface edge.

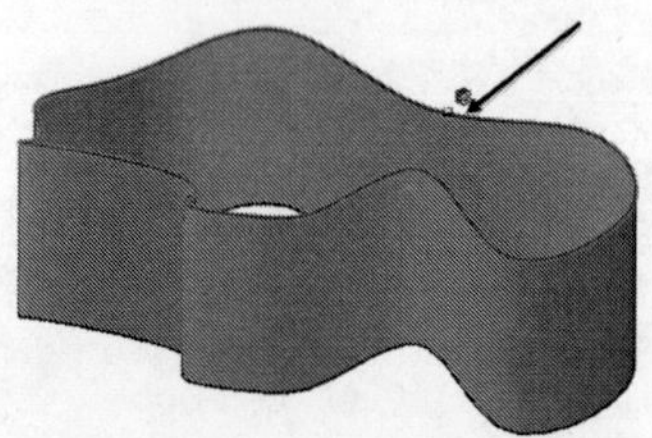

Figure 388 select edge of surface

Step 3: Double Enter.

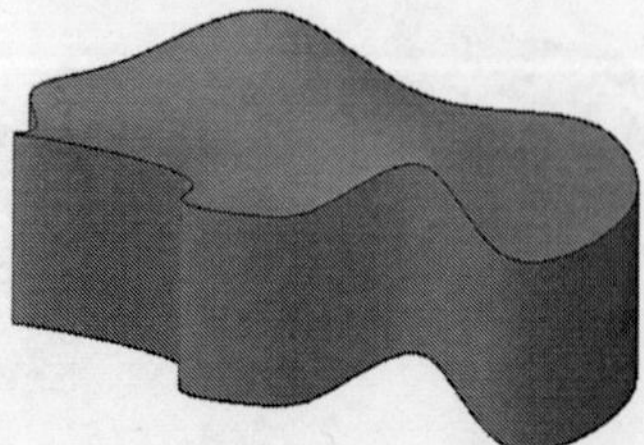

Figure 389 after patch

SURFACE OFFSET

Create a parallel surface or solid by setting an offset distance from a surface.

Step 1: Ribbon ØSurface ➤ Create ØOffset.

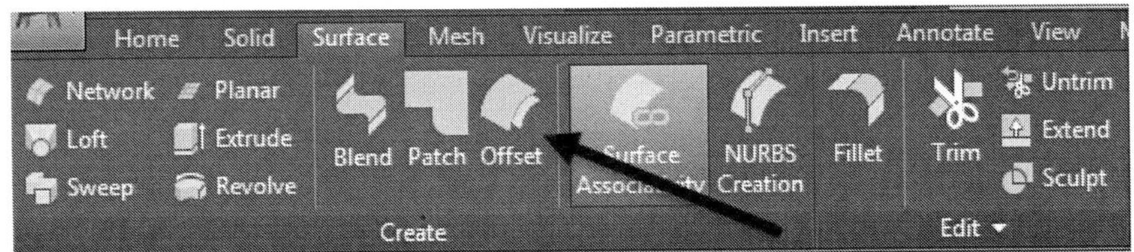

Figure 390 offset tool icon

Step 2: Select Object then enter.

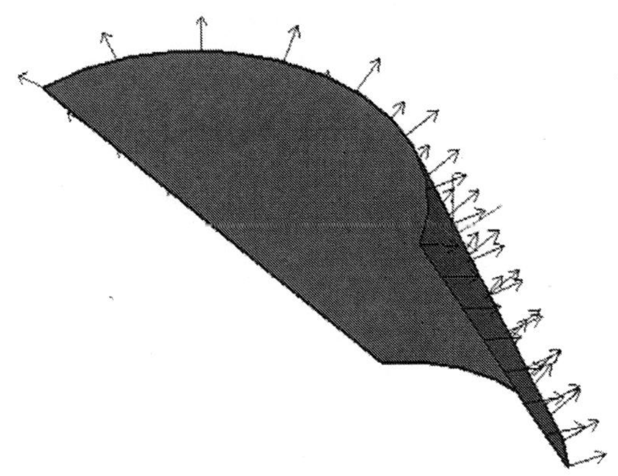

Figure 391 select surface

Step 3: 0.1 Enter for offset distance.

Figure 392 after offset

SURFACE EXTEND

Step 1: Ribbon ØSurface ➢ Edit ➢ Extend.

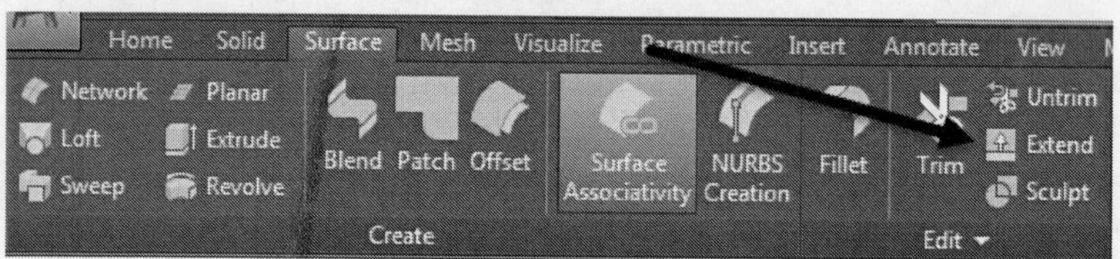

Figure 393 *surface extend tool icon*

Step 2: Select surface edge then enter.

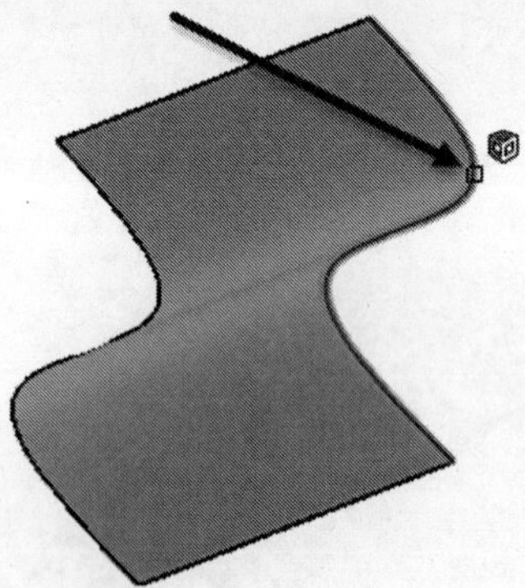

Figure 394 *select edge*

Step 3: 10 Enter for extend distance.

Figure 395 *after extend*

SURFACE TRIM

Step 1: Ribbon ØSurface ➢ Edit ØTrim.

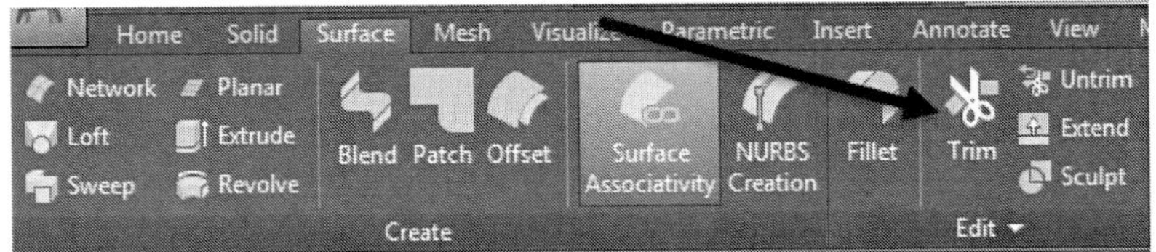

Figure 396 trim tool icon

Step 2: Select surface then enter.

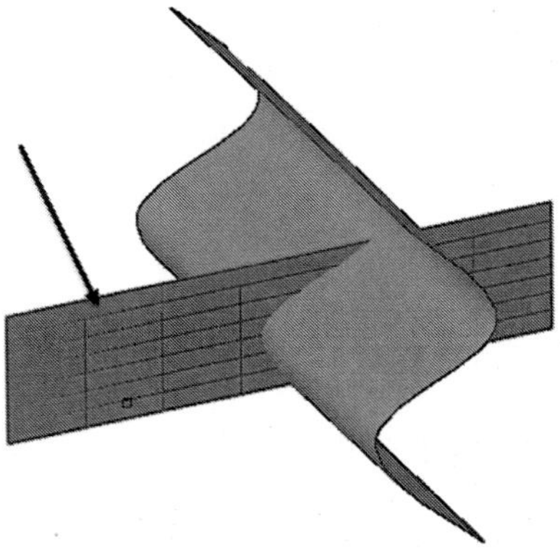

Figure 397 select plane surface

Step 3: Select cutting curves then enter.

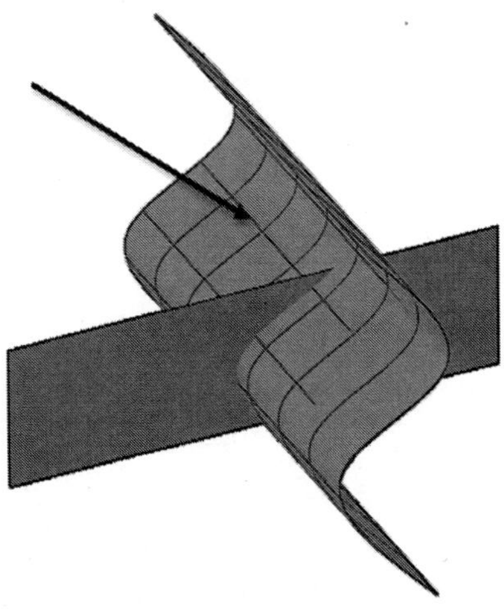

Figure 398 select curve surface

Step 4: Select area to trim.

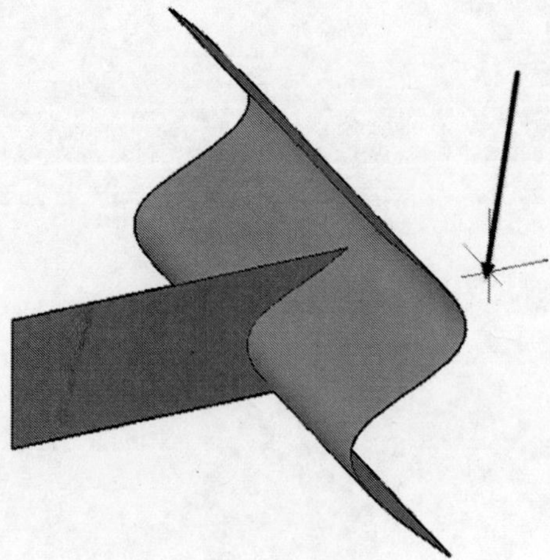

Figure 399 select trim area

SURFACE FILLET

Step 1: Ribbon ØSurface ➢ Edit ➢ Fillet.

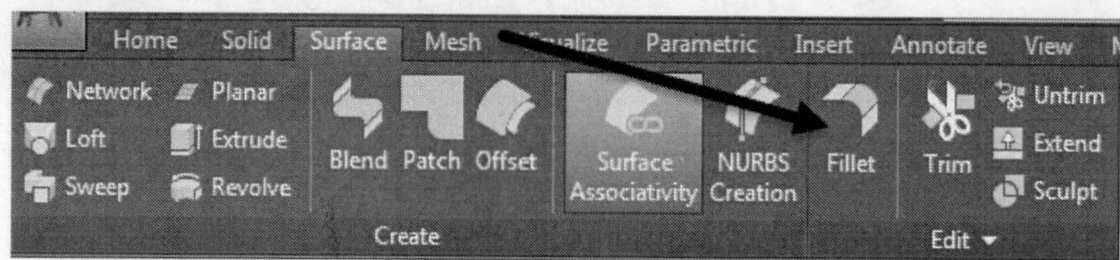

Figure 400 sarface fillet tool icon

Step 2: Select first surface.

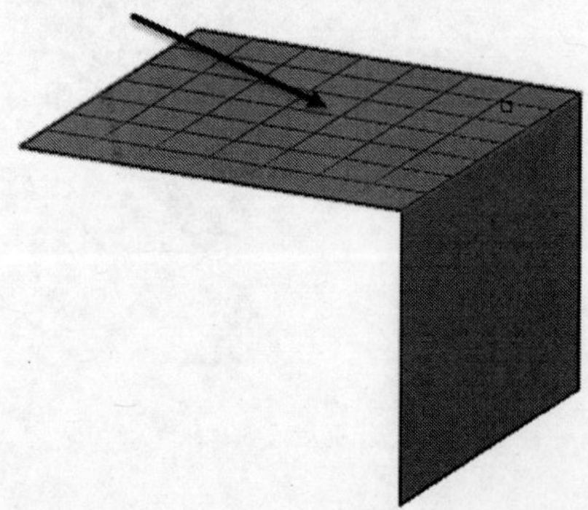

Figure 401 select first surface

Step 3: Select second surface.

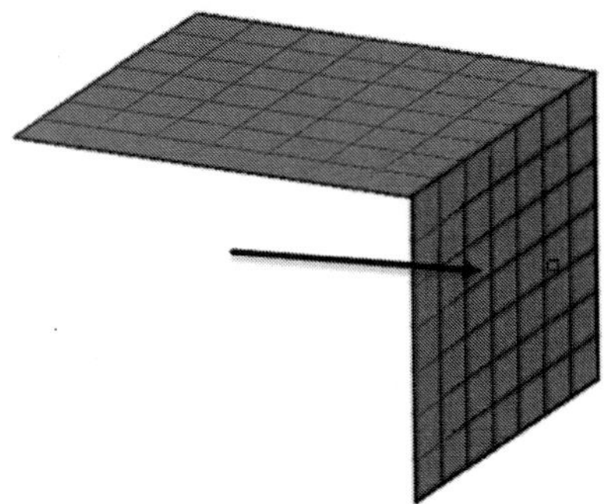

Figure 402 *select second surface*

Step 4: R Enter for radius option.

Step 5: 0.5 Enter for radius then again enter.

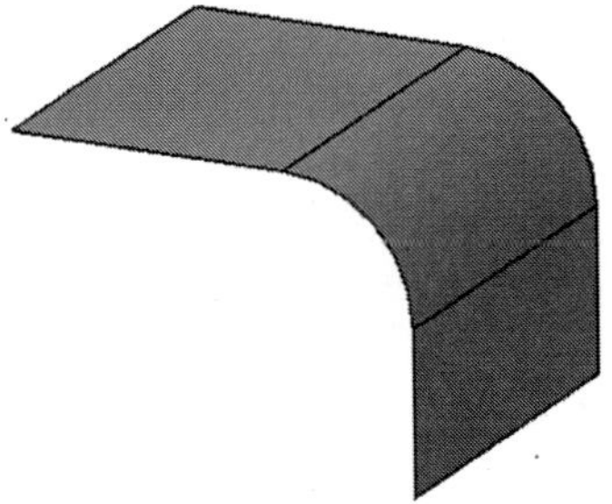

Figure 403 *after fillet*

Chapter 12
What Are the New Features Introduced in AutoCAD 2022?

DWG Compare

Two similar files, in which some changes have been made. To mark them separately or to fabricate both files, the DWG compare tool is used.

Step 1: Ribbon ➢ Collaborate ➢ Compare ➢ DWG compare.

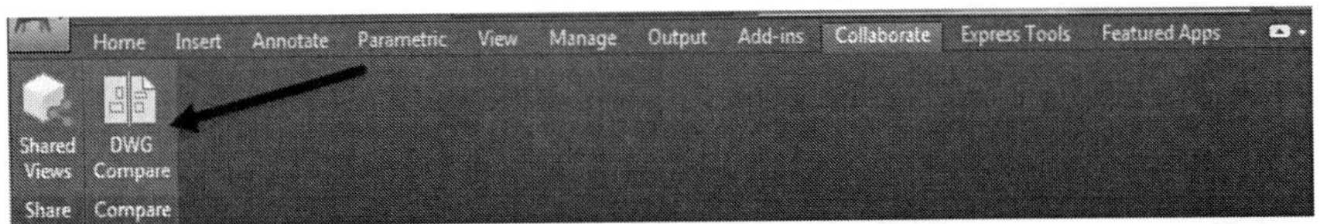

***Figure 404** Dwg compare tool icon*

Step 2: Click on browse button and select first file for comparison.

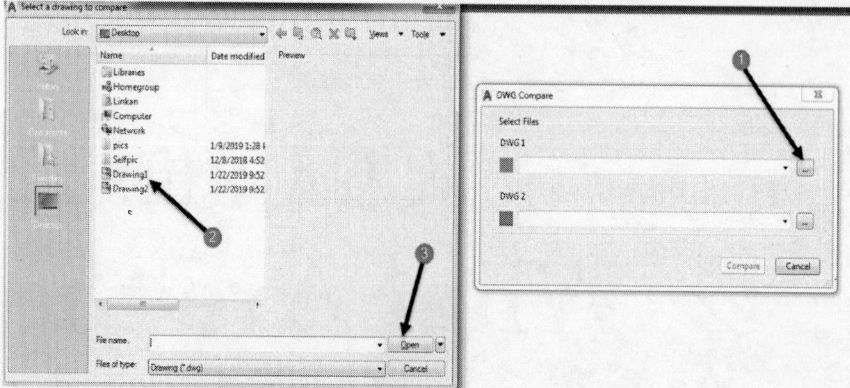

Figure 405 select first file

Step 3: Again click on second browse button and select second file for comparison.

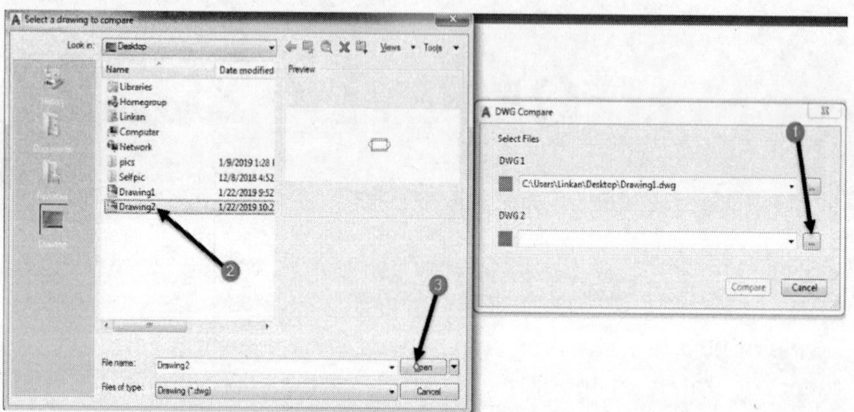

Figure 406 select second file

Step 4: Then click on **Compare** button.

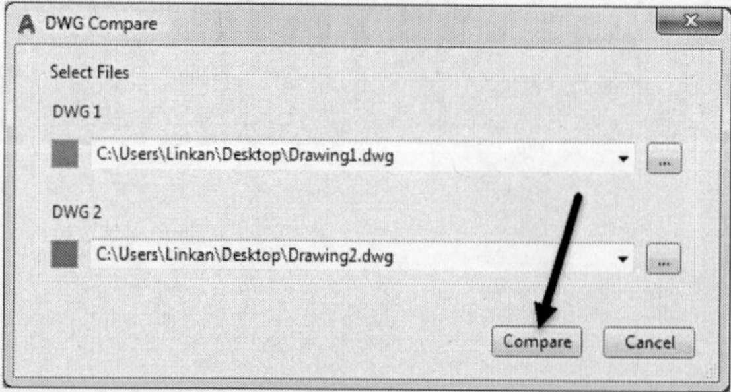

Figure 407 compare tab

Step 5: Now the two different files can be seen.

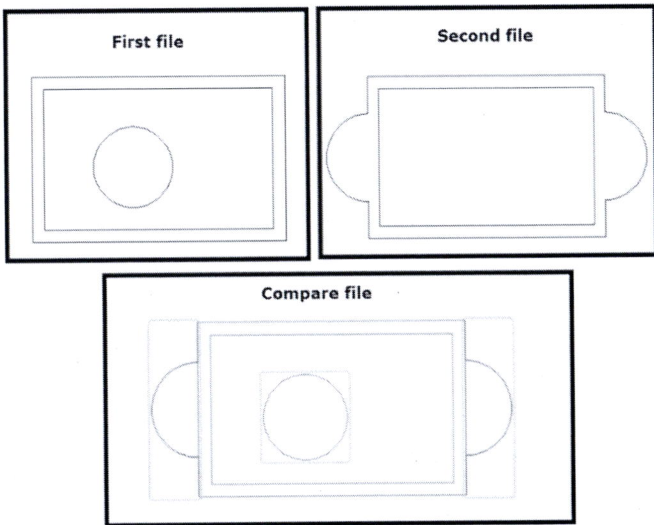

Figure 408 compare file

REVISION CLOUD

Step 1: Ribbon ➤ Home ➤ Draw ØRevision cloud.

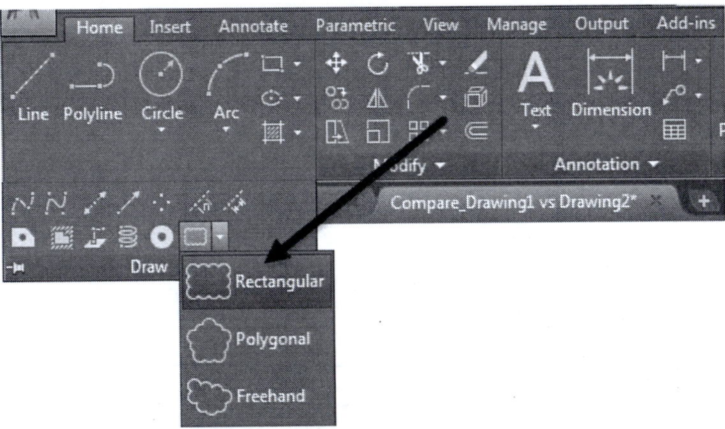

Figure 409 revision cloud tool icon

OR

Command: Revcloud Enter

Step 2: Then enter *R* for rectangle shape of Revision cloud.

Figure 410 *rectangle revision cloud*

OR

P enter for Polygon shape Revision cloud.

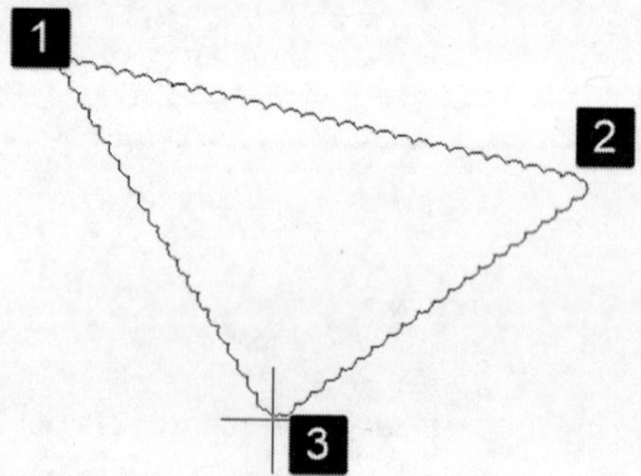

Figure 411 *POLYGON SHAPE REVISION CLOUD*

SMART DIMENSION

To measure the diameter of a circle as to measure the length of a line; two different tools are required for the same, but with the help of smart dimension's new feature both types of dimension's can be measure with the same tool.
I.e. Smart dimension

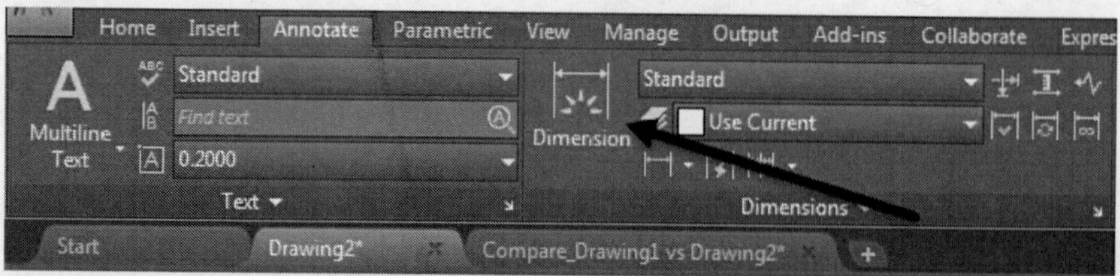

Figure 412 *Smart dimension tool icon*

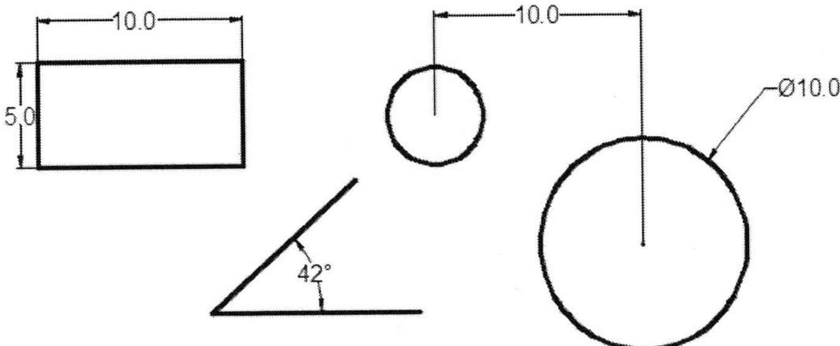

Figure 413 All dimension

GEOMETRIC CENTER (OSNAP)

Geometric any Polygon center point of it is to show. These new features are **Object snapping** (**Osnap**).

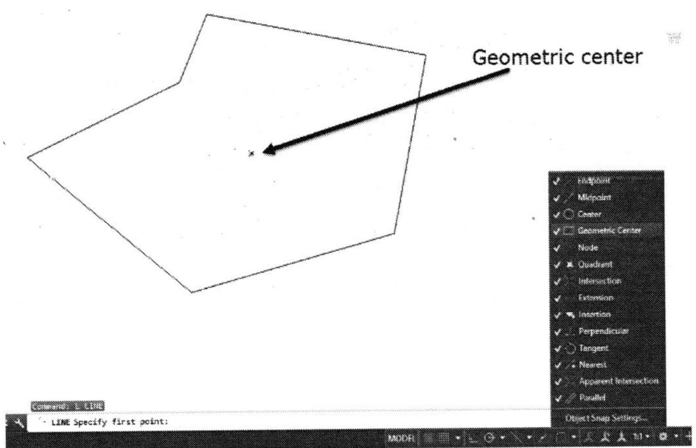

Figure 414 Geometric option

CENTER MARKS AND CENTER LINES

Step 1: Click on **Annotate** tab.

Step 2: Click on Center lines.

Step 3: Select the first line.

Step 4: Select the second line.

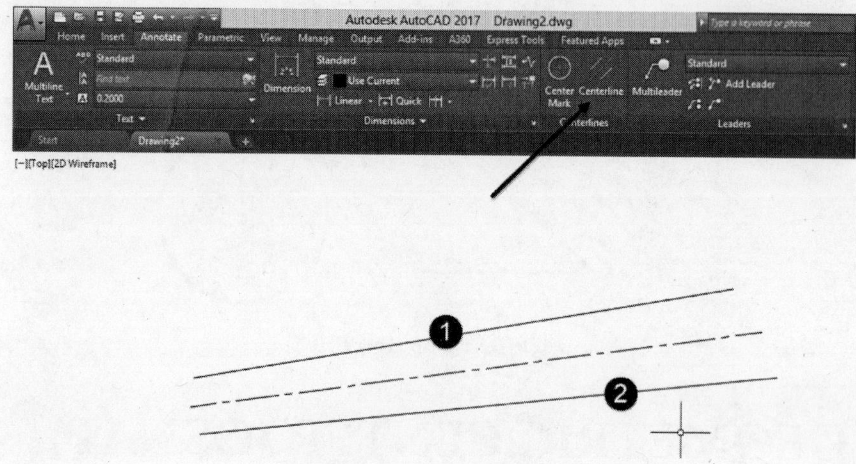

Figure 415 Center line use

OR

Click on the **Center Mark** then select the circle.

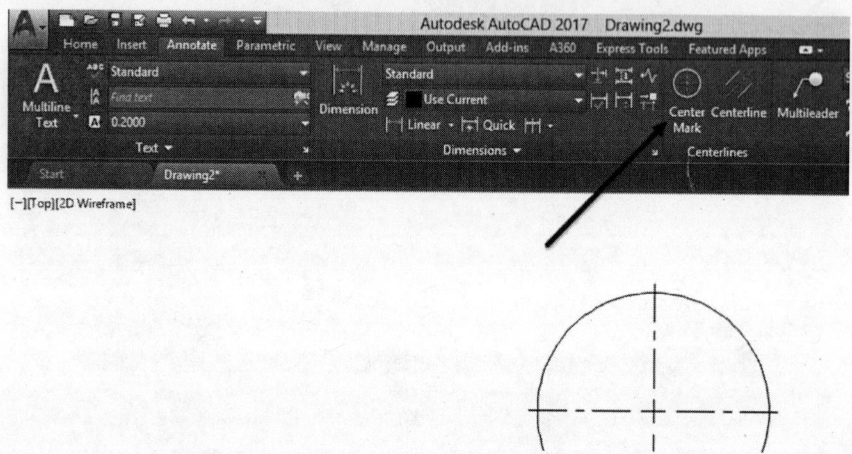

Figure 416 center mark

COUNT

This tool is used to see the count list of blocks in the drawing. And using this, we can also see the position of each block.

Step 1: First of all, open file in which the block is used. If is not block. So, you can also create new blocks.

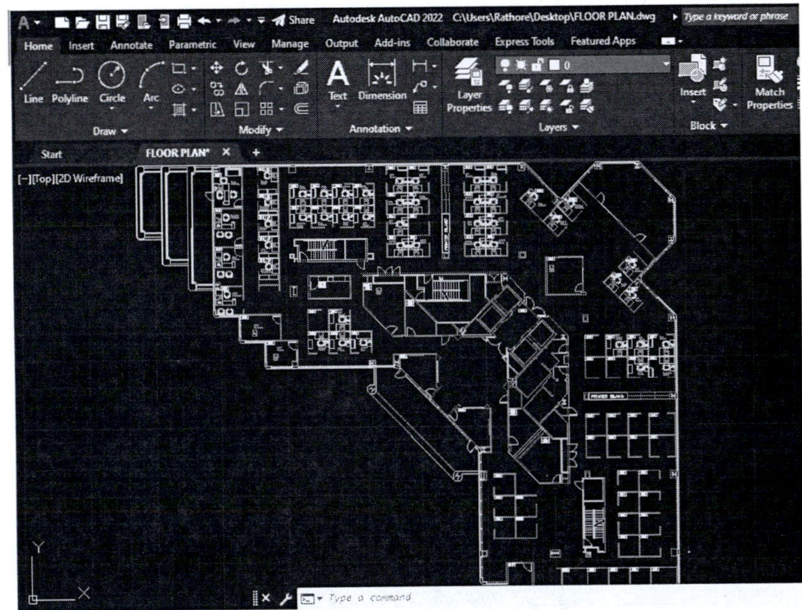

Step 2: Click on View tab Then click on "COUNT" tool.

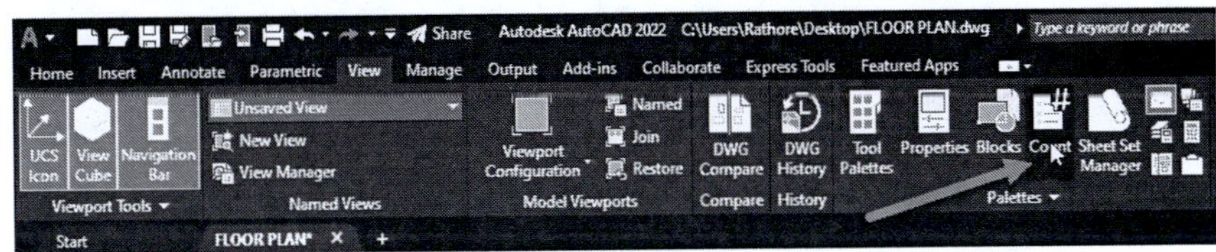

Step 3: Select any block option.

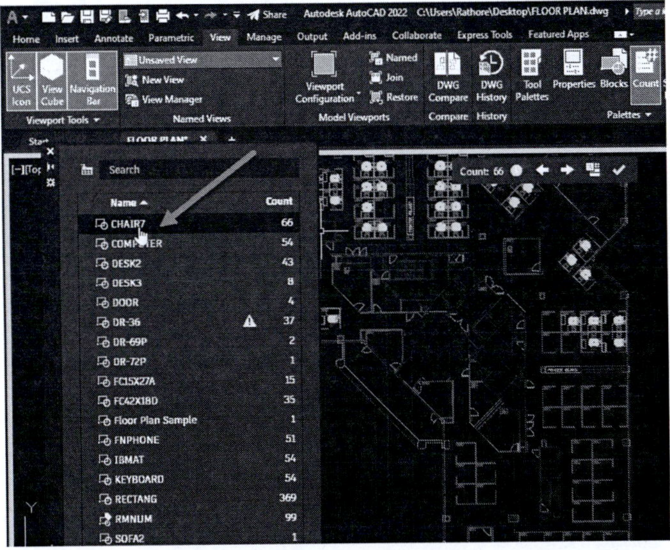

Step 4: After that, you can use any right or left arrow to view the blocks one by one.

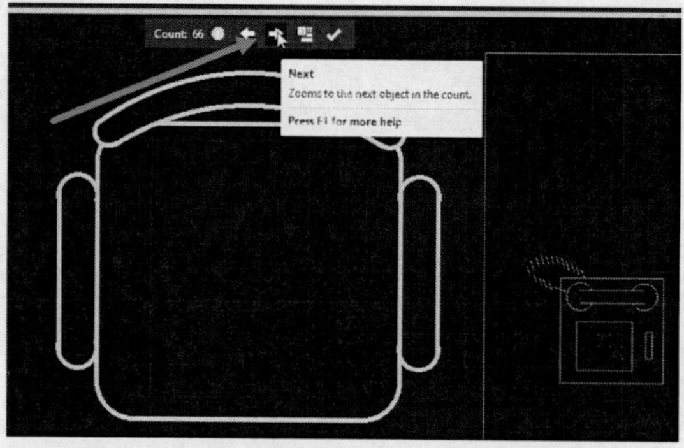

PDF file import

Step 1: Click on **Insert** tab then click on **Pdf Import**.

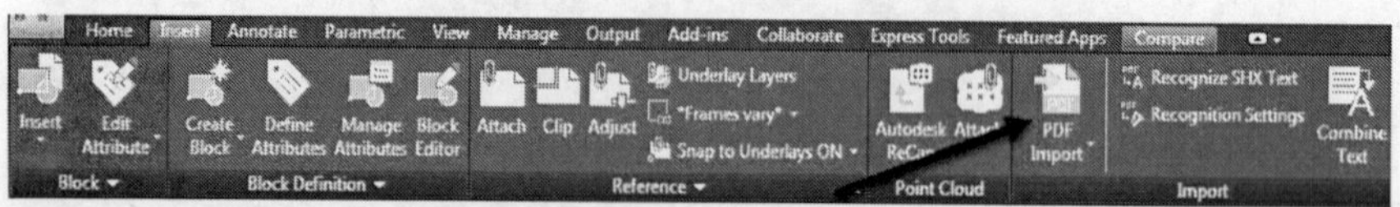

Figure 417 pdf import tool icon

Step 2: Then press enter or right click.

Step 3: Select the file and open.

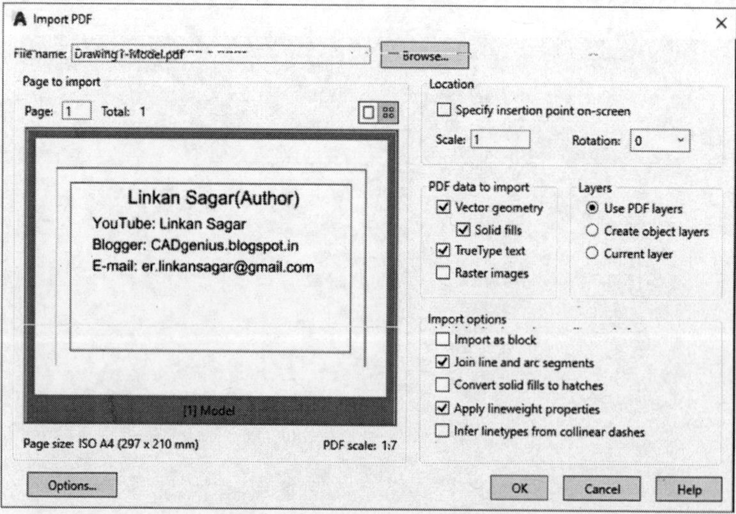

Figure 418 pdf import tab

PRACTICE MODE

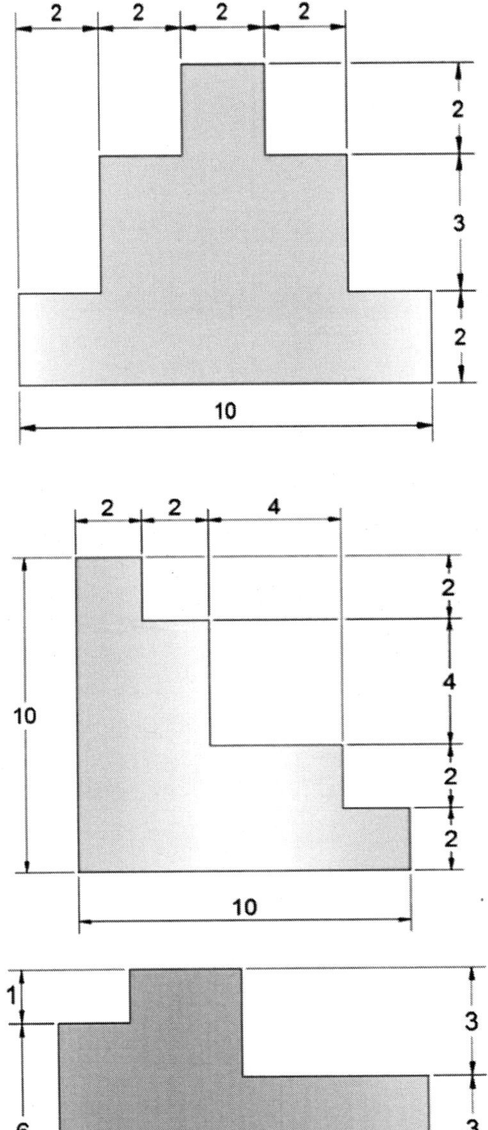

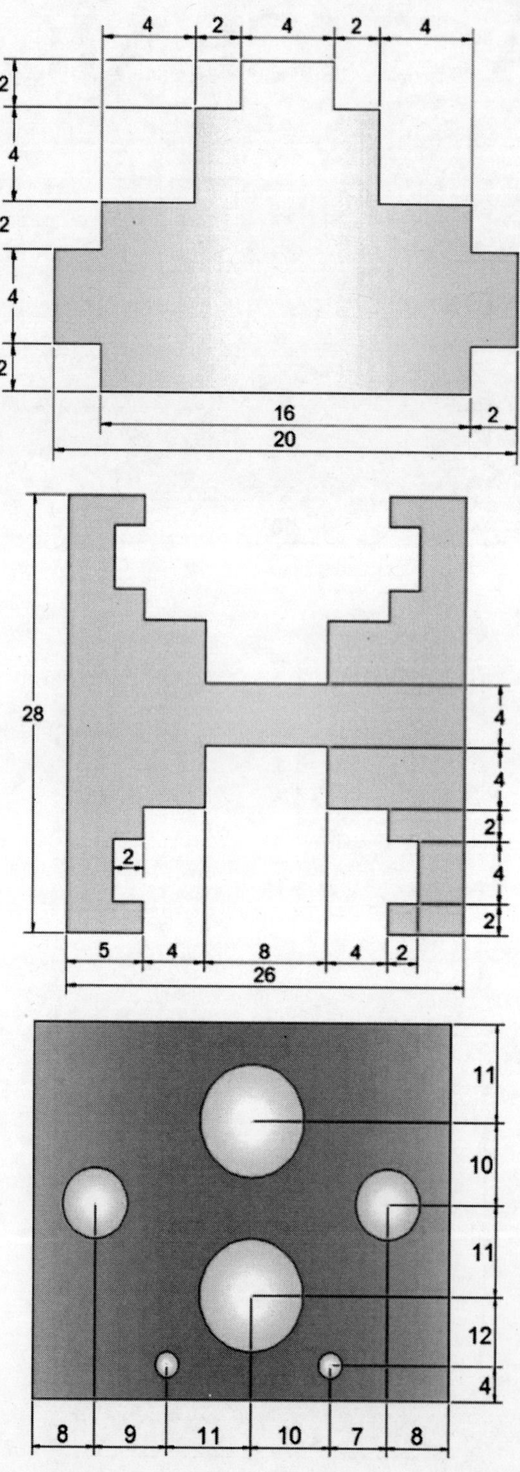
4
2
4
2
4
2
4
2
4
2
16
2
20
28
4
4
2
2
4
2
5
4
8
4
2
26
11
10
11
12
4
8
9
11
10
7
8

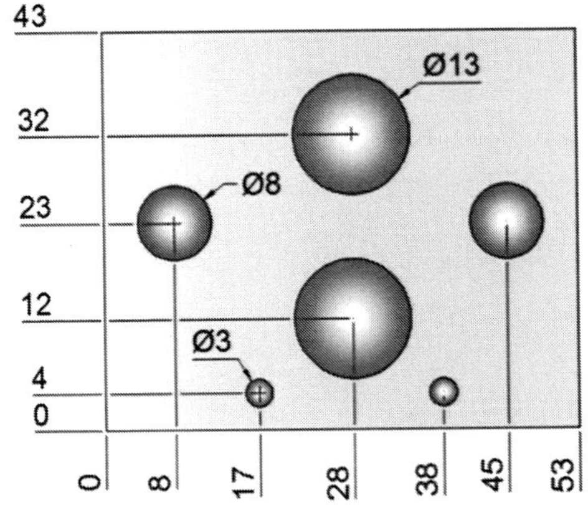
43
32
23
12
4
0
Ø13
Ø8
Ø3
0
8
17
28
38
45
53

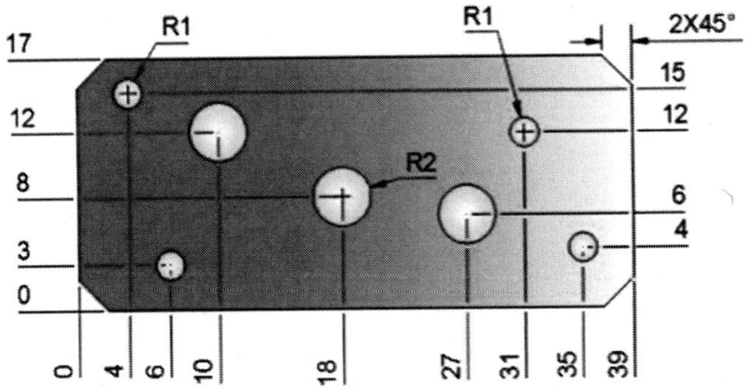
R1
R1
2X45°
17
12
8
3
0
15
12
R2
6
4
0
4
6
10
18
27
31
35
39

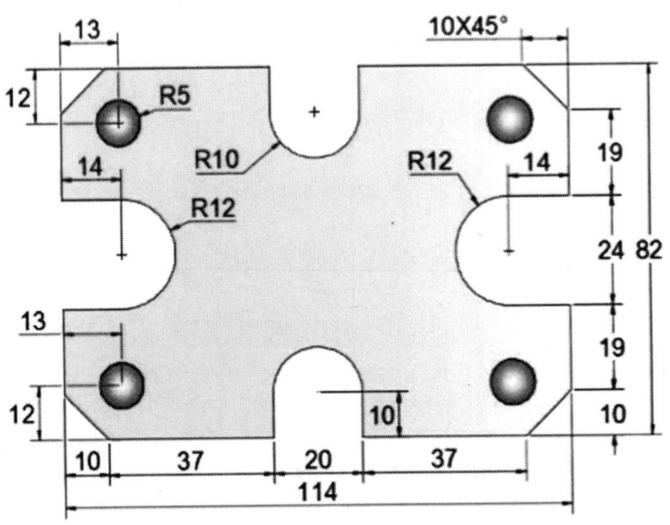
13
10X45°
12
R5
R10
R12
14
14
19
R12
24
82
13
19
12
10
10
10
37
20
37
114

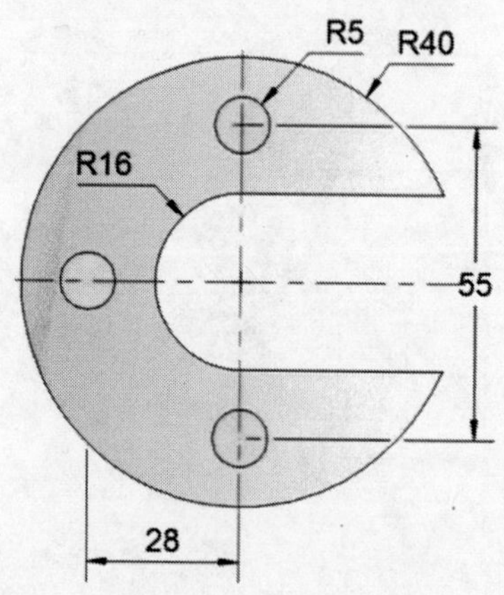
R5
R40
R16
55
28

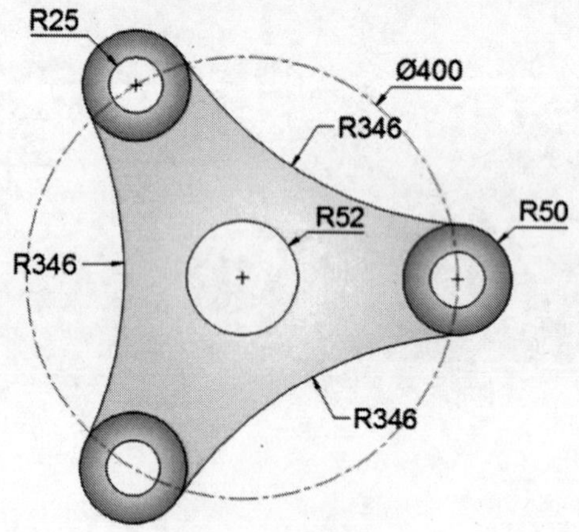
R25
Ø400
R346
R52
R50
R346
R346

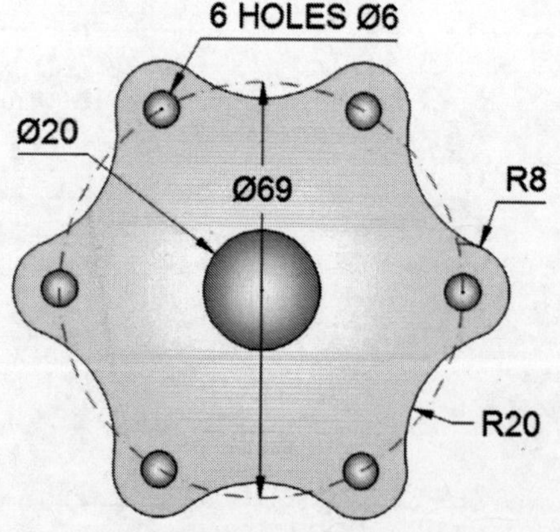
6 HOLES Ø6
Ø20
Ø69
R8
R20

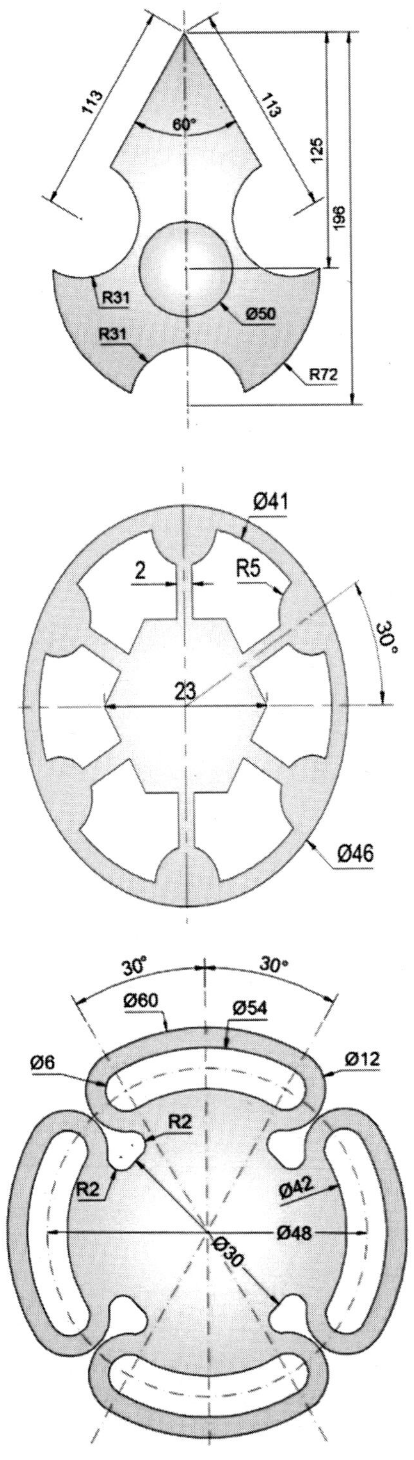
113
113
60°
125
196
R31
Ø50
R31
R72
Ø41
2
R5
30°
23
Ø46
30°
30°
Ø60
Ø54
Ø6
Ø12
R2
R2
Ø42
Ø48
Ø30

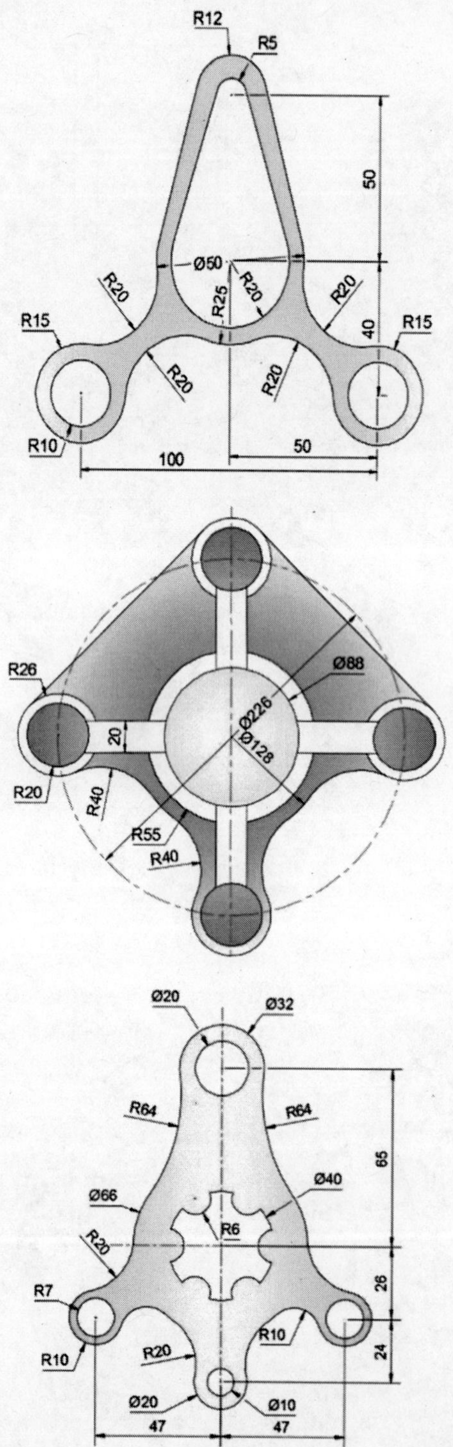
R12
R5
50
Ø50
R20
R20
R20
R25
R15
40
R15
R20
R20
R10
50
100
R26
Ø88
Ø226
20
Ø128
R20
R40
R55
R40
Ø20
Ø32
R64
R64
65
Ø66
Ø40
R6
R20
26
R7
R10
R10
24
R20
Ø20
Ø10
47
47

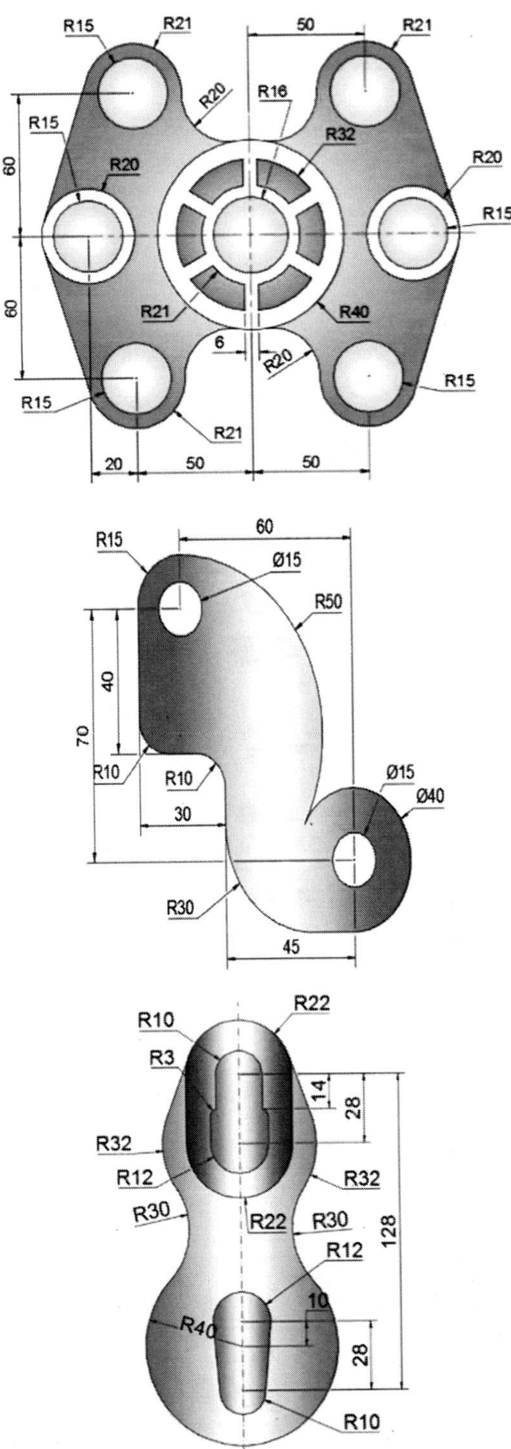
R15
R21
50
R21
R20
R16
R32
R15
60
R20
R20
R15
60
R21
R40
6
R20
R15
R15
R21
20
50
50
60
R15
Ø15
R50
40
70
R10
R10
30
Ø15
Ø40
R30
45
R10
R22
R3
14
28
R32
R12
R32
R30
R22
R30
128
R12
10
R40
28
R10

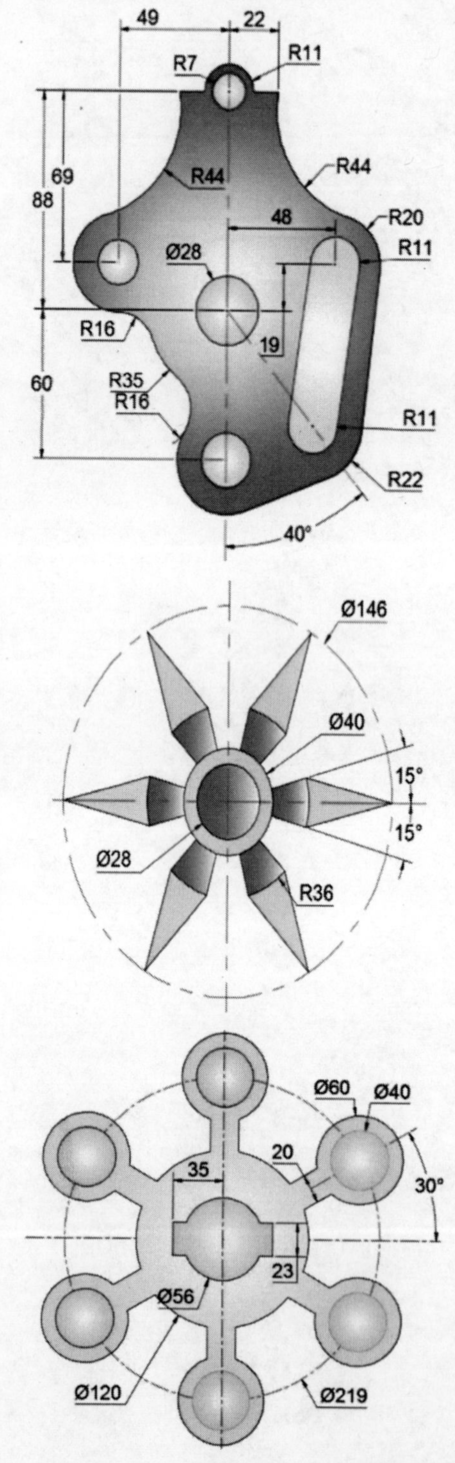
49
22
R7
R11
69
88
R44
R44
48
R20
Ø28
R11
R16
19
60
R35
R16
R11
R22
40°
Ø146
Ø40
15°
15°
Ø28
R36
Ø60
Ø40
20
35
30°
23
Ø56
Ø120
Ø219

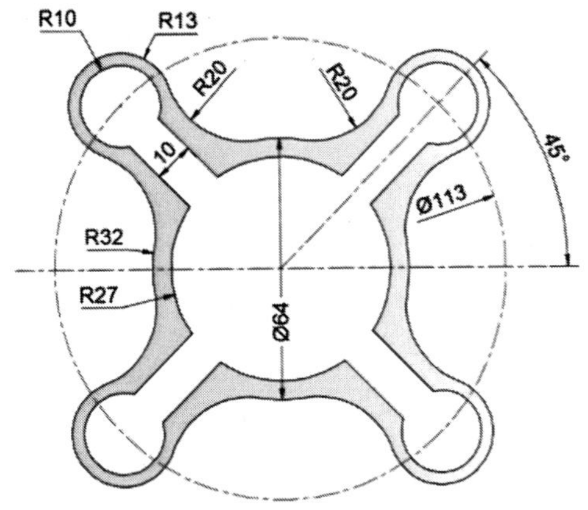
R10
R13
R20
R20
45°
10
Ø113
R32
R27
Ø64

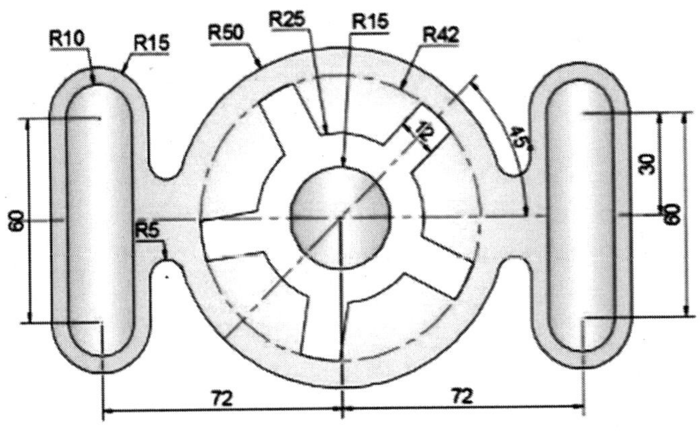
R10
R15
R50
R25
R15
R42
12
45°
30
60
60
R5
72
72

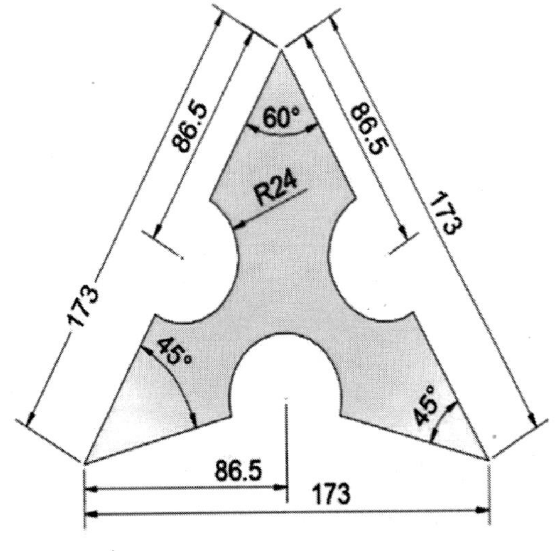
86.5
60°
86.5
R24
173
173
45°
45°
86.5
173

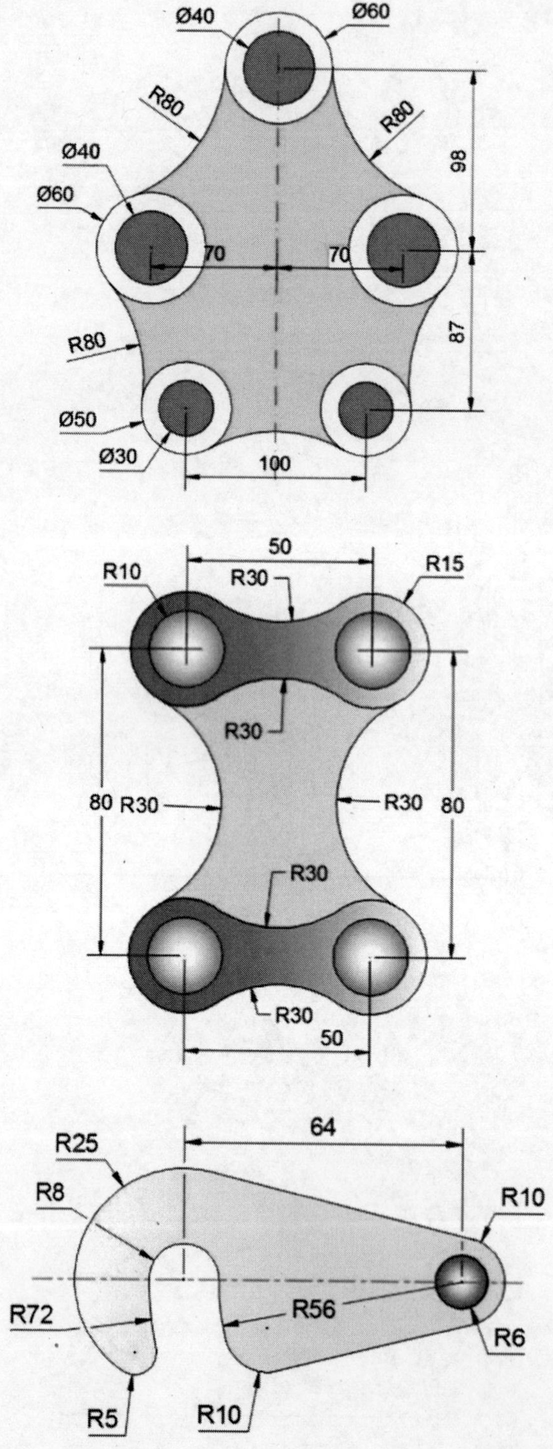
Ø40
Ø60
R80
R80
98
Ø40
Ø60
70
70
87
R80
Ø50
Ø30
100
50
R10
R30
R15
R30
80 R30
R30 80
R30
R30
50
64
R25
R8
R10
R72
R56
R6
R5
R10

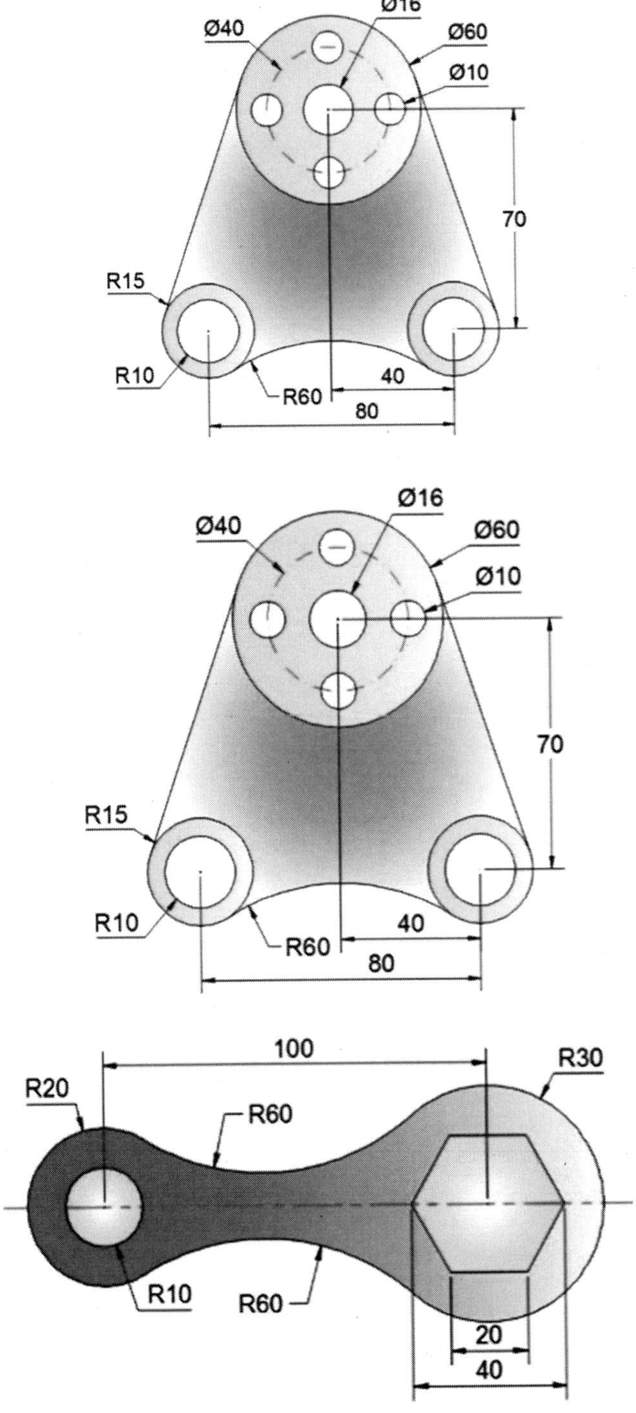
Ø16
Ø40
Ø60
Ø10
70
R15
R10
R60
40
80
Ø16
Ø40
Ø60
Ø10
70
R15
R10
R60
40
80
100
R30
R20
R60
R10
R60
20
40

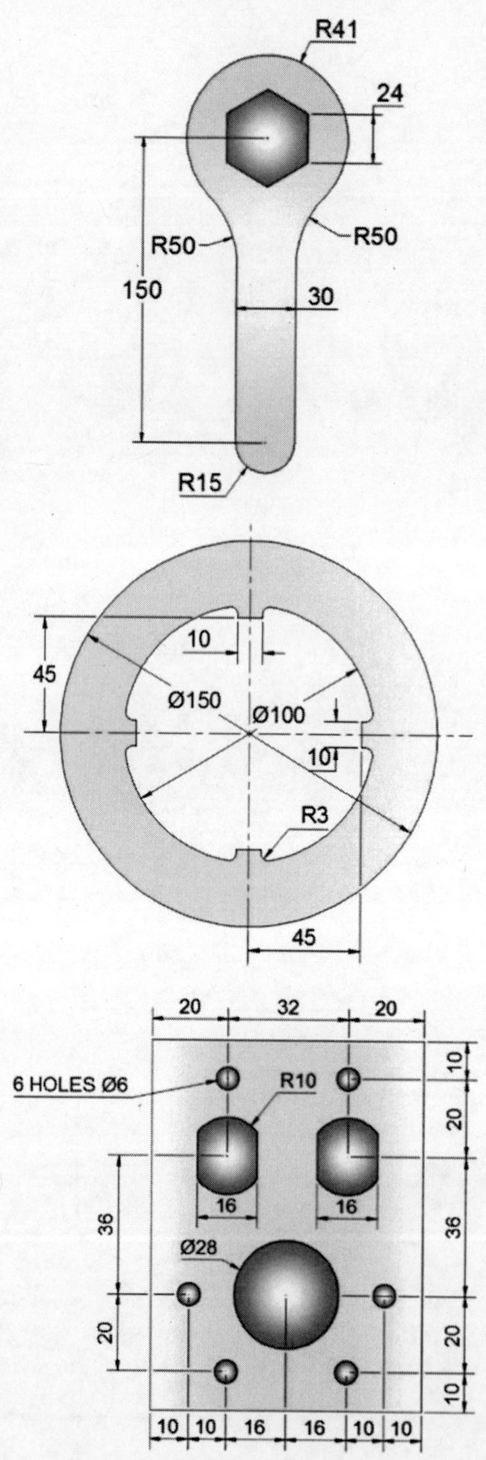
R41
24
R50
R50
150
30
R15
10
45
Ø150
Ø100
10
R3
45
20
32
20
6 HOLES Ø6
R10
10
20
16
16
36
36
Ø28
20
20
10
10
10
16
16
10
10

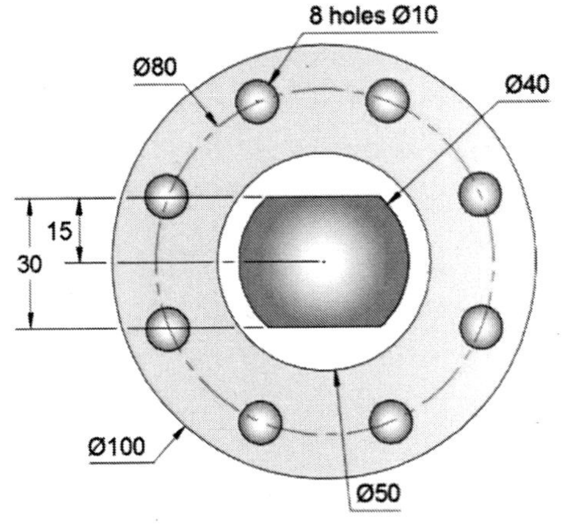
8 holes Ø10
Ø80
Ø40
15
30
Ø100
Ø50

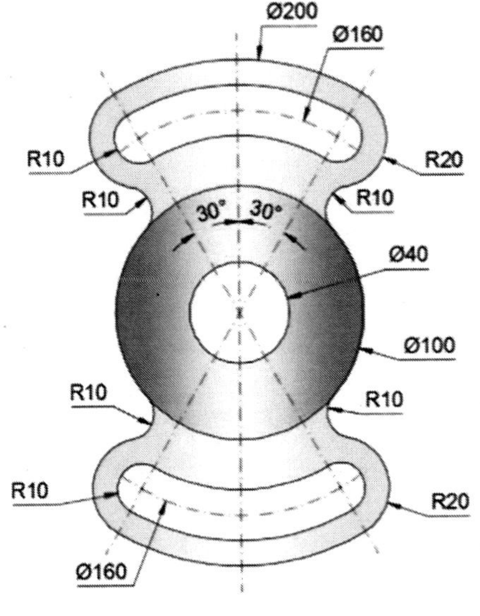
Ø200
Ø160
R10
R20
R10
R10
30°
30°
Ø40
Ø100
R10
R10
R10
R20
Ø160

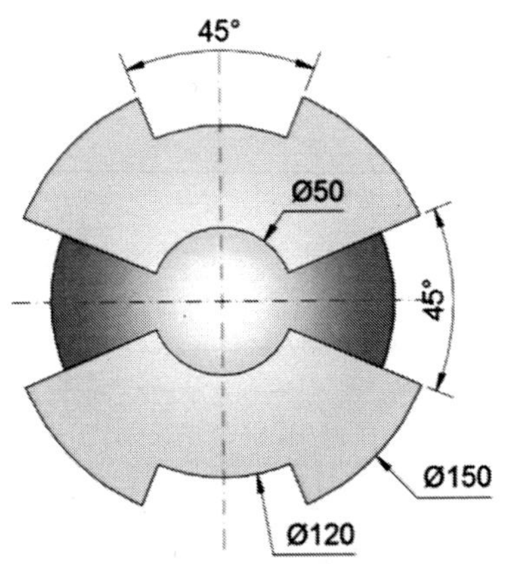
45°
Ø50
45°
Ø150
Ø120

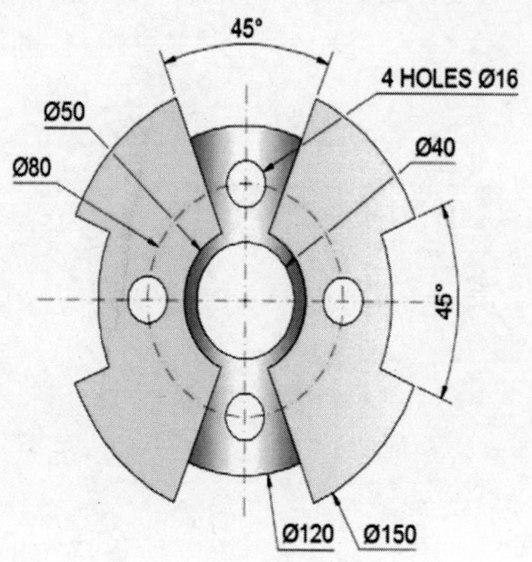
45°
4 HOLES Ø16
Ø50
Ø40
Ø80
45°
Ø120
Ø150

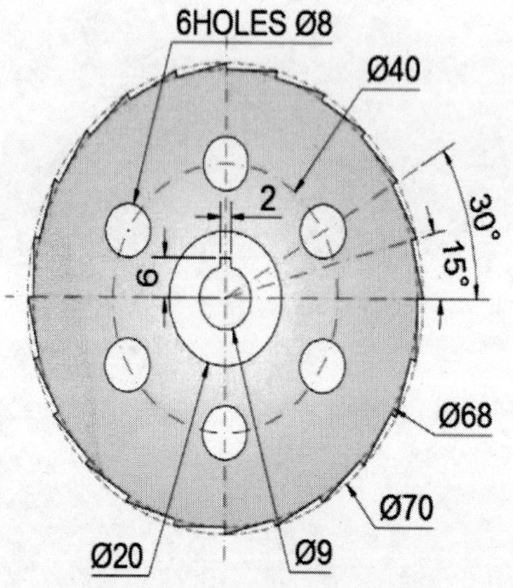
6HOLES Ø8
Ø40
2
30°
6
15°
Ø68
Ø70
Ø20
Ø9

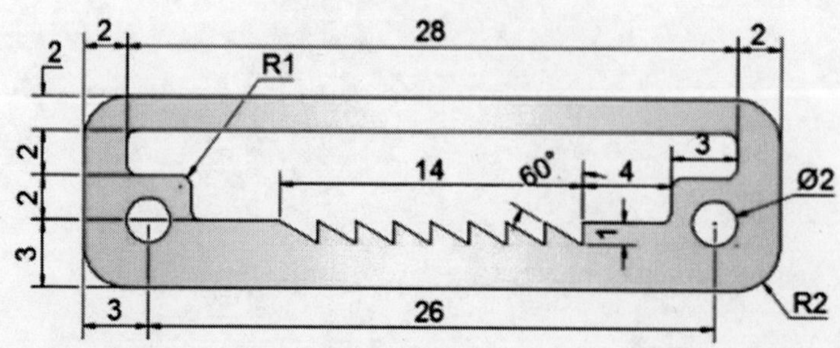
2
28
2
2
R1
3
2
14
60°
4
Ø2
2
1
3
3
26
R2

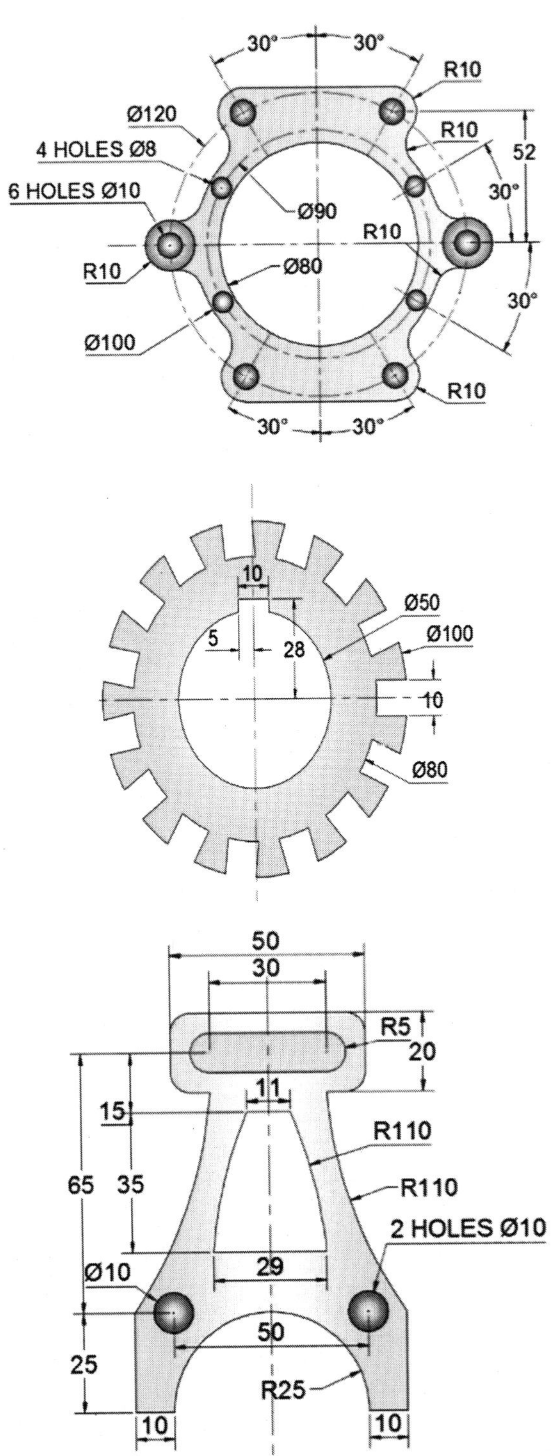
30°
30°
R10
Ø120
R10
4 HOLES Ø8
52
30°
6 HOLES Ø10
Ø90
R10
R10
Ø80
30°
Ø100
R10
30°
30°
10
Ø50
Ø100
5
28
10
Ø80
50
30
R5
20
11
15
R110
65
35
R110
2 HOLES Ø10
Ø10
29
50
25
R25
10
10

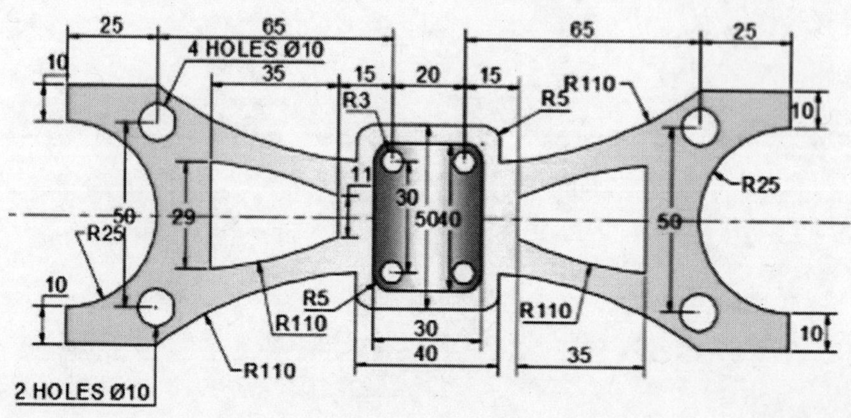
25
65
65
25
4 HOLES Ø10
10
35
15
20
15
R3
R5
R110
10
11
30
5040
R25
50
29
50
R25
10
R5
R110
R110
30
40
35
10
R110
2 HOLES Ø10

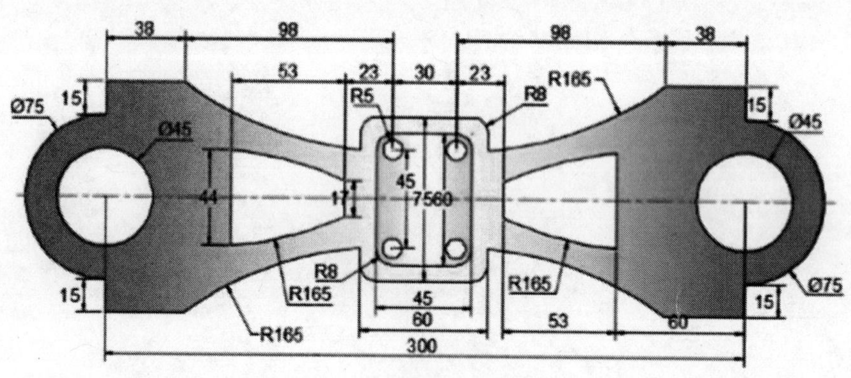
38
98
98
38
53
23
30
23
R5
R8
R165
15
Ø75
Ø45
15
Ø45
44
17
45
7560
R8
R165
R165
15
Ø75
15
45
60
53
60
R165
300

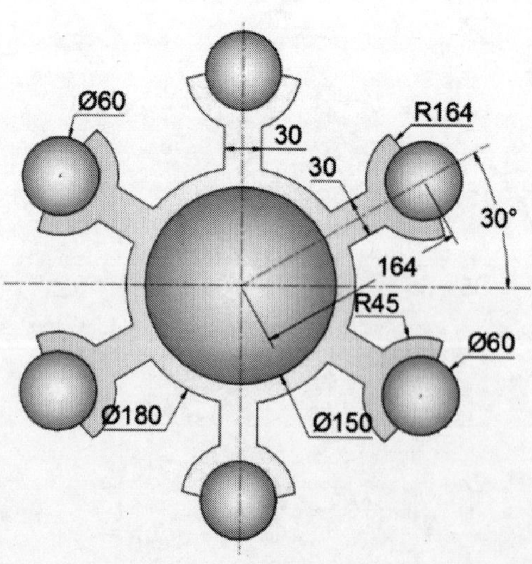
Ø60
R164
30
30
30°
164
R45
Ø60
Ø180
Ø150

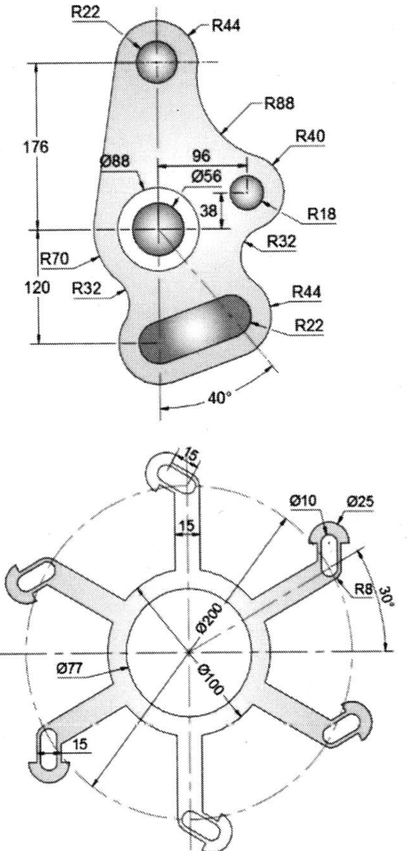
R22
R44
R88
R40
176
96
Ø88
Ø56
R18
38
R32
R70
120
R32
R44
R22
40°
15
Ø10
Ø25
15
R8
30°
Ø200
Ø77
Ø100
15

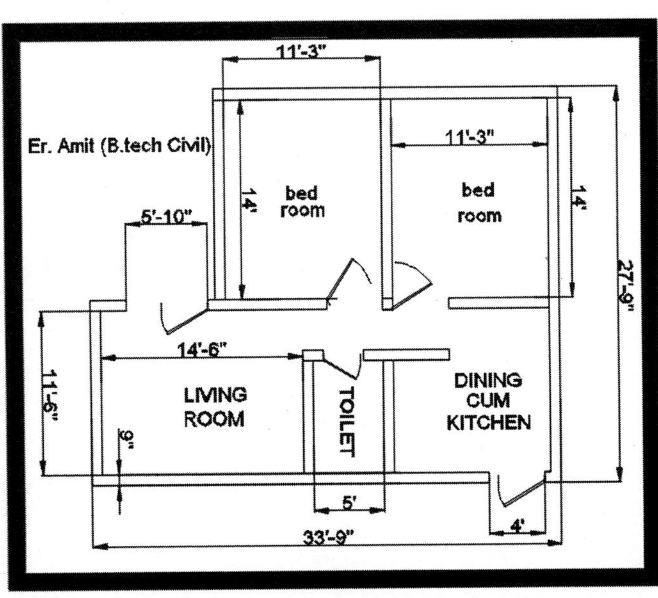
11'-3"
11'-3"
Er. Amit (B.tech Civil)
14'
bed
room
bed
room
14'
5'-10"
27'-9"
14'-6"
11'-6"
LIVING
ROOM
TOILET
DINING
CUM
KITCHEN
9"
5'
4'
33'-9"

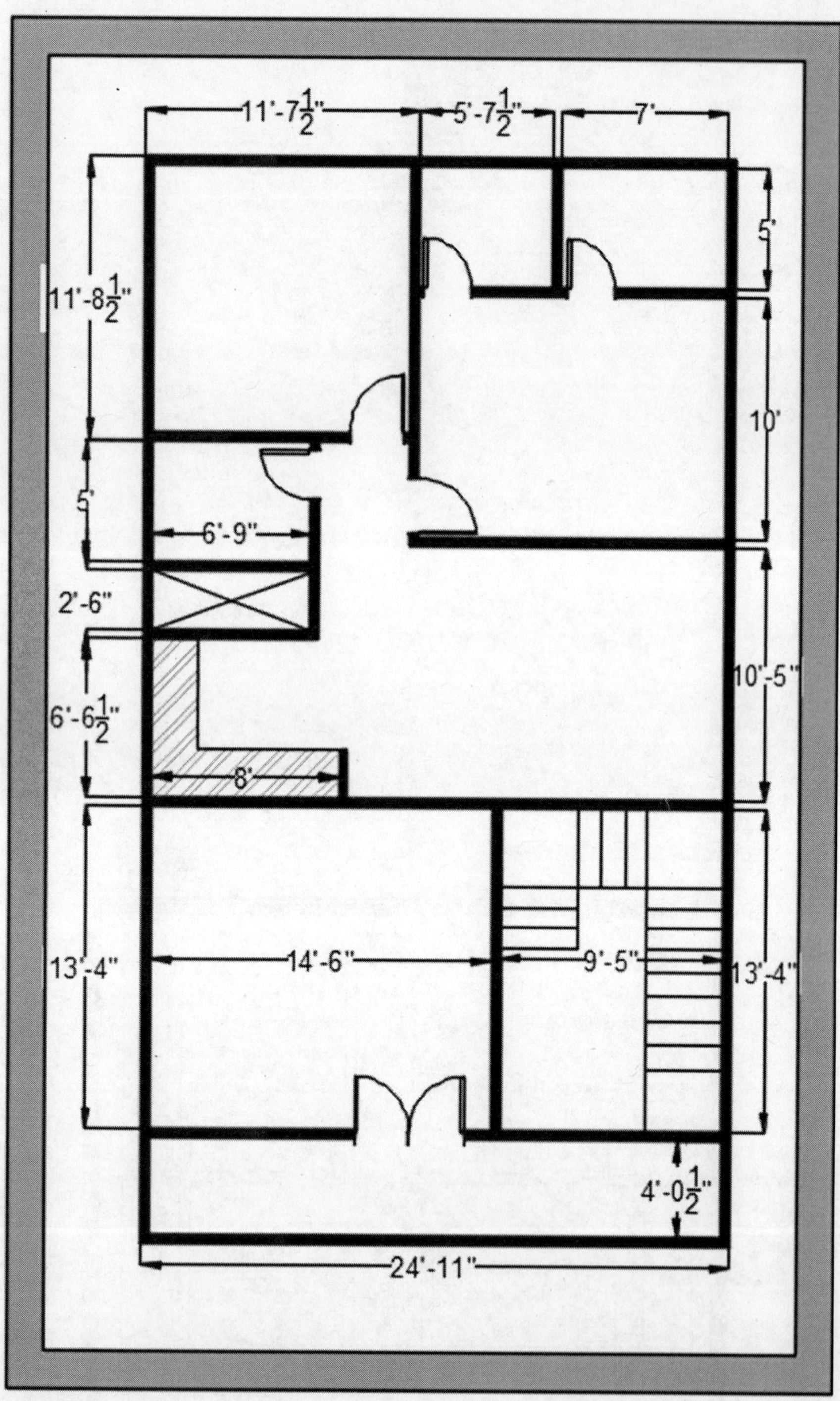
11'-7½"
5'-7½"
7'
5'
11'-8½"
10'
5'
6'-9"
2'-6"
10'-5"
6'-6½"
8'
13'-4"
14'-6"
9'-5"
13'-4"
4'-0½"
24'-11"

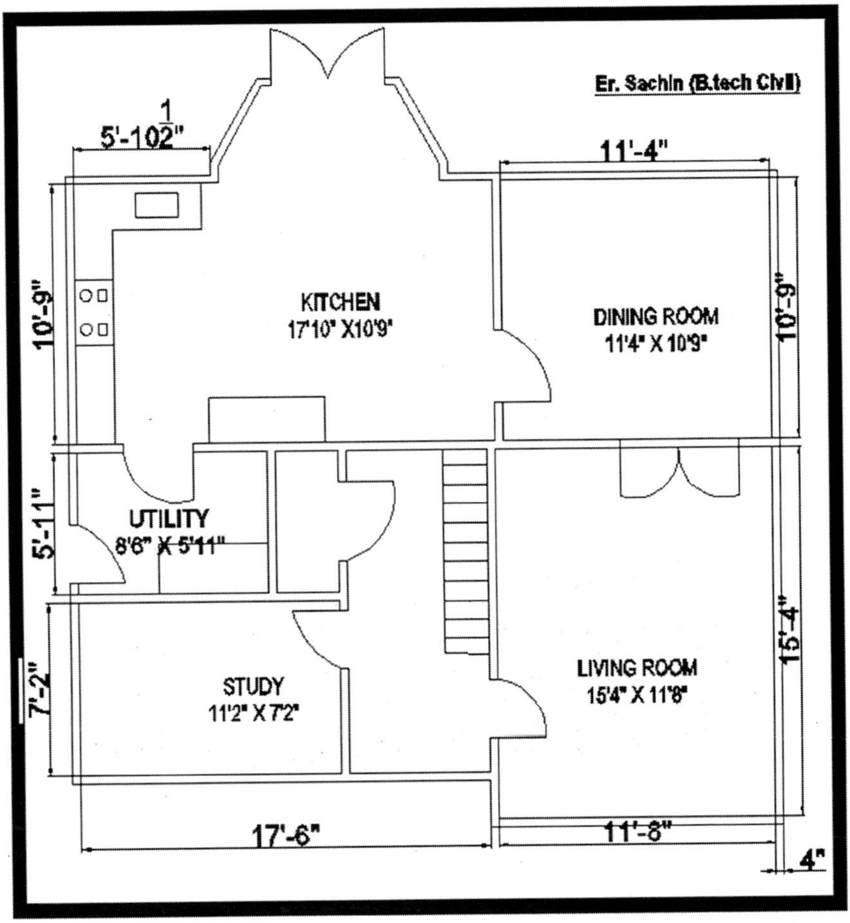

Er. Sachin (B.tech Civil)
5'-10 1/2"
11'-4"
10'-9"
KITCHEN
17'10" X10'9"
DINING ROOM
11'4" X 10'9"
10'-9"
5'-11"
UTILITY
8'6" X 5'11"
7'-2"
STUDY
11'2" X 7'2"
LIVING ROOM
15'4" X 11'8"
15'-4"
17'-6"
11'-8"
4"

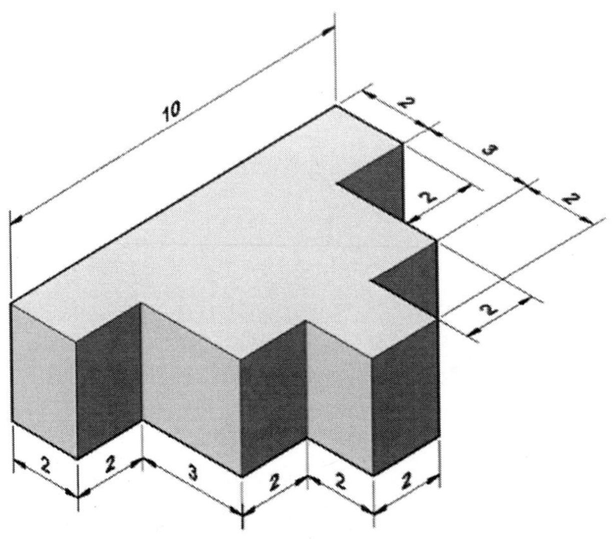
10
2
3
2
2
2
2
2
3
2
2
2

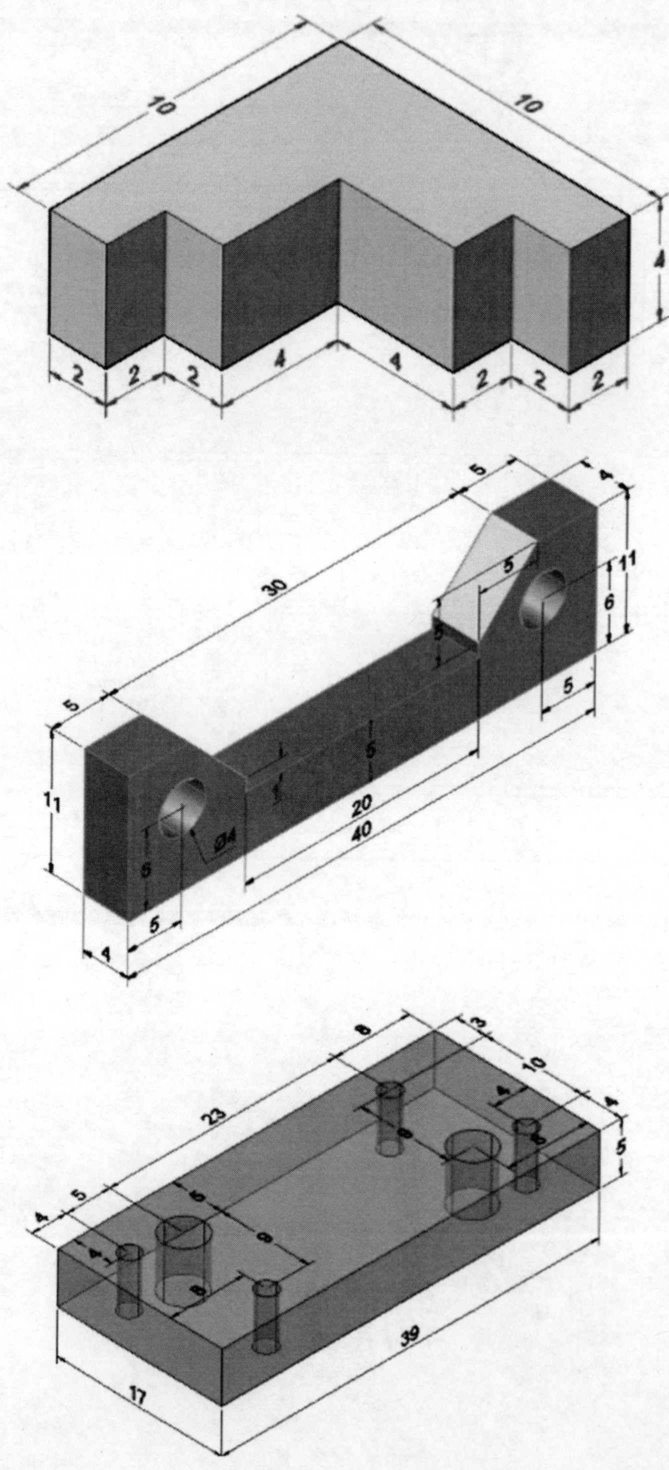
10
10
4
2
2
2
4
4
2
2
2
5
4
30
5
11
6
5
5
5
11
20
40
Ø4
5
4
8
3
10
4
4
23
5
5
4
5
39
17

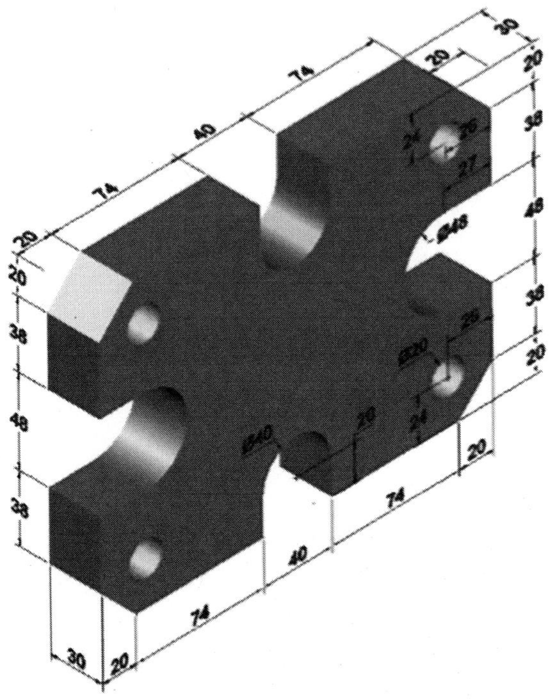
30
20
74
40
74
20
20
38
48
38
20
24
26
27
Ø48
Ø20
Ø40
74
40
74
30
20

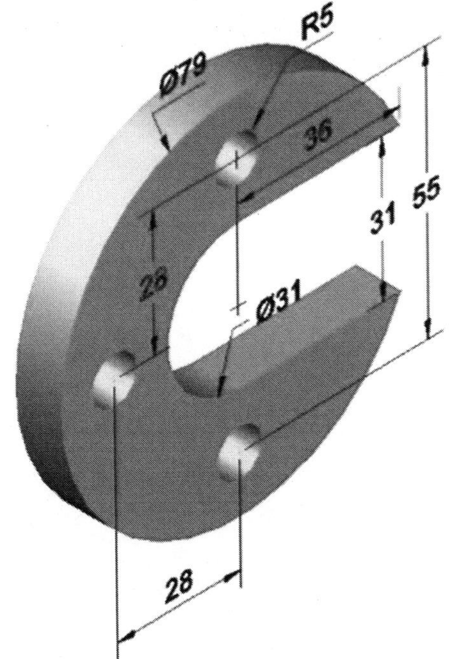
R5
Ø79
36
31
55
26
Ø31
28

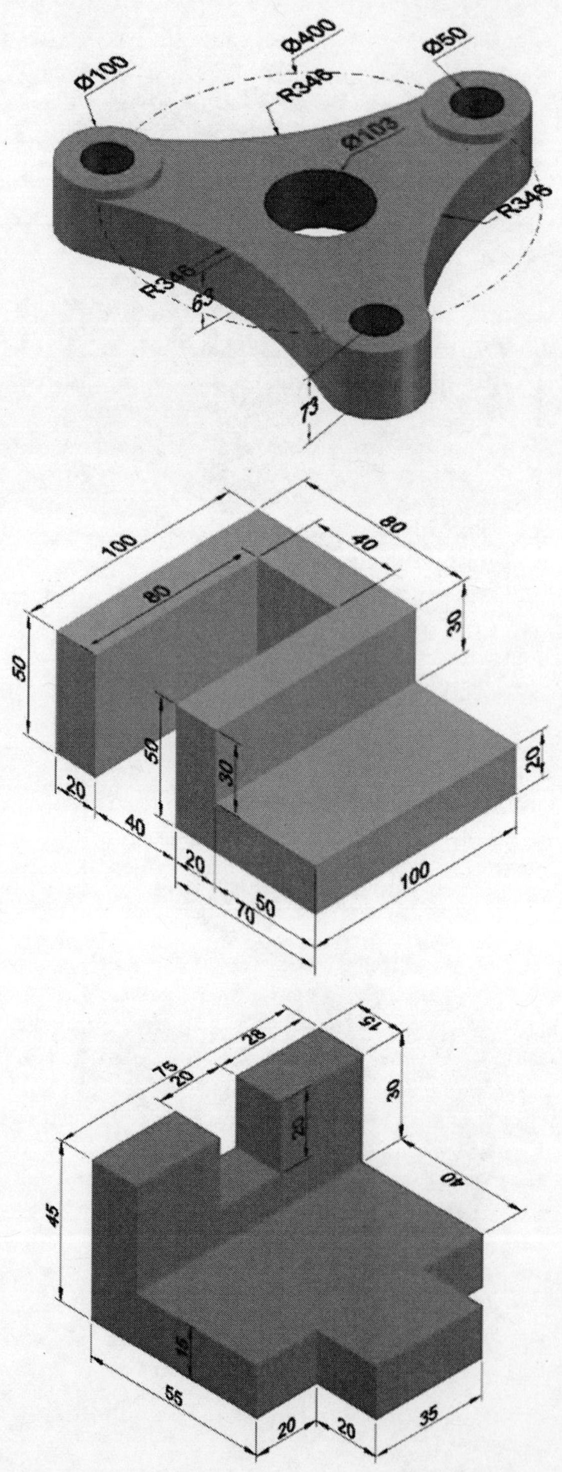
Ø400
Ø100
Ø50
R348
Ø103
R346
R346
63
73
100
80
40
80
30
50
50
30
20
20
40
20
100
50
70
75
28
15
20
30
20
45
40
15
55
20
20
35

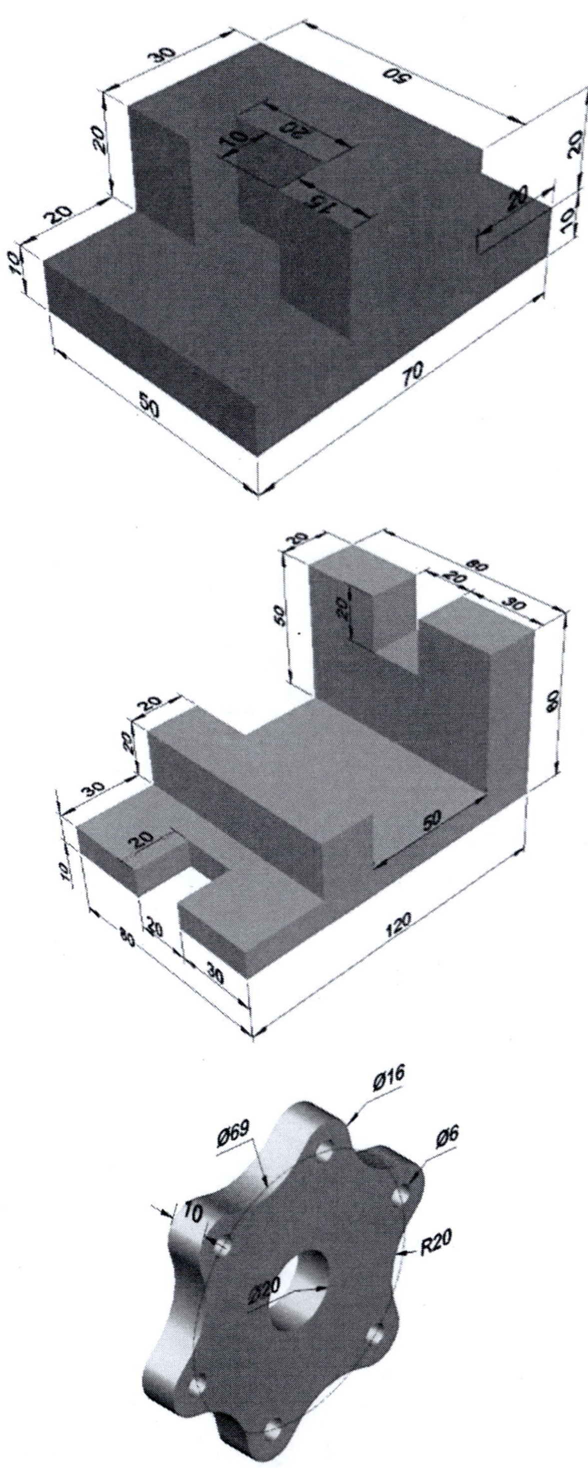
30
50
20
10
20
15
20
20
20
10
10
70
50
20
80
20
30
50
20
80
20
20
30
20
10
50
80
20
120
30
Ø16
Ø69
Ø6
10
R20
Ø20

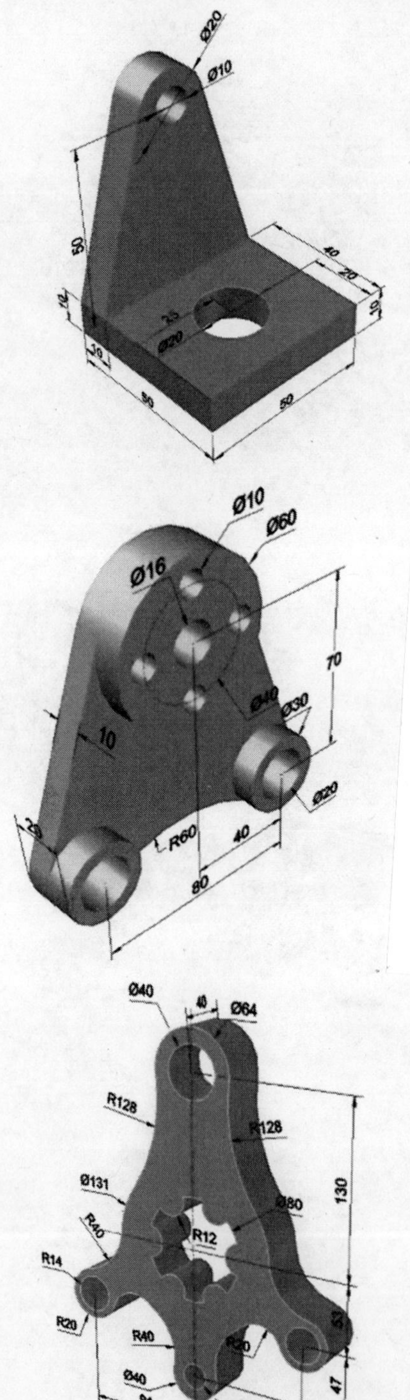

Ø20
Ø10
50
10
25
Ø20
10
50
50
40
20
10
Ø10
Ø60
Ø16
70
Ø40
Ø30
10
Ø20
20
R60
40
80
Ø40
40
Ø64
R128
R128
Ø131
Ø80
R40
R12
130
R14
R20
R40
R20
53
Ø40
94
Ø20
94
47